Add your opinion to our next book

Fill out a survey

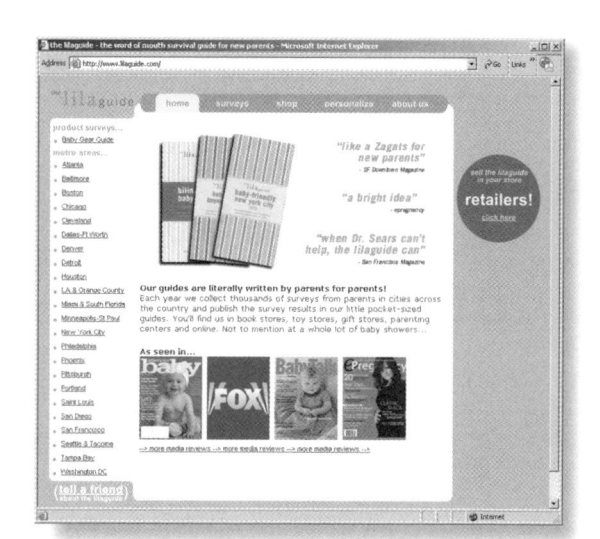

visit www.lilaguide.com

the lilaguide
by PARENTS *for* PARENTS

baby-friendly boston area

NEW PARENT SURVIVAL GUIDE TO SHOPPING, ACTIVITIES, RESTAURANTS AND MORE...

2ND EDITION

LOCAL EDITOR: MAGDA HERNANDEZ

PUBLISHED BY THE LILAGUIDE/OAM SOLUTIONS, INC.
SAN FRANCISCO, CA   WWW.LILAGUIDE.COM

Published by:
OAM Solutions, Inc.
139 Saturn Street
San Francisco, CA 94114, USA
415.252.1300
orders@lilaguide.com
www.lilaguide.com

ISBN. 1-932847-13-8
First Printing: 2005
Printed in the USA
Copyright © 2005 by OAM Solutions, Inc.

All rights reserved. No part of this book may be reproduced or transmitted in any form or by any means, electronic or mechanical, including photocopying, recording or by any information storage and retrieval system, without written permission from the publisher, except for the inclusion of brief quotations in a review.

This book is designed to share parents' opinions regarding baby-related products, services and activities. It is sold with the understanding that the information contained in the book does not represent the publisher's opinion or recommendations. The reviews contained in this guide are based on public opinion surveys and are therefore subjective in nature. The publisher shall have neither liability nor responsibility to any person or entity with respect to any loss or damage caused, or alleged to have been caused, directly or indirectly, by the information contained in this book.

If you do not wish to be bound by the above, you may return this book to the publisher for a full refund.

table of contents

07 about the lilaguide
09 thank yous
10 disclaimer
11 how to use this book

Shopping
13 baby basics & accessories
77 maternity clothing

Fun & Entertainment
97 activities & outings
125 parks & playgrounds
139 restaurants

Health & Support
173 doulas & lactation consultants
177 exercise
191 parent education & support
201 pediatricians

Other Necessities
209 breast pump sales & rentals
215 diaper delivery services
217 haircuts
221 nanny & babysitter referrals
227 photographers

indexes
234 alphabetical
239 by city/neighborhood

about the lilaguide

No, for the last time, the baby does not come with a handbook. And even if there were a handbook, you wouldn't read it. You'd fill out the warranty card, throw out the box, and start playing right away. Until a few hours passed and you were hit with the epiphany of, "Gee whiz honey, what in the wide, wide world of childcare are we doing here?"

Relax. We had that panicked thought when we had our daughter Delilah. And so did **all the parents** we talked to when they had their children. And while we all knew there was no handbook, there was, we found, a whole lot of **word-of-mouth information**. Everyone we talked to had some bit of child rearing advice about what baby gear store is the most helpful. Some **nugget of parenting wisdom** about which restaurant tolerates strained carrots on the floor. It all really seemed to help. Someone, we thought, should write this down.

And that's when, please pardon the pun, the lilaguide was born. The book you're now holding is a guide **written by local parents for local parents**. It's what happens when someone actually does write it down (and organizes it, calculates it, and presents it in an easy-to-use format).

Nearly 8,900 surveys have produced this first edition of **the lilaguide: Baby-Friendly Boston Area**. It provides a truly unique insider's view of over 1,400 "parent-friendly" stores, activities, restaurants, and service providers that are about to become a very big part of your life. And while this guide won't tell you how to change a diaper or how to get by on little or no sleep (that's what grandparents are for), it will tell you what other **local parents have learned** about the amazing things your city and neighborhood have to offer.

As you peruse these reviews, please remember that this guide is **not intended to be a comprehensive directory** since it does not contain every baby store or activity in the area. Rather, it is intended to provide a short-list of places that your neighbors and friends **deemed exciting and noteworthy**. If a place or business is not listed, it simply means that nobody (or not enough people) rated or submitted information about it to us. **Please let us know** about your favorite parent and baby-friendly businesses and service providers by participating in our online survey at **www.lilaguide.com**. We always want your opinions!

So there you have it. Now go make some phone calls, clean up the house, take a nap, or do something on your list before the baby arrives.

Enjoy!

Oli & Elysa

Oli Mittermaier & Elysa Marco, MD

PS

We love getting feedback (good and bad) so don't be bashful. Email us at **lila@lilaguide.com** with your thoughts, comments and suggestions. We'll be sure to try to include them in next year's edition!

thank yous

We'd like to take a moment to offer a heart-felt thank you to all the **parents who participated in our survey** and took the time to share their thoughts and opinions. Without your participation, we would never have been able to create this unique guide.

Thanks to our extra helpful Boston area contributors **Terri Cancelarich**, **Marilyn Cufone**, **Michelle Farrington**, **Julie Fleites**, **Sarah Kemp Fullerton**, **Anu Kothari**, **Leslie Hartman**, **Julie Lanza**, **Param Roychoudhury**, and **Terry Yanulavich** for going above and beyond in the quest for hip tot spots.

Thanks also to **Lisa Barnes**, **Nora Borowsky**, **Todd Cooper**, **Amy Iannone**, **Katy Jacobson**, **Felicity John Odell**, **Shira Johnson**, **Kasia Kappes**, **Jen Krug**, **Dana Kulvin**, **Deborah Schneider**, **Kevin Schwall**, **April Stewart**, and **Nina Thompson** for their tireless editorial eyes, **Satoko Furuta** and **Paul D. Smith** for their beautiful sense of design, and **Lane Foard** for making the words yell.

Special thanks to **Paul D. Smith**, **Ken Miles**, and **Ali Wing** for their consistent support and overall encouragement in all things lilaguide, and of course **our parents** for their unconditional support in this and all our other endeavors.

And last, but certainly not least, thanks to **little Delilah** for inspiring us to embark on this challenging, yet incredibly fulfilling project.

www.lilaguide.com

disclaimer

This book is designed to share parents' opinions regarding baby-related products, services and activities. It is sold with the understanding that the information contained in the book **does not represent the publisher's opinion** or recommendations.

The reviews contained in this guide are based on **public opinion surveys** and are therefore subjective in nature. The publisher shall have neither liability nor responsibility to any person or entity with respect to any loss or damage caused, or alleged to have been caused, directly or indirectly, by the information contained in this book.

ratings

Most listings have stars and numbers as part of their write-up. These symbols mean the following:

- ❺ / ★★★★★   extraordinary
- ❹ / ★★★★☆   very good
- ❸ / ★★★☆☆   good
- ❷ / ★★☆☆☆   fair
- ❶ / ★☆☆☆☆   poor
- ✓   available
- ✗   not available/relevant

If a ☆ is listed instead of ★, it means that the rating is less reliable because a small number of parents surveyed the listing. Furthermore, if a listing has **no stars** or **criteria ratings**, it means that although the listing was rated, the number of surveys submitted was so low that we did not feel it justified an actual rating.

quotes & reviews

The quotes/reviews are taken directly from surveys submitted to us via our web site (**www.lilaguide.com**). Other than spelling and minor grammatical changes, they come to you as they came to us. Quotes were selected based on how well they appeared to represent the collective opinions of the surveys submitted.

fact checking

We have contacted all of the businesses listed to verify their address and phone number, as well as to inquire about their hours, class schedules and web site information. Since some of this information may change after this guide has been printed, we appreciate you letting us know of any errors by notifying us via email at **lila@lilaguide.com**.

how to use the lilaguide

baby basics & accessories

City of Boston

★★★★★
"lila picks"

★ Bonpoint   ★ Red Wagon

April Cornell ★★★½☆
"...beautiful, classic dresses and accessories for special occasions... I love the matching 'mommy and me' outfits... lots of fun knickknacks for sale... great selection of baby wear on their web site... rest assured your baby won't look like every other child in these adorable outfits... very frilly and girlie—beautiful...**"**

Furniture, Bedding & Decor	✗	$$$	Prices
Gear & Equipment	✗	❸	Product availability
Nursing & Feeding	✗	❹	Staff knowledge
Safety & Babycare	✗	❹	Customer service
Clothing, Shoes & Accessories	✓	❹	Decor
Books, Toys & Entertainment	✗		

DOWNTOWN—6 N MARKETPLACE BLDG (AT FANEUIL HALL MARKETPLACE); 617.248.0280; M-SA 10-9, SU 12-6

Baby Belle ★★★★☆
"...a girlie girl spot... friendly staff, and a great location... lots of beautiful and thoughtfully-chosen products... a fairly new boutique with beautiful items... owner is very personable and helpful... close to Starbucks which makes mom happy...**"**

Furniture, Bedding & Decor	✗	$$$$	Prices
Gear & Equipment	✗	❸	Product availability
Nursing & Feeding	✗	❹	Staff knowledge
Safety & Babycare	✗	❹	Customer service
Clothing, Shoes & Accessories	✓	❹	Decor
Books, Toys & Entertainment	✓		

WEST ROXBURY—1780 CENTRE ST (AT WILLOW ST); 617.325.2355; M-W 10-5, TH-F 10-6, SA 10-5

BabyGap/GapKids ★★★★☆
"...colorful baby and toddler clothing in clean, well-lit stores... great return policy... it's the Gap, so you know what you're getting—colorful, cute and well-made clothing... best place for baby hats... prices are reasonable especially since there's always a sale of some sort going on... sales, sales, sales—frequent and fantastic... everything I'm looking for in infant clothing—snap crotches, snaps up the front, all natural fabrics and great styling... fun seasonal selections—a great place to shop for gifts as well as for your own kids... although it can get busy, staff generally seem accommodating and helpful...**"**

Furniture, Bedding & Decor	✗	$$$	Prices
Gear & Equipment	✗	❹	Product availability
Nursing & Feeding	✗	❹	Staff knowledge
Safety & Babycare	✗	❹	Customer service
Clothing, Shoes & Accessories	✓	❹	Decor

Books, Toys & Entertainment .... ✘
WWW.GAP.COM

BACK BAY—201 NEWBURY ST (AT EXETER ST); 617.424.8778; M-TH 10-8, F-SA 10-9, SU 11-6; PARKING LOT

DOWNTOWN—100 HUNTINGTON AVE (AT COPLEY PLACE); 617.424.8778; M-SA 10-8, SU 11-6; PARKING LOT

DOWNTOWN—200 STATE ST (AT PURCHASE ST); 617.439.7844; M-SA 10-9, SU 12-7; PARKING IN FRONT OF BLDG

Bonpoint ★★★★★

"...stylish, elegant clothes for the trendy toddler and child... gorgeous European workmanship... a great splurge for your little one... make sure you get the right size as they run small... black silk dresses for girls, as well as tailored pants and jumpers for boys... good for the oohs and aahs..."

Furniture, Bedding & Decor .... ✘	$$$$	Prices
Gear & Equipment .... ✘	❹	Product availability
Nursing & Feeding .... ✘	❹	Staff knowledge
Safety & Babycare .... ✘	❹	Customer service
Clothing, Shoes & Accessories .... ✓	❹	Decor
Books, Toys & Entertainment .... ✓		

WWW.BONPOINT.COM

BACK BAY—18 ARLINGTON ST (AT NEWBURY ST); 617.267.1717; M-SA 10-6; STREET PARKING

Children's Place, The ★★★½☆

"...great bargains on cute clothing... shoes, socks, swimsuits, sunglasses and everything in between... lots of '3 for $20' type deals on sleepers, pants and mix-and-match separates... so much more affordable than the other 'big chains'... don't expect the most unique stuff here, but it wears and washes well... cheap clothing for cheap prices... you can leave the store with bags full of clothes without putting a huge dent in your wallet..."

Furniture, Bedding & Decor .... ✘	$$	Prices
Gear & Equipment .... ✘	❹	Product availability
Nursing & Feeding .... ✘	❹	Staff knowledge
Safety & Babycare .... ✘	❹	Customer service
Clothing, Shoes & Accessories .... ✓	❹	Decor
Books, Toys & Entertainment .... ✓		

WWW.CHILDRENSPLACE.COM

DOWNTOWN—349-351 WASHINGTON ST (AT BLUE HILL AVE); 617.426.9524; M-SA 9:30-7, SU 11-6; PARKING LOT

Copley Flair ★★★★½

"...unique card shop with the most whimsical collection of stuff... all kinds of cards from the classic to the off-beat eccentric... great for gifts for baby and mom—soaps, photo albums, frames, decor... lots of options for product in a variety of price ranges... tight aisles... I love all the collectible and home decor products... good place for housewarming items and children's accessories... the most gorgeous gift wrap paper and ribbons anywhere..."

Furniture, Bedding & Decor .... ✘	$$$	Prices
Gear & Equipment .... ✘	❹	Product availability
Nursing & Feeding .... ✘	❹	Staff knowledge
Safety & Babycare .... ✘	❹	Customer service
Clothing, Shoes & Accessories .... ✘	❹	Decor
Books, Toys & Entertainment .... ✓		

WWW.COPLEYFLAIR.COM

BACK BAY—583 BOYLSTON ST (AT DARTMOUTH ST); 617.247.1648; M-F 8:30-7, SA 9-7, SU 12-5; PARKING LOT

www.lilaguide.com

DOWNTOWN—11 SCHOOL ST (AT WASHINGTON ST); 617.367.7170; M-F 8:30-6:30, SA 10-5; GARAGE ON WASHINGTON ST

DOWNTOWN—617.737.2420; M-F 8-6:30; GARAGE ON FEDERAL ST

Gymboree ★★★★☆

❝...beautiful clothing and great quality... colorful and stylish baby and kids wear... lots of fun birthday gift ideas... easy exchange and return policy... items usually go on sale pretty quickly... save money with Gymbucks... many stores have a play area which makes shopping with my kids fun (let alone feasible)...❞

Furniture, Bedding & Decor	✗	$$$	Prices
Gear & Equipment	✗	❹	Product availability
Nursing & Feeding	✗	❹	Staff knowledge
Safety & Babycare	✗	❹	Customer service
Clothing, Shoes & Accessories	✓	❹	Decor
Books, Toys & Entertainment	✓		

WWW.GYMBOREE.COM

BACK BAY—100 HUNTINGTON AVE (AT COPLEY PLACE); 617.437.1191; M-SA 10-9, SU 11-6; PARKING LOT

H & M ★★★⯪☆

❝...wonderful prices for trendy baby and toddler clothes... it's the 'Euro' Target... buy for yourself and for your kids... a fun shopping experience as long as your child doesn't mind the bright lights and loud music... decent return policy... incredible sale prices... store can get messy at peak hours... busy and hectic, but their inventory is fun and worth the visit...❞

Furniture, Bedding & Decor	✗	$$	Prices
Gear & Equipment	✗	❸	Product availability
Nursing & Feeding	✗	❸	Staff knowledge
Safety & Babycare	✗	❸	Customer service
Clothing, Shoes & Accessories	✓	❸	Decor
Books, Toys & Entertainment	✓		

WWW.HM.COM

DOWNTOWN—350 WASHINGTON ST (AT FRANKLIN ST); 617.482.7001; M-SA 10-8, SU 11-7; PAID GARAGES

Jacadi ★★★★☆

❝...beautiful French clothes, baby bumpers and quilts... elegant and perfect for special occasions... quite expensive, but the clothing is hip and the quality really good... many handmade clothing and bedding items... take advantage of their sales... more of a store to buy gifts than practical, everyday clothes... beautiful, special clothing—especially for newborns and toddlers... velvet pajamas, coordinated nursery items... stores are as pretty as the clothes... they have a huge (half-off everything) sale twice a year that makes it very affordable...❞

Furniture, Bedding & Decor	✓	$$$$	Prices
Gear & Equipment	✗	❹	Product availability
Nursing & Feeding	✗	❹	Staff knowledge
Safety & Babycare	✗	❹	Customer service
Clothing, Shoes & Accessories	✓	❹	Decor
Books, Toys & Entertainment	✓		

WWW.JACADIUSA.COM

BACK BAY—310 BOYLSTON ST (AT CHARLES ST); 617.574.8833; M-SA 10-6 SU 12-5; STREET PARKING

JP Boing's Toy Shop ★★★★☆

❝...terrific neighborhood toy store... hands-on play with the toys in the store... fun place to shop for kids with kids... always worth the trip to see the toys and talk with knowledgeable staff... unique, atypical toys

you won't find at the chain stores... educational and fun for newborns through middle school aged kids... something for everyone... "

Furniture, Bedding & Decor	✗	$$$	Prices
Gear & Equipment	✗	❹	Product availability
Nursing & Feeding	✗	❹	Staff knowledge
Safety & Babycare	✗	❹	Customer service
Clothing, Shoes & Accessories	✗	❹	Decor
Books, Toys & Entertainment	✓		

WWW.BOINGTOYS.COM

JAMAICA PLAIN—729 CENTRE ST (AT HARRIS AVE); 617.522.7800; M-T 10-6, W-F 10-8, SA 10-7 SU 12-6; PARKING BEHIND BLDG

Kids R Kids ★★★★½

"*...lots of unique items... good dress-up clothes for girls... great selection of books, crafts, and puzzles you won't find at chains... pricey, but overall a great experience... staff is super helpful and they offer free gift wrapping... a bit small, so leave stroller home ...* "

Furniture, Bedding & Decor	✗	$$$	Prices
Gear & Equipment	✗	❹	Product availability
Nursing & Feeding	✗	❹	Staff knowledge
Safety & Babycare	✗	❹	Customer service
Clothing, Shoes & Accessories	✗	❹	Decor
Books, Toys & Entertainment	✓		

WEST ROXBURY—1952 CENTRE ST (AT MT VERNON ST); 617.323.3991; M-W 9-6, TH 9-8, F-SA 9-6, SU 11-4; STREET OR CVS PARKING LOT

Lester Harry's ★★★★☆

"*...upscale boutique with a good selection of different high-end product lines... they carry brands I've only ever been able to find online... exquisite, trendy items... staff is wonderful, they really know their great clothes and linens for kids... wonderful gifts here, from gorgeously unique blankets to the Bugaboo Frog... expensive, but well worth it... great place to go for a unique gift or a European touch...* "

Furniture, Bedding & Decor	✓	$$$$	Prices
Gear & Equipment	✓	❹	Product availability
Nursing & Feeding	✗	❹	Staff knowledge
Safety & Babycare	✗	❹	Customer service
Clothing, Shoes & Accessories	✓	❹	Decor
Books, Toys & Entertainment	✓		

WWW.LESTERHARRYS.COM

BACK BAY—115 NEWBURY ST (AT CLARENDON ST); 617.927.5400; M-SA 10-6, SU 12-6; GARAGE BTWN DARTMOUTH & NEWBURY

Macy's ★★★½☆

"*...Macy's has it all and I never leave empty-handed... if you time your visit right you can find some great deals... go during the week so you don't get overwhelmed with the weekend crowd... good for staples as well as beautiful party dresses for girls... lots of brand-names like Carter's, Guess, and Ralph Lauren... not much in terms of assistance... newspaper coupons and sales help keep the cost down... some stores are better organized and maintained than others... if you're going to shop at a department store for your baby, then Macy's is a safe bet...* "

Furniture, Bedding & Decor	✓	$$$	Prices
Gear & Equipment	✗	❸	Product availability
Nursing & Feeding	✗	❸	Staff knowledge
Safety & Babycare	✗	❸	Customer service
Clothing, Shoes & Accessories	✓	❸	Decor
Books, Toys & Entertainment	✓		

WWW.MACYS.COM

DOWNTOWN—450 WASHINGTON ST (AT STORES AT 500 WASHINGTON); 617.357.3000; M-SA 9:30-8, SU 10-7; PARKING LOT

Mass General Gift Shop ★★★★☆

"...surprising treasures to be found amid the greeting cards, and balloons... great for a last minute gift... I've found some of the best stuffed animals, slippers, raincoats and hats when browsing to kill time before my OB appointment... lots of gifts for the new mom as well as baby... a great resource for inexpensive gifts—especially on your way to visit a newborn upstairs...**"**

Furniture, Bedding & Decor ✗	$$$	Prices
Gear & Equipment ✓	❹	Product availability
Nursing & Feeding ✓	❸	Staff knowledge
Safety & Babycare ✗	❹	Customer service
Clothing, Shoes & Accessories ✓	❸	Decor
Books, Toys & Entertainment ✓		

WWW.MGHGENERALSTORE.COM

BEACON HILL/WEST END—55 FRUIT ST BLAKE 155 (AT CHARLES ST); 617.726.2227; M-F 8:30-7:30, SA-SU 10-6; GARAGE PARKING

Mulberry Road ★★★★☆

"...small upscale shop that has a nice selection of clothes, gift items and toys for very young babies... custom made bedding... special order gliders... adorable nursery decor and unique handcrafted sweaters and blankets... lots of personal service and amazing gift wrapping... a great place to find gifts that will be remembered—especially for newborns... there are stairs up to the door...**"**

Furniture, Bedding & Decor ✓	$$$$	Prices
Gear & Equipment ✗	❹	Product availability
Nursing & Feeding ✗	❹	Staff knowledge
Safety & Babycare ✗	❹	Customer service
Clothing, Shoes & Accessories ✓	❹	Decor
Books, Toys & Entertainment ✓		

WWW.MULBERRYROAD.COM

BACK BAY—46 GLOUCESTER ST (AT PUBLIC ALLEY 442); 617.859.5861; M-T SA 11-5, TH 11-7, F 11-6, SU 1-4; STREET PARKING

Oilily ★★★★½

"...exclusive shop with fun, colorful clothing... prices are a bit steep, but if you value unique, well-designed clothes, this is the place... better selection for girls than boys but there are special items for either sex... your tot will definitely stand out from the crowd in these unique pieces... my kids love wearing their 'cool' clothes... whimsical items for mom, too...**"**

Furniture, Bedding & Decor ✗	$$$$	Prices
Gear & Equipment ✗	❹	Product availability
Nursing & Feeding ✗	❹	Staff knowledge
Safety & Babycare ✗	❹	Customer service
Clothing, Shoes & Accessories ✓	❹	Decor
Books, Toys & Entertainment ✗		

WWW.OILILYUSA.COM

BACK BAY—32 NEWBURY ST (AT BERKELEY ST); 617.247.2386; M-SA 10-6, TH 10-7, SU 12-5

Old Navy ★★★★☆

"...hip and 'in' clothes for infants and tots... plenty of steals on clearance items... T-shirts and pants for $10 or less... busy, busy, busy—long lines, especially on weekends... nothing fancy and you won't mind when your kids get down and dirty in these clothes... easy to wash, decent quality... you can shop for your baby, your toddler, your teen and yourself all at the same time... clothes are especially *affordable when you hit their sales (post-holiday sales are amazing!)...* "

Furniture, Bedding & Decor .... ✗	$$ .... Prices
Gear & Equipment .... ✗	❹ .... Product availability
Nursing & Feeding .... ✗	❸ .... Staff knowledge
Safety & Babycare .... ✗	❸ .... Customer service
Clothing, Shoes & Accessories....... ✓	❸ .... Decor
Books, Toys & Entertainment .... ✗	

WWW.OLDNAVY.COM

DORCHESTER—8 ALLSTATE RD (AT MASSACHUSETTS AVE); 617.989.9950; M-SA 9-9:30, SU 10-7; PARKING LOT

Payless Shoe Source ★★★☆☆

"*...a good place for deals on children's shoes... staff is helpful with sizing... the selection and prices for kids' shoes can't be beat, but the quality isn't always spectacular... good leather shoes for cheap... great variety of all sizes and widths... I get my son's shoes here and don't feel like I'm wasting my money since he'll outgrow them in 3 months anyway...*"

Furniture, Bedding & Decor .... ✗	$$ .... Prices
Gear & Equipment .... ✗	❸ .... Product availability
Nursing & Feeding .... ✗	❸ .... Staff knowledge
Safety & Babycare .... ✗	❸ .... Customer service
Clothing, Shoes & Accessories....... ✓	❸ .... Decor
Books, Toys & Entertainment .... ✗	

WWW.PAYLESS.COM

DOWNTOWN—367 WASHINGTON ST (AT FRANKLIN ST); 617.451.1871; M-SA 9-7, SU 12-6

EAST BOSTON—32 CENTRAL SQ (AT SARATOGA ST); 617.561.7714; M-SA 9-7, SU 12-5

SOUTH BOSTON—425 W BROADWAY (AT F ST); 617.464.0108; M-SA 10-7, SU 12-5

Petit Bateau ★★★★☆

"*...the ultimate in European styled baby clothes—wonderful French design and quality... great place for a 'going home' outfit as they have small sizes... lots of pastel... so soft and lasts forever... outfits gets less expensive if you average the cost out over a couple of kids... some outfits require hand washing... love the cotton onesies and sleepers... full array of baby clothes along with clothes for older children and women... great end of season sales...*"

Furniture, Bedding & Decor .... ✗	$$$$ .... Prices
Gear & Equipment .... ✗	❹ .... Product availability
Nursing & Feeding .... ✗	❹ .... Staff knowledge
Safety & Babycare .... ✗	❹ .... Customer service
Clothing, Shoes & Accessories....... ✓	❹ .... Decor
Books, Toys & Entertainment .... ✗	

WWW.PETIT-BATEAU.COM

BACK BAY—171 NEWBURY ST (AT DARTMOUTH ST); 617.425.0042; M-F 10-7, SA 10-6, SU 12-5; PARKING LOT

Red Wagon ★★★★★

"*...clothes and shoes for the well-heeled infant and toddler... their sister store Pixie Stix has items for the older set... trendy items that are adorable and pricey... a little small for carting in a stroller, so go with the girls on a shopping trip to the city... one of the best baby stores in Boston for getting something special... try to hit the annual sales... great gifts for all things baby...*"

Furniture, Bedding & Decor .... ✗	$$$$ .... Prices
Gear & Equipment .... ✗	❹ .... Product availability

Nursing & Feeding	✗	❹	Staff knowledge
Safety & Babycare	✗	❹	Customer service
Clothing, Shoes & Accessories	✓	❹	Decor
Books, Toys & Entertainment	✓		

WWW.THEREDWAGON.COM

BEACON HILL/WEST END—69 CHARLES ST (AT MT VERNON ST); 617.523.9402; M-SA 10-7, SU 11-5; PARKING LOT

Talbots Kids ★★★½☆

"...a nice alternative to the typical department store experience... expensive, but fantastic quality... great for holiday and special occasion outfits including christening outfits... well-priced, conservative children's clothing... cute selections for infants, toddlers and kids... sales are fantastic—up to half off at least a couple times a year... the best part is, you can also shop for yourself while shopping for baby..."

Furniture, Bedding & Decor	✗	$$$$	Prices
Gear & Equipment	✗	❹	Product availability
Nursing & Feeding	✗	❹	Staff knowledge
Safety & Babycare	✗	❹	Customer service
Clothing, Shoes & Accessories	✓	❹	Decor
Books, Toys & Entertainment	✗		

WWW.TALBOTS.COM

BACK BAY—800 BOYLSTON ST (AT THE SHOPS AT PRUDENTIAL CTR); 617.266.9400; M-SA 10-9, SU 11-6

Target ★★★★☆

"...our favorite place to shop for kids' stuff—good selection and very affordable... guilt-free shopping—kids grow so fast so I don't want to pay high department-store prices... everything from diapers and sippy cups to car seats and strollers... easy return policy... generally helpful staff, but you don't go for the service—you go for the prices... decent registry that won't freak your friends out with outrageous prices... easy, convenient shopping for well-priced items... all the big-box brands available—Graco, Evenflo, Eddie Bauer, etc...."

Furniture, Bedding & Decor	✓	$$	Prices
Gear & Equipment	✓	❹	Product availability
Nursing & Feeding	✓	❸	Staff knowledge
Safety & Babycare	✓	❸	Customer service
Clothing, Shoes & Accessories	✓	❸	Decor
Books, Toys & Entertainment	✓		

WWW.TARGET.COM

DORCHESTER—7 ALLSTATE RD (AT MASSACHUSETTS AVE); 617.602.1921; M-SA 8-10, SU 8-9; PARKING IN FRONT OF BLDG

Toys R Us ★★★½☆

"...not just toys, but also tons of gear and supplies including diapers and formula... a hectic shopping experience but the prices make it all worthwhile... I've experienced good and bad service at the same store on the same day... the stores are huge and can be overwhelming... most big brand-names available... leave the kids at home unless you want to end up with a cart full of toys..."

Furniture, Bedding & Decor	✓	$$$	Prices
Gear & Equipment	✓	❹	Product availability
Nursing & Feeding	✓	❸	Staff knowledge
Safety & Babycare	✓	❸	Customer service
Clothing, Shoes & Accessories	✓	❸	Decor
Books, Toys & Entertainment	✓		

WWW.TOYSRUS.COM

DORCHESTER—14 ALLSTATE RD (AT BAKER CT); 617.445.5159; M-SA 10-9, SU 11-6; PARKING LOT

Northern Suburbs

★★★★★ "lila picks"

- ★ Babystyle
- ★ Barefoot Books
- ★ Boston Baby
- ★ Stellabella Toys

baby basics

April Cornell ★★★½☆

"...beautiful, classic dresses and accessories for special occasions... I love the matching 'mommy and me' outfits... lots of fun knickknacks for sale... great selection of baby wear on their web site... rest assured your baby won't look like every other child in these adorable outfits... very frilly and girlie—beautiful..."

Furniture, Bedding & Decor .... ✗	$$$ .... Prices
Gear & Equipment .... ✗	❸ .... Product availability
Nursing & Feeding .... ✗	❹ .... Staff knowledge
Safety & Babycare .... ✗	❹ .... Customer service
Clothing, Shoes & Accessories ...... ✓	❹ .... Decor
Books, Toys & Entertainment .... ✗	

CAMBRIDGE—43 BRATTLE ST (AT HARVARD SQ); 617.661.8910; M-SA 10-7, SU 12-6

Babies R Us ★★★★☆

"...everything baby under one roof... they have a wide selection and carry most 'mainstream' items such as Graco, Fisher-Price, Avent and Britax... great customer service—given how big the stores are, I was pleasantly surprised at how attentive the staff was... easy return policy... super busy on weekends so try to visit on a weekday for the best service... keep an eye out for great coupons, deals and frequent sales... easy and comprehensive registry... shopping here is so easy—you've got to check it out..."

Furniture, Bedding & Decor .... ✓	$$$ .... Prices
Gear & Equipment .... ✓	❹ .... Product availability
Nursing & Feeding .... ✓	❹ .... Staff knowledge
Safety & Babycare .... ✓	❹ .... Customer service
Clothing, Shoes & Accessories ...... ✓	❹ .... Decor
Books, Toys & Entertainment .... ✓	

WWW.BABIESRUS.COM

EVERETT—12 MYSTIC VIEW RD (AT GATEWAY SHOPPING CTR); 617.381.1537; M-SA 9:30-9:30, SU 11-7; MALL PARKING

PEABODY—300 ANDOVER ST (AT PROSPECT ST); 978.532.0400; M-SA 9:30-9:30, SU 11-7; PARKING IN FRONT OF BLDG

Baby Depot At Burlington Coat Factory ★★★½☆

"...a large, 'super store' layout with a ton of baby gear... wide aisles, packed shelves, barely existent customer service and awesome prices... everything from bottles, car seats and strollers to gliders, cribs and

www.lilaguide.com

clothes... I always find something worth getting... a little disorganized and hard to locate items you're looking for... the staff is not always knowledgeable about their merchandise... return policy is store credit only... "

Furniture, Bedding & Decor	✓	$$	Prices
Gear & Equipment	✓	❸	Product availability
Nursing & Feeding	✓	❸	Staff knowledge
Safety & Babycare	✓	❸	Customer service
Clothing, Shoes & Accessories	✓	❸	Decor
Books, Toys & Entertainment	✓		

WWW.BABYDEPOT.COM

BILLERICA—480 BOSTON RD (AT TOWER FARM RD); 978.663.0405; M-SA 10-9, SU 11-6; PARKING LOT

PEABODY—310 ANDOVER ST (AT MACARTHUR BLVD); 978.531.8822; M-SA 9:30-9:30, SU 11-6; PARKING LOT

Baby Furniture Warehouse Store ★★★★☆

"*...great selection of cribs and furniture... everything you could need under one roof... very helpful staff and the owner himself is on the floor to assist shoppers... warehouse atmosphere, but the selection is what it's all about... worth a drive for the prices and variety of items... some items are pricey, but you get what you pay for in quality... they can order what they don't have on display...* "

Furniture, Bedding & Decor	✓	$$$	Prices
Gear & Equipment	✓	❹	Product availability
Nursing & Feeding	✗	❹	Staff knowledge
Safety & Babycare	✗	❹	Customer service
Clothing, Shoes & Accessories	✗	❸	Decor
Books, Toys & Entertainment	✗		

WWW.BABYFURNITUREWAREHOUSE.COM

READING—128 MARKET PL (AT 1 GENERAL WY); 781.942.7978; M 10-3, T TH10-8, F-SA 10-5:30, SU 12-5; PARKING LOT

BabyGap/GapKids ★★★★☆

"*...colorful baby and toddler clothing in clean, well-lit stores... great return policy... it's the Gap, so you know what you're getting—colorful, cute and well-made clothing... best place for baby hats... prices are reasonable especially since there's always a sale of some sort going on... sales, sales, sales—frequent and fantastic... everything I'm looking for in infant clothing—snap crotches, snaps up the front, all natural fabrics and great styling... fun seasonal selections—a great place to shop for gifts as well as for your own kids... although it can get busy, staff generally seem accommodating and helpful...* "

Furniture, Bedding & Decor	✗	$$$	Prices
Gear & Equipment	✗	❹	Product availability
Nursing & Feeding	✗	❹	Staff knowledge
Safety & Babycare	✗	❹	Customer service
Clothing, Shoes & Accessories	✓	❹	Decor
Books, Toys & Entertainment	✗		

WWW.GAP.COM

BURLINGTON—1 MALL RD (AT MIDDLESEX TPKE); 781.273.0550; M-SA 10-9, SU 11-7; MALL PARKING

BURLINGTON—75 MIDDLESEX TPKE (AT OLD CONCORD RD); 781.221.6711; M-SA 10-10, SU 11-7; PARKING IN FRONT OF BLDG

CAMBRIDGE—100 CAMBRIDGESIDE PL (AT CAMBRIDGESIDE GALLERIA); 617.494.9181; M-SA 10-9:30, SU 11-7; PARKING LOT

PEABODY—210 ANDOVER ST (AT PROSPECT ST); 617.558.3237; M-SA 10-9:30, SU 11-6; PARKING LOT

SAUGUS—1201 BROADWAY (AT SQUARE ONE MALL); 781.233.9200; M-SA 10-10, SU 11-6; MALL PARKING

Babystyle ★★★★★

"...they offer a wonderful range of children's clothing, educational toys, gear and even maternity items... the atmosphere is great for babies—you really feel the staff there want you to be comfortable... great, friendly service... unfortunately what is on their web site is not always in the store... if you are looking for a special occasion gift or a really chic diaper bag then you should come here... their line of baby and toddler clothing is really cute and wears well..."

Furniture, Bedding & Decor ✓	$$$$	Prices
Gear & Equipment ✓	❹	Product availability
Nursing & Feeding ✓	❹	Staff knowledge
Safety & Babycare ✓	❹	Customer service
Clothing, Shoes & Accessories ✓	❹	Decor
Books, Toys & Entertainment ✓		

WWW.BABYSTYLE.COM

BURLINGTON—75 MIDDLESEX TURNPIKE (AT BURLINGTON MALL); 781.653.0004; M-SA 10-9, SU 11-6

Barefoot Books ★★★★★

"...fantastic books and great decor... a lovely place to spend an hour browsing and letting your child flip through the books in the play area... loved the books my daughter received for her birthday... they also sell artwork in the store... storytelling and other activities for children... staff members are wonderful and offer great suggestions for different age groups... they even publish their own collection called The Bear Series..."

Furniture, Bedding & Decor ✗	$$$	Prices
Gear & Equipment ✗	❹	Product availability
Nursing & Feeding ✗	❺	Staff knowledge
Safety & Babycare ✗	❺	Customer service
Clothing, Shoes & Accessories ✗	❺	Decor
Books, Toys & Entertainment ✓		

WWW.BAREFOOTBOOKS.COM

CAMBRIDGE—1771 MASSACHUSETTS AVE (AT FOREST ST); 617.349.1610; M-SA 10-6 TH 10-7 SU 12-5 ; PARKING LOT

Boston Baby ★★★★★

"...a great place for first-time parents... an amazing array of baby furniture... they used to carry lots of gear too, but don't anymore... the staff was always available to answer any questions... great selection of cribs and other items for the nursery... good variety of high-end stuff which is hard to find elsewhere... wonderful displays and prices are reasonable given the quality... a great place to see lots of baby furniture under one roof..."

Furniture, Bedding & Decor ✓	$$$$	Prices
Gear & Equipment ✓	❹	Product availability
Nursing & Feeding ✗	❹	Staff knowledge
Safety & Babycare ✗	❹	Customer service
Clothing, Shoes & Accessories ✗	❹	Decor
Books, Toys & Entertainment ✓		

WWW.BOSTONBABY.COM

DANVERS—10 NEWBURY ST (AT ARCHMEADOW DR); 978.777.1414; M-T-F-SA 10-6, W-TH 10-8, SU 12-5; PARKING LOT

Calliope ★★★★☆

"...I adore their selection of the newest and softest stuffed animals, infant toys and bath accessories... they keep the toys of yesteryear alive... great salespeople, who always were willing to help with

www.lilaguide.com

questions... a little cozy, but still a very fun place to browse and their window displays are the best... unique and beautiful children's clothes and shoes that are priced accordingly... lots of European and hard to find brands... charming inventory in the middle of Harvard Square... **"**

Furniture, Bedding & Decor	✗	$$$$	Prices
Gear & Equipment	✗	❸	Product availability
Nursing & Feeding	✗	❹	Staff knowledge
Safety & Babycare	✗	❹	Customer service
Clothing, Shoes & Accessories	✓	❹	Decor
Books, Toys & Entertainment	✓		

CAMBRIDGE—33 BRATTLE ST (AT CHURCH ST); 617.876.4149; M-SA 10-6:30, SU 12-5; DISCOUNTED PARKING AT CHARLES HOTEL GARAGE

Casa De Moda Clothing Dance & Gifts ★★★½☆

"*...their dance section has the basics and the fantastic... perfect for preparing for the first dance or gymnastics class... as a mother of twins, I loved that they had devoted a whole area to twin things—cards, gifts, calendar... high-quality and fun... selection is limited, but a good place to find a gift for a little ballerina...* **"**

Furniture, Bedding & Decor	✗	$$	Prices
Gear & Equipment	✗	❸	Product availability
Nursing & Feeding	✗	❹	Staff knowledge
Safety & Babycare	✗	❹	Customer service
Clothing, Shoes & Accessories	✗	❹	Decor
Books, Toys & Entertainment	✗		

WWW.CASADEMODA.COM

BEVERLY—272 CABOT ST (AT WINTER ST); 978.922.8100; M-W 9:30-6, TH-F 9:30-8, SA 9:30-6, SU 12-4; PARKING LOT

Chamberi Shoes ★★★★½

"*...wonderful selection of mostly Spanish infant/children's shoes... real leather shoes that are breathable and better for a growing baby's feet... terrific selection for boys and girls... my children get all their shoes here... well worth the money... great quality and very comfortable shoes...* **"**

Furniture, Bedding & Decor	✗	$$$	Prices
Gear & Equipment	✗	❹	Product availability
Nursing & Feeding	✗	❹	Staff knowledge
Safety & Babycare	✗	❹	Customer service
Clothing, Shoes & Accessories	✓	❹	Decor
Books, Toys & Entertainment	✗		

WWW.CHAMBERISHOES.COM

WOBURN—364 CAMBRIDGE RD (AT SOUTHDALE SHOPPING CTR); 781.938.4107; M-SA 10-7, SU 12-5

Children's Orchard ★★★½☆

"*...a friendly resale boutique... the clothes and gear are super clean and sold at amazing prices... amazing prices on clothing that is hardly used and practically brand new... shoes, toys, furniture, hair pretties, crib sets, etc... fantastic deals on well-selected used items... prices are great and you can pretty much always find something useful... a great place to buy those everyday play outfits... a lot of name brands at steeply discounted prices...* **"**

Furniture, Bedding & Decor	✓	$$	Prices
Gear & Equipment	✓	❸	Product availability
Nursing & Feeding	✓	❹	Staff knowledge
Safety & Babycare	✓	❹	Customer service
Clothing, Shoes & Accessories	✓	❸	Decor
Books, Toys & Entertainment	✓		

WWW.CHILDRENSORCHARD.COM

BILLERICA—446 BOSTON RD (AT CHARNSTAFFE LN); 978.671.0008; M-SA 9:30-6, SU 12-5; PARKING LOT

DANVERS—139 ENDICOTT ST (AT ENDICOTT PLAZA); 978.777.3355; M-SA 10-6, SU 12-5; PARKING LOT

NEWBURYPORT—1 MERRIMAC ST (AT INN ST MALL); 978.462.5437; M-SA 9-6, SU 12-5; MALL PARKING

Children's Place, The ★★★½☆

"...great bargains on cute clothing... shoes, socks, swimsuits, sunglasses and everything in between... lots of '3 for $20' type deals on sleepers, pants and mix-and-match separates... so much more affordable than the other 'big chains'... don't expect the most unique stuff here, but it wears and washes well... cheap clothing for cheap prices... you can leave the store with bags full of clothes without putting a huge dent in your wallet..."

Furniture, Bedding & Decor	✗	$$ .... Prices
Gear & Equipment	✗	❹ .... Product availability
Nursing & Feeding	✗	❹ .... Staff knowledge
Safety & Babycare	✗	❹ .... Customer service
Clothing, Shoes & Accessories	✓	❹ .... Decor
Books, Toys & Entertainment	✓	

WWW.CHILDRENSPLACE.COM

BURLINGTON—1016 BURLINGTON MALL RD (AT BRULINGTON MALL); 781.229.6678; M-SA 10-10, SU 11-7; MALL PARKING

CAMBRIDGE—100 CAMBRIDGESIDE PLACE (AT CAMBRIDGE GALLERIA); 617.494.6085; M-SA 10-9:30 SU 11-6:30; PARKING LOT

PEABODY—152 ANDOVER ST (AT HWY 128); 978.532.5494; M-SA 10-10, SU 11-6; PARKING LOT

SAUGUS—1277 BROADWAY DR (AT SQUARE ONE MALL); 781.231.9515; M-SA 10-10, SU 11-6; PARKING LOT

Costco ★★★½☆

"...dependable place for bulk diapers, wipes and formula at discount prices... clothing selection is very hit-or-miss... avoid shopping there during nights and weekends if possible, because parking and checkout lines are brutal... they don't have a huge selection of brands, but the brands they do have are almost always in stock and at a great price... lowest prices around for diapers and formula... kid's clothing tends to be picked through, but it's worth looking for great deals on name-brand items like Carter's..."

Furniture, Bedding & Decor	✓	$$ .... Prices
Gear & Equipment	✓	❸ .... Product availability
Nursing & Feeding	✓	❸ .... Staff knowledge
Safety & Babycare	✓	❸ .... Customer service
Clothing, Shoes & Accessories	✓	❷ .... Decor
Books, Toys & Entertainment	✓	

WWW.COSTCO.COM

DANVERS—11 NEWBURY ST; 978.850.1000; M-F 11-8:30, SA 9:30-6, SU 10-6

EVERETT—2 MYSTIC VIEW RD; 617.544.4806; M-F 11-8:30, SA 9:30-6, SU 10-6

Curious George Goes To Wordsworth ★★★★½

"...wow—this bookstore has it all... not just books, they have toys and boardgames, too... they know their children's books and are always ready with an excellent, age-appropriate recommendation... fun store... staff always helps me find the perfect gifts and makes it very easy to

special order items too... this is my favorite children's book store and web site... **"**

Furniture, Bedding & Decor............ ✗	$$... Prices
Gear & Equipment .... ✗	❹ .... Product availability
Nursing & Feeding .... ✗	❺ .... Staff knowledge
Safety & Babycare .... ✗	❺ ....Customer service
Clothing, Shoes & Accessories .... ✗	❺ .... Decor
Books, Toys & Entertainment .... ✓	

WWW.CURIOUSG.COM

CAMBRIDGE—1 JFK ST (AT ELIOT ST); 617.498.0062; DAILY 9-7; STREET PARKING

Frida Bee ★★★★☆

"...*terrific resale shop... bright and clean... a must for parents hoping to save some money on clothing for kids and babies... name brands at consignment shop prices... great selection and unbeatable prices... many of the best brands are available in a great variety of sizes... friendly, helpful neighborhood atmosphere... I found the selection well-washed and in great condition... good location with access to other kids stores in Huron Village...* **"**

Furniture, Bedding & Decor............ ✓	$$... Prices
Gear & Equipment .... ✓	❹ .... Product availability
Nursing & Feeding .... ✗	❹ .... Staff knowledge
Safety & Babycare .... ✗	❹ ....Customer service
Clothing, Shoes & Accessories ...... ✓	❹ .... Decor
Books, Toys & Entertainment .... ✓	

WWW.FRIDABEE.COM

CAMBRIDGE—360 HURON AVE (AT WYMAN RD); 617.547.1145; M-SA 10-6; PARKING LOT

Goodhearts ★★★☆☆

"...*special occasion shop with lovely clothes... Zutano, Petit Bateau, Cozy Toes... staff is always helpful whether it's choosing a size or helping with gift ideas... the back room has sale items, but they are nonreturnable so be careful... too expensive for day-to-day shopping... limited bathroom access so go before you get there...* **"**

Furniture, Bedding & Decor............ ✗	$$$$.. Prices
Gear & Equipment .... ✗	❹ .... Product availability
Nursing & Feeding .... ✗	❹ .... Staff knowledge
Safety & Babycare .... ✗	❹ ....Customer service
Clothing, Shoes & Accessories .... ✗	❹ .... Decor
Books, Toys & Entertainment .... ✗	

WWW.GOODHEARTSSHOP.COM

READING—642 MAIN ST (AT HARNDEN ST); 781.942.9700; M-SA 10-5 ; PARKING BEHIND BLDG

Gymboree ★★★★☆

"...*beautiful clothing and great quality... colorful and stylish baby and kids wear... lots of fun birthday gift ideas... easy exchange and return policy... items usually go on sale pretty quickly... save money with Gymbucks... many stores have a play area which makes shopping with my kids fun (let alone feasible)...* **"**

Furniture, Bedding & Decor............ ✗	$$$... Prices
Gear & Equipment .... ✗	❹ .... Product availability
Nursing & Feeding .... ✗	❹ .... Staff knowledge
Safety & Babycare .... ✗	❹ ....Customer service
Clothing, Shoes & Accessories ...... ✓	❹ .... Decor
Books, Toys & Entertainment .... ✓	

WWW.GYMBOREE.COM

participate in our survey at

BURLINGTON—1 BURLINGTON MALL (AT CAMBRIDGE ST); 781.272.0967; M-SA 10-10, SU 11-7; MALL PARKING

PEABODY—RTE 128 & 114 (AT FOREST ST); 978.532.6644; M-SA 10-10, SU 11-6; PARKING LOT

SAUGUS—1201 BROADWAY RTE ONE SOUTH (AT SQUARE ONE MALL); 781.233.3572; M-SA 10-10, SU 11-6; MALL PARKING

Haus ★★★★½

"...hand-picked selection of hard to find European children's lines like Selecta wooden toys, Icky and Zutano... the handmade German receiving blankets are the best... I always shop here for baby showers gifts... everything is so unique that each gift is well-received... gifts from here are a sure thing... the owner always has the perfect suggestion... stop by, you'll love it..."

Furniture, Bedding & Decor	✗	$$$ ... Prices
Gear & Equipment	✗	❺ ... Product availability
Nursing & Feeding	✗	❺ ... Staff knowledge
Safety & Babycare	✗	❺ ... Customer service
Clothing, Shoes & Accessories	✓	❺ ... Decor
Books, Toys & Entertainment	✓	

WWW.HAUS-LOWELL.COM

LOWELL—17 SHATTUCK ST (AT DUTTON ST); 978.458.4287; T-F 11-5, SA 10-5; STREET PARKING

Henry Bear's Park ★★★★☆

"...a wonderful resource for fun and imaginative children's toys, books, and doo-dads... tons of choices for evey age and developmental stage... adorable store with great selection of gifts and toys... we are there regularly to shop, play or enjoy their weekly story time... a great change from chain stores... thoughtful selection of children's books... an added bonus is the neighborhood bulletin board, which gets a lot of use..."

Furniture, Bedding & Decor	✗	$$$ ... Prices
Gear & Equipment	✗	❹ ... Product availability
Nursing & Feeding	✗	❹ ... Staff knowledge
Safety & Babycare	✗	❹ ... Customer service
Clothing, Shoes & Accessories	✗	❹ ... Decor
Books, Toys & Entertainment	✓	

WWW.HENRYBEAR.COM

ARLINGTON—685 MASSACHUSETTS AVE (AT WATER ST); 781.646.9400; M-T 9:30-6, W-F 9:30-7, SA 9:30-6, SU 11-5; PARKING LOT

CAMBRIDGE—361 HURON AVE (AT STANDISH ST); 617.547.8424; M-T 9:30-6, W-F 9:30-7, SA 9:30-6, SU 11-5; STREET PARKING

Jordan's Furniture ★★★★☆

"...you can't beat Jordan's when shopping for quality furniture you want to last... reasonable prices and great selection... perfect for 'big kid' beds and furniture sets... my son loves the taxi-car strollers... customer service shines at Jordan's... all kinds of furniture for all budgets... they stand behind all of their products... their displays are amazing and they have fun events to keep the kids entertained while shopping... more than a furniture store it's an adventure for the kids..."

Furniture, Bedding & Decor	✓	$$$ ... Prices
Gear & Equipment	✗	❹ ... Product availability
Nursing & Feeding	✗	❹ ... Staff knowledge
Safety & Babycare	✗	❹ ... Customer service
Clothing, Shoes & Accessories	✗	❹ ... Decor
Books, Toys & Entertainment	✗	

WWW.JORDANS.COM

READING—50 WALKERS BROOK DR (AT NEWCROSSING RD); 781.944.9090; M-SA 10-10, SU 12-6; PARKING LOT

KB Toys ★★★☆☆

"...hectic and always buzzing... wall-to-wall plastic and blinking lights... more Fisher-Price, Elmo and Sponge Bob than the eye can handle... a toy super store with discounted prices... they always have some kind of special sale going on... if you're looking for the latest and greatest popular toy, then look no further—not the place for unique or unusual toys... perfect for bulk toy shopping—especially around the holidays..."

Furniture, Bedding & Decor........... ✗	$$ .... Prices
Gear & Equipment .... ✗	❸ .... Product availability
Nursing & Feeding .... ✗	❸ .... Staff knowledge
Safety & Babycare .... ✗	❸ .... Customer service
Clothing, Shoes & Accessories .... ✗	❸ .... Decor
Books, Toys & Entertainment .... ✓	

WWW.KBTOYS.COM

BURLINGTON—75 MIDDLESEX ST (AT BURLINGTON MALL); 781.273.3867; M-SA 10-10 SU 11-7; MALL PARKING

CAMBRIDGE—1ST & COMMERCE ST (AT CAMBRIDGESIDE GALLERIA); 617.494.8519; M-SA 10-9:30 SU 11-7; PARKING LOT

CHELMSFORD—288 CHELMSFORD ST (AT EASTGATE PLAZA); 978.250.8058; M-SA 9:30-9 SU 10-6; PARKING LOT

METHUEN—90 PLEASANT VALLEY ST (AT THE LOOP); 978.683.2539; DAILY 10-9; MALL PARKING

SALEM—263 HIGHLAND AVE (AT HIGHLANDER PLAZA); 978.741.2990; M-SA 9:30-9, SU 10-6; PARKING LOT

SAUGUS—1277 BROADWAY DR (AT SQUARE ONE MALL); 781.231.9466; DAILY 10-9; MALL PARKING

STONEHAM—ROUTE 28, MAIN ST (AT REDSTONE SHOPPING CTR); 781.438.7986; M-SA 9:30-9, SU 10-6; PARKING LOT

Kids En Vogue ★★★☆☆

"...fancy, but fabulous... if you want to dress your kid like a rock star, this store is for you... the cutest flair pants around... all the top kid's lines... trendy shoes, too... it ain't cheap... perfect for standing out in a crowd or a super special gift..."

Furniture, Bedding & Decor........... ✓	$$$ .... Prices
Gear & Equipment .... ✗	❹ .... Product availability
Nursing & Feeding .... ✗	❹ .... Staff knowledge
Safety & Babycare .... ✗	❹ .... Customer service
Clothing, Shoes & Accessories ...... ✓	❹ .... Decor
Books, Toys & Entertainment .... ✗	

WWW.KIDSENVOGUE.COM

PEABODY—215 NEWBURY ST (AT LOWELL ST); 978.536.0740; T-SA 10-5; PARKING LOT

Klassy Kids

Furniture, Bedding & Decor........... ✗	✗ .... Gear & Equipment
Nursing & Feeding .... ✗	✗ .... Safety & Babycare
Clothing, Shoes & Accessories ...... ✓	✓ .... Books, Toys & Entertainment

MELROSE—515 MAIN ST (AT FOSTER ST); 781.662.1737; M-SA 10-5; PARKING LOT

Kohl's ★★★★☆

"...nice one-stop shopping for the whole family—everything from clothing to baby gear... great sales on clothing and a good selection of higher-end brands... stylish, inexpensive clothes for babies through 24 months... very easy shopping experience... dirt-cheap sales and

participate in our survey at

clearance prices... nothing super fancy, but just right for those everyday romper outfits... Graco, Eddie Bauer and other well-known brands... "

Furniture, Bedding & Decor	✓	$$	Prices
Gear & Equipment	✓	❸	Product availability
Nursing & Feeding	✓	❸	Staff knowledge
Safety & Babycare	✓	❸	Customer service
Clothing, Shoes & Accessories	✓	❸	Decor
Books, Toys & Entertainment	✓		

WWW.KOHLS.COM

BURLINGTON—150 LEXINGTON ST (AT BURLINGTON MALL RD); 781.229.6494; M-SA 8-10, SU 10-8; MALL PARKING

CHELMSFORD—265-10 CHELMSFORD ST (AT MANAHAN ST); 978.250.0054; M-SA 8-10, SU 10-8; FREE PARKING

DANVERS—50 INDEPENDENCE WY (AT LIBERTY TREE MALL); 978.774.6199; M-SA 8-10, SU 10-8; MALL PARKING

MEDFORD—3850 MYSTIC VALLEY PKWY (AT MEADOW GLEN MALL); 781.395.6001; M-SA 8-10, SU 10-8; MALL PARKING

SAUGUS—333 BROADWAY (AT NEWBURYPORT TPKE); 781.941.8145; M-SA 8-10, SU 10-8; FREE PARKING

WOBURN—425 WASHINGTON ST (AT MISHAWUM RD); 781.376.1222; M-SA 8-10, SU 10-8; PARKING LOT

Learning Tree Store ★★★★★

" *...outstanding for their nature-oriented learning and exploration... reasonable prices... cool store with a real mission to helping parents and the community... we love to go to their special events... this story makes our home teaching so much easier and more fun... I highly recommend this store to other parents with children with special needs...* "

Furniture, Bedding & Decor	✗	$$$	Prices
Gear & Equipment	✗	❹	Product availability
Nursing & Feeding	✗	❹	Staff knowledge
Safety & Babycare	✗	❺	Customer service
Clothing, Shoes & Accessories	✗	❹	Decor
Books, Toys & Entertainment	✓		

WWW.TLTREE.COM

STONEHAM—62-B MONTVALE AVE (AT MAPLE ST); 781.438.8101; M 10-6, T-TH 10-8, F 10-6, SA 10-5, SU 12-5; PARKING LOT

Lester Harry's ★★★★☆

" *...upscale boutique with a good selection of different high-end product lines... they carry brands I've only ever been able to find online... exquisite, trendy items... staff is wonderful, they really know their great clothes and linens for kids... wonderful gifts here, from gorgeously unique blankets to the Bugaboo Frog... expensive, but well worth it... great place to go for a unique gift or a European touch...* "

Furniture, Bedding & Decor	✓	$$$$	Prices
Gear & Equipment	✗	❹	Product availability
Nursing & Feeding	✗	❹	Staff knowledge
Safety & Babycare	✗	❹	Customer service
Clothing, Shoes & Accessories	✓	❹	Decor
Books, Toys & Entertainment	✗		

WWW.LESTERHARRYS.COM

MARBLEHEAD—140 WASHINGTON ST (AT DARLING ST); 781.631.4343; M-SA 10-6, SU 12-5; STREET PARKING

Macy's ★★★★½☆

" *...Macy's has it all and I never leave empty-handed... if you time your visit right you can find some great deals... go during the week so you don't get overwhelmed with the weekend crowd... good for staples as* *well as beautiful party dresses for girls... lots of brand-names like Carter's, Guess, and Ralph Lauren... not much in terms of assistance... newspaper coupons and sales help keep the cost down... some stores are better organized and maintained than others... if you're going to shop at a department store for your baby, then Macy's is a safe bet...* **"**

Furniture, Bedding & Decor	✓	$$$ .... Prices
Gear & Equipment	✗	❸ ...... Product availability
Nursing & Feeding	✗	❸ ...... Staff knowledge
Safety & Babycare	✗	❸ ...... Customer service
Clothing, Shoes & Accessories	✓	❸ ...... Decor
Books, Toys & Entertainment	✓	

WWW.MACYS.COM

BURLINGTON—1300 MIDDLESEX TURNPIKE (AT THE MITRE); 781.272.6000; M-SA 10-10, SU 11-7; PARKING LOT

PEABODY—NORTH SHORE PEABODY MALL (AT NORTH SHORE PEABODY MALL); 978.531.9000; M-SA 10-10, SU 11-7; MALL PARKING

Marblehead Toy Shop, The ★★★★½

"*...the un-Toys R Us... a toy store with old world charm... toys, books, puzzles... enough arts and crafts projects to keep your kid busy for a year... quality toys... open every day... just a fun place to visit and of course you always end up with something... I usually end up with a gift for me and my daughter...* **"**

Furniture, Bedding & Decor	✗	$$$ .... Prices
Gear & Equipment	✗	❹ ...... Product availability
Nursing & Feeding	✗	❹ ...... Staff knowledge
Safety & Babycare	✗	❹ ...... Customer service
Clothing, Shoes & Accessories	✗	❹ ...... Decor
Books, Toys & Entertainment	✓	

MARBLEHEAD—46 ATLANTIC AVE (AT COMMERCIAL ST); 781.631.9900; M-W 9:30-5:30, TH 9:30-8, F 9:30-5:30, SA 9-5:30, SU 12-5; PARKING LOT

Maxima Gift Center ★★★★½

"*...unique gifts and toys for all ages—including some hard-to-find items... great Seuss collection... plenty of new baby gifts like fun onesies and bibs... recently expanded to include a large children's selection... a great shop to get an artistic gift... lots of great books as well as Manhattan toys and Lizzy Bee toys... good ideas for making your own gifts...* **"**

Furniture, Bedding & Decor	✗	$$$ .... Prices
Gear & Equipment	✗	❹ ...... Product availability
Nursing & Feeding	✗	❹ ...... Staff knowledge
Safety & Babycare	✗	❹ ...... Customer service
Clothing, Shoes & Accessories	✗	❺ ...... Decor
Books, Toys & Entertainment	✓	

WWW.MAXIMACENTER.COM

ARLINGTON—212 MASSACHUSETTS AVE (AT LAKE ST); 781.646.6835; M-T 10-7, W-TH 10-8, F-SA 10-10, SU 12-6; STREET PARKING

Mud Puddle Toys ★★★☆☆

"*...this store will take care of your gift needs all year long... fun, interactive games... cute and a bit pricey... watch out for the return policy... free gift wrapping and they will put together the expensive items for you—now that's service!...* **"**

Furniture, Bedding & Decor	✗	$$$ .... Prices
Gear & Equipment	✗	❸ ...... Product availability
Nursing & Feeding	✗	❸ ...... Staff knowledge
Safety & Babycare	✗	❹ ...... Customer service
Clothing, Shoes & Accessories	✗	❹ ...... Decor
Books, Toys & Entertainment	✓	

WWW.MUDPUDDLETOYS.COM

MARBLEHEAD—1 PLEASANT ST (AT WASHINGTON ST); 781.631.0814; M-W 10-5, TH-SA 10-6, SU 11:30-5; STREET PARKING

Old Navy ★★★★☆

"...hip and 'in' clothes for infants and tots... plenty of steals on clearance items... T-shirts and pants for $10 or less... busy, busy, busy—long lines, especially on weekends... nothing fancy and you won't mind when your kids get down and dirty in these clothes... easy to wash, decent quality... you can shop for your baby, your toddler, your teen and yourself all at the same time... clothes are especially affordable when you hit their sales (post-holiday sales are amazing!)... **"**

Furniture, Bedding & Decor	✗	$$ .... Prices
Gear & Equipment	✗	❹ .... Product availability
Nursing & Feeding	✗	❸ .... Staff knowledge
Safety & Babycare	✗	❸ .... Customer service
Clothing, Shoes & Accessories	✓	❸ .... Decor
Books, Toys & Entertainment	✗	

WWW.OLDNAVY.COM

BURLINGTON—43 MIDDLESEX TPKE (AT ADAMS ST); 781.229.0996; M-SA 9-9 SU 11-6; PARKING LOT

CAMBRIDGE—100 CAMBRIDGESIDE PL (AT CAMBRIDGESIDE GALLERIA); 617.577.0070; M-SA 10-9:30, SU 11-7; PARKING LOT

DANVERS—100 INDEPENDENCE WY (AT LIBERTY TREE MALL); 978.762.4700; M-SA 9-9:30, SU 11-6; PARKING LOT

EVERETT—9 MYSTIC VIEW RD (AT REVERE BEACH PKWY); 617.387.1422; M-SA 9-9, SU 10-6; PARKING LOT

METHUEN—90 PLEASANT VALLEY ST (AT MILK ST); 978.689.9066; M-SA 10-9, SU 11-7; PARKING LOT

Payless Shoe Source ★★★☆☆

"...a good place for deals on children's shoes... staff is helpful with sizing... the selection and prices for kids' shoes can't be beat, but the quality isn't always spectacular... good leather shoes for cheap... great variety of all sizes and widths... I get my son's shoes here and don't feel like I'm wasting my money since he'll outgrow them in 3 months anyway... **"**

Furniture, Bedding & Decor	✗	$$ .... Prices
Gear & Equipment	✗	❸ .... Product availability
Nursing & Feeding	✗	❸ .... Staff knowledge
Safety & Babycare	✗	❸ .... Customer service
Clothing, Shoes & Accessories	✓	❸ .... Decor
Books, Toys & Entertainment	✗	

WWW.PAYLESS.COM

CAMBRIDGE—100 CAMBRIDGESIDE PL (AT CAMBRIDGESIDE GALLERIA MALL); 617.225.0517; M-SA 9:30-9:30, SU 11-7

CAMBRIDGE—599 MASSACHUSETTS AVE (AT ESSEX ST); 617.864.4529; M-SA 9-8, SU 9-6

Port O'Call Exchange

Furniture, Bedding & Decor	✗	✗ .... Gear & Equipment
Nursing & Feeding	✗	✗ .... Safety & Babycare
Clothing, Shoes & Accessories	✓	✓ .... Books, Toys & Entertainment

GLOUCESTER—67 MAIN ST (AT CHURCH ST); 978.283.4899; M-S 10-4; STREET PARKING

Pottery Barn Kids ★★★★½

"...stylish furniture, rugs, rockers and much more... they've found the right mix between quality and price... finally a company that stands

behind what they sell—their customer service is great... gorgeous baby decor and furniture that will make your nursery to-die-for... the play area is so much fun—my daughter never wants to leave... a beautiful store with tons of ideas for setting up your nursery or kid's room... bright colors and cute patterns with basics to mix and match... if you see something in the catalog, but not in the store, just ask because they often have it in the back... **"**

Furniture, Bedding & Decor ✓	$$$$ .... Prices
Gear & Equipment ✗	❹ .... Product availability
Nursing & Feeding ✗	❹ .... Staff knowledge
Safety & Babycare ✗	❹ .... Customer service
Clothing, Shoes & Accessories ✗	❺ .... Decor
Books, Toys & Entertainment ✓	

WWW.POTTERYBARNKIDS.COM

BURLINGTON—75 MIDDLESEX TURNPIKE (AT WHEELER RD); 781.221.5833; M-SA 10-10, SU 11-7; PARKING LOT

Priceless Kids ★★★½☆

"*...inexpensive clothes and shoes even with brand-name labels... especially helpful for the early months as babies grow quickly... great place for t-shirt, socks and accessories... affordable and cute clothes, but quality can vary... good when you're not looking for anything in particular... great bargains and interesting variety of clothing...* **"**

Furniture, Bedding & Decor ✗	$$ .... Prices
Gear & Equipment ✗	❸ .... Product availability
Nursing & Feeding ✗	❸ .... Staff knowledge
Safety & Babycare ✗	❸ .... Customer service
Clothing, Shoes & Accessories ✓	❸ .... Decor
Books, Toys & Entertainment ✗	

WWW.PRICELESSKIDS.COM

SAUGUS—635 BROADWAY (AT THOMAS ST); 781.233.5029; M-SA 10-9, SU 12-6; PARKING LOT

Rugged Bear ★★★★☆

"*...their merchandise is truly top quality... employees go above and beyond to help... a little pricey, but the the durability of the clothes and shoes are worth it... top brands as well as their own which we have had very good luck with... if they don't have the size/style you are looking for they are more than happy to call other stores and have it sent to you... go and get great outdoor wear for your kids... sales near the end of the season are the best times to go...* **"**

Furniture, Bedding & Decor ✗	$$$ .... Prices
Gear & Equipment ✓	❹ .... Product availability
Nursing & Feeding ✗	❹ .... Staff knowledge
Safety & Babycare ✗	❹ .... Customer service
Clothing, Shoes & Accessories ✓	❹ .... Decor
Books, Toys & Entertainment ✗	

WWW.RUGGEDBEAR.COM

ANDOVER—34 PARK ST (AT BARTLETT ST); 978.474.0666; M-T-W-F-SA 9:30-5:30, TH 9:30-8, SU 12-5; PARKING LOT

BEVERLY—2-4 ENON ST (AT DODGE ST); 978.927.9212; M-SA 9:30-5:30, SU 12-5; PARKING LOT

Sears ★★★☆☆

"*...a decent selection of clothes and basic baby equipment... check out the Kids Club program—it's a great way to save money... you go to Sears to save money, not to be pampered... the quality of their merchandise is better than Wal-Mart, but don't expect anything too special or different... not much in terms of gear, but tons of well-priced baby and toddler clothing...* **"**

participate in our survey at

Furniture, Bedding & Decor ✓	$$ .... Prices
Gear & Equipment ✓	❸ .... Product availability
Nursing & Feeding ✓	❸ .... Staff knowledge
Safety & Babycare ✓	❸ .... Customer service
Clothing, Shoes & Accessories ✓	❸ .... Decor
Books, Toys & Entertainment ✓	

WWW.SEARS.COM

BURLINGTON—1100 MIDDLESEX TPKE (AT BULINGTON MALL); 781.221.4900; M-SA 9:30-10, SU 11-5; MALL PARKING

CAMBRIDGE—100 CAMBRIDGESIDE PL (AT CAMBRIDGESIDE GALLERIA); 617.252.9001; M-SA 10-9, SU 10-6 ; MALL PARKING

PEABODY—HWYS 114 & 128 (AT HWY 128); 978.977.7500; M-SA 9-10, SU 11-7

SAUGUS—1325 BROADWAY (AT SQUARE ONE MALL); 781.231.4500; M-SA 9:30-10, SU 11-7; MALL PARKING

Stellabella Toys ★★★★★

"...great selection of educational toys... the environment is very kid-friendly... nice play area and love the sing-alongs... knowledgeable staff who are happy to see the kids take interest in new toys and games... fun location that's worth a visit when you're in the area...I appreciate the child-can-touch atmosphere... creative and unique items... great selection of non-commercial toys..."

Furniture, Bedding & Decor ✗	$$$ .... Prices
Gear & Equipment ✗	❹ .... Product availability
Nursing & Feeding ✗	❹ .... Staff knowledge
Safety & Babycare ✗	❹ .... Customer service
Clothing, Shoes & Accessories ✗	❹ .... Decor
Books, Toys & Entertainment ✓	

CAMBRIDGE—1360 CAMBRIDGE ST (AT SPRINGFIELD ST); 617.491.6290; M-SA 9:30-7, SU 10-5; LOT AT SPRINGFIELD ST/METERED STREET PARKING

Stride Rite Shoes ★★★★½☆

"...wonderful selection of baby and toddler shoes... sandals, sneakers, and even special-occasion shoes... decent quality shoes that last... they know a lot about kids' shoes and take the time to get it right—they always measure my son's feet before fittings... store sizes vary, but they always have something in stock that works... they've even special ordered shoes for my daughter... a fun 'first shoe' buying experience..."

Furniture, Bedding & Decor ✗	$$$ .... Prices
Gear & Equipment ✗	❹ .... Product availability
Nursing & Feeding ✗	❹ .... Staff knowledge
Safety & Babycare ✗	❹ .... Customer service
Clothing, Shoes & Accessories ✓	❹ .... Decor
Books, Toys & Entertainment ✗	

WWW.STRIDERITE.COM

BURLINGTON—95 MALL RD (AT LEXINGTON ST); 781.272.7994; M-SA 10-10, SU 11-7; MALL PARKING

PEABODY—137-ROUTES 128 & 114 (AT NORTHSHORE MALL); 978.531.3770; M-SA 10-10, SU 11-6; MALL PARKING

PEABODY—RTE 128 (AT NOTHSHORE SHOPPING CTR); 978.531.3770

Talbots Kids ★★★★½☆

"...a nice alternative to the typical department store experience... expensive, but fantastic quality... great for holiday and special occasion outfits including christening outfits... well-priced, conservative children's clothing... cute selections for infants, toddlers and kids... sales are fantastic—up to half off at least a couple times a year... the best part is, you can also shop for yourself while shopping for baby..."

Furniture, Bedding & Decor	✗	$$$$	Prices
Gear & Equipment	✗	❹	Product availability
Nursing & Feeding	✗	❹	Staff knowledge
Safety & Babycare	✗	❹	Customer service
Clothing, Shoes & Accessories	✓	❹	Decor
Books, Toys & Entertainment	✗		

WWW.TALBOTS.COM

BURLINGTON—1125 BURLINGTON MALL (AT THE BURLINGTON MALL); 781.270.9500; M-SA 10-10, SU 11-7; MALL PARKING

PEABODY—STATE HWY 128 N AT ANDOVER ST (AT N SHORE RD); 978.977.9355; M-SA 10-10, SU 11-6; PARKING LOT

Target ★★★★☆

"...our favorite place to shop for kids' stuff—good selection and very affordable... guilt-free shopping—kids grow so fast so I don't want to pay high department-store prices... everything from diapers and sippy cups to car seats and strollers... easy return policy... generally helpful staff, but you don't go for the service—you go for the prices... decent registry that won't freak your friends out with outrageous prices... easy, convenient shopping for well-priced items... all the big-box brands available—Graco, Evenflo, Eddie Bauer, etc.... "

Furniture, Bedding & Decor	✓	$$	Prices
Gear & Equipment	✓	❹	Product availability
Nursing & Feeding	✓	❸	Staff knowledge
Safety & Babycare	✓	❸	Customer service
Clothing, Shoes & Accessories	✓	❸	Decor
Books, Toys & Entertainment	✓		

WWW.TARGET.COM

DANVERS—240 INDEPENDENCE WY (AT LIBERTY TREE MALL); 978.762.4439; M-SA 8-10, SU 8-9; PARKING IN FRONT OF BLDG

EVERETT—1 MYSTIC VIEW RD (AT REVERE BEACH PKWY); 617.420.0000; M-SA 8-10, SU 8-9; PARKING IN FRONT OF BLDG

SALEM—227 HIGHLAND AVE (AT FARRELL CT); 978.224.4000; M-SA 8-10, SU 8-9; PARKING IN FRONT OF BLDG

SAUGUS—400 LYNN FELLS PKWY (AT FOREST ST); 781.307.0000; M-SA 8-10, SU 8-9; PARKING IN FRONT OF BLDG

SOMERVILLE—180 SOMERVILLE AVE (AT NANSFIELD ST); 617.776.4036; M-SA 8-10, SU 8-9; PARKING IN FRONT OF BLDG

WOBURN—101 COMMERCE WY (AT ATLANTIC AVE); 781.904.0002; M-SA 8-10, SU 8-9; PARKING IN FRONT OF BLDG

Toys R Us ★★★★½☆

"...not just toys, but also tons of gear and supplies including diapers and formula... a hectic shopping experience but the prices make it all worthwhile... I've experienced good and bad service at the same store on the same day... the stores are huge and can be overwhelming... most big brand-names available... leave the kids at home unless you want to end up with a cart full of toys... "

Furniture, Bedding & Decor	✓	$$$	Prices
Gear & Equipment	✓	❹	Product availability
Nursing & Feeding	✓	❸	Staff knowledge
Safety & Babycare	✓	❸	Customer service
Clothing, Shoes & Accessories	✓	❸	Decor
Books, Toys & Entertainment	✓		

WWW.TOYSRUS.COM

CAMBRIDGE—200 ALEWIFE BROOK PKWY (AT TERMINAL RD); 617.576.8697; M-SA 10-9, SU 11-6; PARKING LOT

MEDFORD—630 FELLSWAY PKWY (AT WELLINGTON RD); 781.396.6885; M-SA 10-9, SU 11-6; PARKING LOT

PEABODY—NORTHSHORE SHOPPING CTR (AT SAWYER ST); 978.532.0978; M-SA 10-9, SU 11-6; PARKING LOT

REVERE—66 SQUIRE RD (AT FERRAGAMO WAY); 781.289.1181; M-SA 10-9, SU 11-6

WOBURN—366 CAMBRIDGE ST (AT NEW VILLAGE RD); 781.935.7654; M-SA 10-9, SU 10-6; PARKING LOT

Western Suburbs

★★★★★ "lila picks"

- ★ Babystyle
- ★ Barneys New York
- ★ Boston Baby
- ★ Concord Toy Shoppe
- ★ Isis Maternity
- ★ Magic Beans
- ★ Village Baby

Abigail's Children's Boutique ★★★★☆
"...fancy, high-end, special occasion clothing... the clothes are absolutely gorgeous, but quite expensive... check out the end of season sales... customer service is wonderful... there are stairs which makes it challenging with a stroller... quality of clothes is exceptional... good store to browse... good gifts for both boys and girls..."

Furniture, Bedding & Decor ✗	$$$$	Prices
Gear & Equipment ✗	❹	Product availability
Nursing & Feeding ✗	❹	Staff knowledge
Safety & Babycare ✗	❹	Customer service
Clothing, Shoes & Accessories ✓	❹	Decor
Books, Toys & Entertainment ✓		

WWW.ABIGAILSCHILDRENSBTQ.COM
WELLESLEY—93 CENTRAL ST (AT WESTON RD); 800.477.1181; M-SA 10-6; STREET PARKING

April Cornell ★★★★☆
"...beautiful, classic dresses and accessories for special occasions... I love the matching 'mommy and me' outfits... lots of fun knickknacks for sale... great selection of baby wear on their web site... rest assured your baby won't look like every other child in these adorable outfits... very frilly and girlie—beautiful..."

Furniture, Bedding & Decor ✗	$$$	Prices
Gear & Equipment ✗	❸	Product availability
Nursing & Feeding ✗	❹	Staff knowledge
Safety & Babycare ✗	❹	Customer service
Clothing, Shoes & Accessories ✓	❹	Decor
Books, Toys & Entertainment ✗		

NEWTON—199 BOYLSTON ST (AT THE MALL AT CHESTNUT HILL); 617.965.1126; M-F 10-9:30, SA 10-8, SU 12-6

Babies R Us ★★★★☆
"...everything baby under one roof... they have a wide selection and carry most 'mainstream' items such as Graco, Fisher-Price, Avent and Britax... great customer service—given how big the stores are, I was pleasantly surprised at how attentive the staff was... easy return policy... super busy on weekends so try to visit on a weekday for the best service... keep an eye out for great coupons, deals and frequent

sales... easy and comprehensive registry... shopping here is so easy—you've got to check it out... "

Furniture, Bedding & Decor	✓	$$$ .... Prices
Gear & Equipment	✓	❹ .... Product availability
Nursing & Feeding	✓	❹ .... Staff knowledge
Safety & Babycare	✓	❹ .... Customer service
Clothing, Shoes & Accessories	✓	❹ .... Decor
Books, Toys & Entertainment	✓	

WWW.BABIESRUS.COM

FRAMINGHAM—1 WORCESTER RD (AT SHOPPPERS WORLD PLZ); 508.872.9358; M-SA 9:30-9:30, SU 11-7; PARKING IN FRONT OF BLDG

Baby Depot At Burlington Coat Factory ★★★½☆

"*...a large, 'super store' layout with a ton of baby gear... wide aisles, packed shelves, barely existent customer service and awesome prices... everything from bottles, car seats and strollers to gliders, cribs and clothes... I always find something worth getting... a little disorganized and hard to locate items you're looking for... the staff is not always knowledgeable about their merchandise... return policy is store credit only...*"

Furniture, Bedding & Decor	✗	$$ .... Prices
Gear & Equipment	✗	❸ .... Product availability
Nursing & Feeding	✗	❸ .... Staff knowledge
Safety & Babycare	✗	❸ .... Customer service
Clothing, Shoes & Accessories	✗	❸ .... Decor
Books, Toys & Entertainment	✗	

WWW.BABYDEPOT.COM

NATICK—321 SPEEN ST (AT MARLBORO PIKE); 508.651.2526; M-SA 9:30-9, SU 11-6; PARKING LOT

Baby Place, The ★★★★☆

"*...if you want top of the line baby stuff, this is the place... for a small store they have good variety... great store for hard to find items... very customer service-oriented with knowledgeable sales staff... good place for gifts-they will gift wrap everything for you... every crib is the best in the line, every bedding set is exclusive... Pali, Stokke, Peg Perego, Bugaboo, Maclaren... although a little expensive you can get everything for the nursery in one store... you can register online here too... nice selection of things you don't see in other stores...*"

Furniture, Bedding & Decor	✓	$$$$ .... Prices
Gear & Equipment	✓	❹ .... Product availability
Nursing & Feeding	✓	❹ .... Staff knowledge
Safety & Babycare	✓	❹ .... Customer service
Clothing, Shoes & Accessories	✓	❹ .... Decor
Books, Toys & Entertainment	✓	

WWW.THEBABYPLACE.COM

NATICK—50 WORCESTER RD (AT BYRON RD); 508.655.5305; M-SA 10-5:30, SU 12-5; PARKING LOT

BabyGap/GapKids ★★★★☆

"*...colorful baby and toddler clothing in clean, well-lit stores... great return policy... it's the Gap, so you know what you're getting—colorful, cute and well-made clothing... best place for baby hats... prices are reasonable especially since there's always a sale of some sort going on... sales, sales, sales—frequent and fantastic... everything I'm looking for in infant clothing—snap crotches, snaps up the front, all natural fabrics and great styling... fun seasonal selections—a great place to shop for gifts as well as for your own kids... although it can get busy, staff generally seem accommodating and helpful...*"

Furniture, Bedding & Decor	✗
Gear & Equipment	✗
Nursing & Feeding	✗
Safety & Babycare	✗
Clothing, Shoes & Accessories	✓
Books, Toys & Entertainment	✗

$$$ .... Prices
❹ .... Product availability
❹ .... Staff knowledge
❹ .... Customer service
❹ .... Decor

WWW.GAP.COM

BELLINGHAM—249 HARTFORD AVE (AT DEERFIELD LN); 508.966.9300; M-SA 9-9, SU 11-6; PARKING LOT

BROOKLINE—306 HARVARD ST (AT BABCOCK ST); 617.738.6625; M-SA 10-9, SU 11-6; PARKING IN FRONT OF BLDG

CHESTNUT HILL—300 BOYLSTON ST (AT FLORENCE ST); 617.964.1190; M-SA 10-9:30, SU 11-6; PARKING LOT

NATICK—1245 WORCESTER ST (AT NATICK MALL); 508.653.4198; M-SA 10-10, SU 11-6; MALL PARKING

WATERTOWN—550 ARSENAL ST (AT ARSENAL MALL); 617.923.1966; M-SA M-SA 9:30-9 SU 11-6; MALL PARKING

Babystyle ★★★★★

"...they offer a wonderful range of children's clothing, educational toys, gear and even maternity items... the atmosphere is great for babies—you really feel the staff there want you to be comfortable... great, friendly service... unfortunately what is on their web site is not always in the store... if you are looking for a special occasion gift or a really chic diaper bag then you should come here... their line of baby and toddler clothing is really cute and wears well..."

Furniture, Bedding & Decor	✓
Gear & Equipment	✓
Nursing & Feeding	✓
Safety & Babycare	✓
Clothing, Shoes & Accessories	✓
Books, Toys & Entertainment	✓

$$$$ .... Prices
❹ .... Product availability
❹ .... Staff knowledge
❹ .... Customer service
❹ .... Decor

WWW.BABYSTYLE.COM

CHESTNUT HILL—300 BOYLSTON ST (AT ATRIUM MALL); 617.796.8982; M-F 10-9:30, SA 10-9:30, SU 11-6

Bambini Design ★★★½☆

"...fabulous stuff for those looking for modern and brightly colored European goodies of all shapes and size... perfect place to buy gifts or decorate a child's room... the owner is very helpful and knowledgeable... great place for blankets... expensive, but unique and fun decor items... some really fantastic and original items in this store... worth a visit if only to browse... everything from design to installation of your baby's room..."

Furniture, Bedding & Decor	✓
Gear & Equipment	✗
Nursing & Feeding	✗
Safety & Babycare	✗
Clothing, Shoes & Accessories	✓
Books, Toys & Entertainment	✓

$$$$ .... Prices
❹ .... Product availability
❹ .... Staff knowledge
❹ .... Customer service
❹ .... Decor

WWW.BAMBINI-DESIGN.COM

BROOKLINE—82 BOYLESTON ST (AT WASHINGTON ST); 617.730.4114; M-W 10-6, TH 11-7, F-SA 10-6, SU 12-6; PARKING LOT

Barber Bros ★★★★½

"...a great store to get lost in... they have a children's section stocked with some favorites like Legos and Groovy Girls... a beautiful store with creative and original baby gifts... they even have a cozy cafe... you pay for the atmosphere, but it's a wonderful shopping experience... nice

selection of invitations and birth announcement choices... lots of toys and other items you can't get at mainstream stores... 99

Furniture, Bedding & Decor	✗	$$$$ .... Prices
Gear & Equipment	✗	❹ .... Product availability
Nursing & Feeding	✗	❹ .... Staff knowledge
Safety & Babycare	✗	❹ .... Customer service
Clothing, Shoes & Accessories	✗	❺ .... Decor
Books, Toys & Entertainment	✓	

WWW.BARBERBROS.COM
NATICK—215 W CENTRAL ST (AT WELLESLEY AVE); 508.653.8378; M-SA 9-9, SU 9-6; PARKING LOT

Barn ★★★★☆

...great selection of shoes and they work hard to find what is just right for your child... the most cost-effective children's shoes in the area... get there early in the season because the good stuff moves quickly... I've gotten shoes there since I was just a kid... great sales rack... great foot measuring for the little ones, very patient staff and good parking... shoes for the whole family... staff is extremely helpful and very well trained... an ever-changing selection of shoes... 99

Furniture, Bedding & Decor	✗	$$$ .... Prices
Gear & Equipment	✗	❹ .... Product availability
Nursing & Feeding	✗	❹ .... Staff knowledge
Safety & Babycare	✗	❹ .... Customer service
Clothing, Shoes & Accessories	✓	❸ .... Decor
Books, Toys & Entertainment	✗	

NEWTON—25 KEMPTON PL (AT WASHINGTON ST); 617.332.6300; M-F 9:30-9, SA 9-6, SU 12-5; PARKING LOT

Barneys New York ★★★★★

...pretty much what you would expect from Barneys—totally decadent, sensationally cool, big price tags... adorable designer clothes for tots... you can find wonderful little gifts at reasonable prices... a great place for gifts—my friends get so excited when they see the Barneys box... when you're in the mood to impress, Barneys is a sure bet... yes it's pricey, but the experience is so wonderful... 99

Furniture, Bedding & Decor	✓	$$$$ .... Prices
Gear & Equipment	✗	❹ .... Product availability
Nursing & Feeding	✓	❹ .... Staff knowledge
Safety & Babycare	✗	❹ .... Customer service
Clothing, Shoes & Accessories	✓	❹ .... Decor
Books, Toys & Entertainment	✓	

WWW.BARNEYS.COM
CHESTNUT HILL—199 BOYLSTON ST; 617.969.5354; M-F 10-9:30, SA 10-8, SU 12-6; PARKING LOT

Bella ★★★★☆

...cool and unusual outfits, toys and accessories for baby... a great place for special, unique baby gifts and new mom gifts... helpful staff... uncommon items... high-end niceties for your nursery... not an abundance of clothing and bedding brands, but what they do have is lovely... baby stuff is downstairs so you have to leave your stroller upstairs... expensive, but worth it... 99

Furniture, Bedding & Decor	✓	$$$$ .... Prices
Gear & Equipment	✓	❹ .... Product availability
Nursing & Feeding	✗	❹ .... Staff knowledge
Safety & Babycare	✗	❹ .... Customer service
Clothing, Shoes & Accessories	✓	❹ .... Decor
Books, Toys & Entertainment	✓	

BELMONT—59 LEONARD ST (AT CHANNING RD); 617.489.9944; M-SA 10-6; PARKING LOT

NEWTON—65 UNION ST (AT BEACON ST); 617.558.1212; M-SA 10-6; PARKING LOT

Bellini ★★★★☆

"...high-end furniture for a gorgeous nursery... if you're looking for the kind of furniture you see in magazines then this is the place to go... excellent quality... yes, it's pricey, but the quality is impeccable... free delivery and setup... their furniture is built to withstand the abuse my tots dish out... they sell very unique merchandise, ranging from cribs to bedding and even some clothes... our nursery design was inspired by their store decor... I wish they had more frequent sales..."

Furniture, Bedding & Decor .... ✓	$$$$ .... Prices
Gear & Equipment .... ✗	❹ .... Product availability
Nursing & Feeding .... ✗	❹ .... Staff knowledge
Safety & Babycare .... ✗	❹ .... Customer service
Clothing, Shoes & Accessories .... ✗	❹ .... Decor
Books, Toys & Entertainment .... ✓	

WWW.BELLINI.COM

WELLESLEY—999 WORCESTER ST (AT OVERBROOK DR); 781.235.2800; M-W F-SA 10-6, TH 10-8, SU 12-5; PARKING LOT

Boston Baby ★★★★★

"...a great place for first-time parents... an amazing array of baby furniture... they used to carry lots of gear too, but don't anymore... the staff was always available to answer any questions... great selection of cribs and other items for the nursery... good variety of high-end stuff which is hard to find elsewhere... wonderful displays and prices are reasonable given the quality... a great place to see lots of baby furniture under one roof..."

Furniture, Bedding & Decor .... ✓	$$$$ .... Prices
Gear & Equipment .... ✓	❹ .... Product availability
Nursing & Feeding .... ✗	❹ .... Staff knowledge
Safety & Babycare .... ✗	❹ .... Customer service
Clothing, Shoes & Accessories .... ✗	❹ .... Decor
Books, Toys & Entertainment .... ✓	

WWW.BOSTONBABY.COM

NEWTON—30 TOWER RD (AT NEEDHAM ST); 617.332.1400; M-T F-SA 10-6, W-TH 10-8, SU 12-5; PARKING LOT

Carter's ★★★★☆

"...always a great selection of inexpensive baby basics—everything from clothing to linens... I always find something at 'giveaway prices' during one of their frequent sales... busy and crowded—it can be a chaotic shopping experience... 30 to 50 percent less than what you would pay at other boutiques... I bought five pieces of baby clothing for less than $40... durable, adorable and affordable... most stores have a small play area for kids in center of store so you can get your shopping done..."

Furniture, Bedding & Decor .... ✓	$$ .... Prices
Gear & Equipment .... ✗	❹ .... Product availability
Nursing & Feeding .... ✗	❹ .... Staff knowledge
Safety & Babycare .... ✗	❹ .... Customer service
Clothing, Shoes & Accessories ...... ✓	❹ .... Decor
Books, Toys & Entertainment .... ✓	

WWW.CARTERS.COM

WATERTOWN—550 ARSENAL ST (AT ARSENAL MALL); 617.924.7251; M-SA 10-9, SU 11-6; MALL PARKING

participate in our survey at

Children's Orchard ★★★★☆

"...a friendly resale boutique... the clothes and gear are super clean and sold at amazing prices... amazing prices on clothing that is hardly used and practically brand new... shoes, toys, furniture, hair pretties, crib sets, etc... fantastic deals on well-selected used items... prices are great and you can pretty much always find something useful... a great place to buy those everyday play outfits... a lot of name brands at steeply discounted prices..."

Furniture, Bedding & Decor	✓	$$	Prices
Gear & Equipment	✓	❸	Product availability
Nursing & Feeding	✓	❹	Staff knowledge
Safety & Babycare	✓	❹	Customer service
Clothing, Shoes & Accessories	✓	❸	Decor
Books, Toys & Entertainment	✓		

WWW.CHILDRENSORCHARD.COM

CHESTNUT HILL—807 BOYLSTON ST (AT RESERVOIR RD); 617.277.3006; M-F 9-6, SA 10-5, SU 12-5; PARKING LOT

FRAMINGHAM—786 WATER ST (AT EDSELL RD); 508.788.0072; M-F 9:30-6, SA 10-5, SU 12-5; PARKING LOT

MILFORD—196 E MAIN ST (AT MEDWAY ST); 508.473.3383; M-W 9:30-5, TH 9:30-7, F-SA 9:30-5, SU 12-5; PARKING LOT

NATICK—132 E CENTRAL ST (AT WALKUP CT); 508.651.9386; M-F 10-6, SA 10-5, SU 12-5; PARKING LOT

Children's Place, The ★★★★☆

"...great bargains on cute clothing... shoes, socks, swimsuits, sunglasses and everything in between... lots of '3 for $20' type deals on sleepers, pants and mix-and-match separates... so much more affordable than the other 'big chains'... don't expect the most unique stuff here, but it wears and washes well... cheap clothing for cheap prices... you can leave the store with bags full of clothes without putting a huge dent in your wallet..."

Furniture, Bedding & Decor	✗	$$	Prices
Gear & Equipment	✗	❹	Product availability
Nursing & Feeding	✗	❹	Staff knowledge
Safety & Babycare	✗	❹	Customer service
Clothing, Shoes & Accessories	✓	❹	Decor
Books, Toys & Entertainment	✓		

WWW.CHILDRENSPLACE.COM

BROOKLINE—302 HARVARD ST (AT BABCOCK ST); 617.738.2912; M-SA 10-8, SU 11-6; PARKING LOT

MARLBOROUGH—580 DONALD LYNCH BLVD (AT SALMON POND MALL); 508.303.0277; M-SA 10-9:30, SU 11-7; MALL PARKING

NATICK—1324 WORCESTER RD (AT SPEEN RD IN SHERWOOD PLZ); 508.647.0063; M-SA 10-9, SU 11-6; PARKING LOT

WATERTOWN—455 ARSENAL ST (AT ARSENAL COURT DR); 617.924.6605; M-SA 10-9:30, SU 11-6; PARKING LOT

Concord Toy Shoppe ★★★★★

"...the quintessential toy store in a quintessential New England town... wonderful selection of dolls, stuffed animals, toy trains and craft items... classic and unusual toys you won't find anyplace else—where else can you find a Viking hat... knowledgeable and friendly staff... a little tough to navigate with a stroller... worth a drive to see... like an old fashioned toy store... a lot packed in, but fun to look around..."

Furniture, Bedding & Decor	✗	$$$$	Prices
Gear & Equipment	✗	❹	Product availability
Nursing & Feeding	✗	❹	Staff knowledge
Safety & Babycare	✗	❹	Customer service

| Clothing, Shoes & Accessories | ✗ | ❹ | Decor |
| Books, Toys & Entertainment | ✓ | | |

WWW.CONCORDTOYS.COM

CONCORD—4 WALDEN ST (AT HWY 2A); 978.369.2553; M-F 9:30-5:30, SA 9-5, SU 12-5; PARKING LOT

Costco ★★★⯪☆

❝...dependable place for bulk diapers, wipes and formula at discount prices... clothing selection is very hit-or-miss... avoid shopping there during nights and weekends if possible, because parking and checkout lines are brutal... they don't have a huge selection of brands, but the brands they do have are almost always in stock and at a great price... lowest prices around for diapers and formula... kid's clothing tends to be picked through, but it's worth looking for great deals on name-brand items like Carter's...❞

Furniture, Bedding & Decor	✓	$$	Prices
Gear & Equipment	✓	❸	Product availability
Nursing & Feeding	✓	❸	Staff knowledge
Safety & Babycare	✓	❸	Customer service
Clothing, Shoes & Accessories	✓	❷	Decor
Books, Toys & Entertainment	✓		

WWW.COSTCO.COM

WALTHAM—71 2ND AVE; 781.622.3883; M-F 11-8:30, SA 9:30-6, SU 10-6

Foot Stock ★★★★☆

❝...I would not go anywhere else for children's shoes... great playroom in back... high-quality European shoes... good selection and the staff is very helpful... my daughter went from being terrified at buying shoes to loving it... I found the service can be hit or miss... they really do try to find the right shoes for my son's feet...❞

Furniture, Bedding & Decor	✗	$$$$	Prices
Gear & Equipment	✗	❹	Product availability
Nursing & Feeding	✗	❹	Staff knowledge
Safety & Babycare	✗	❹	Customer service
Clothing, Shoes & Accessories	✓	❹	Decor
Books, Toys & Entertainment	✗		

WWW.FOOTSTOCKSHOES.COM

CONCORD—46 MAIN ST (AT WALDEN ST); 978.287.4034; M-SA 9:30-6, TH 9:30-7, SU 11-6; PARKING LOT

WELLESLEY—35 CENTRAL ST (AT ABBOTT ST); 781.431.1655; M-SA 9:30-6, TH 9:30-7, SU 11-6; PARKING LOT

Green Planet

Furniture, Bedding & Decor	✗	✗	Gear & Equipment
Nursing & Feeding	✗	✗	Safety & Babycare
Clothing, Shoes & Accessories	✗	✓	Books, Toys & Entertainment

WWW.THEGREENPLANET.COM

NEWTON—22 LINCOLN ST (AT WALNUT ST); 617.332.7841; M-F 10-6, SA 10-5; PARKING LOT

Gymboree ★★★★☆

❝...beautiful clothing and great quality... colorful and stylish baby and kids wear... lots of fun birthday gift ideas... easy exchange and return policy... items usually go on sale pretty quickly... save money with Gymbucks... many stores have a play area which makes shopping with my kids fun (let alone feasible)...❞

Furniture, Bedding & Decor	✗	$$$	Prices
Gear & Equipment	✗	❹	Product availability
Nursing & Feeding	✗	❹	Staff knowledge
Safety & Babycare	✗	❹	Customer service

Clothing, Shoes & Accessories....... ✓ ❹ .... Decor
Books, Toys & Entertainment .... ✓
WWW.GYMBOREE.COM

CHESTNUT HILL—199 BOYLESTON ST (AT THE MALL AT CHESTNUT HILL);
617.969.9936; M-F 9-9:30, SA 9-9, SU 11-6; MALL PARKING

NATICK—1245 WORCESTER ST (AT NATICK MALL); 508.651.1123; M-SA 10-10, SU 11-6; MALL PARKING

Henry Bear's Park ★★★★☆

"...*a wonderful resource for fun and imaginative children's toys, books, and doodads... lots to offer in products for different ages... adorable store with great selection of gifts and toys... we are there regularly to shop, play or enjoy their weekly story time... a great change from chain stores... excellent selection of stimulating toys... very good, thoughtful selection of children's books... an added bonus is the neighborhood bulletin board, which seems to get a lot of use...* **"**

Furniture, Bedding & Decor .... ✗ $$$ .... Prices
Gear & Equipment .... ✗   ❹ .... Product availability
Nursing & Feeding .... ✗   ❹ .... Staff knowledge
Safety & Babycare .... ✗   ❹ .... Customer service
Clothing, Shoes & Accessories....... ✗   ❹ .... Decor
Books, Toys & Entertainment .... ✓
WWW.HENRYBEAR.COM

BROOKLINE—19 HARVARD ST (AT WASHINGTON ST); 617.264.2422; M-W F 9:30-7, TH 9:30-8, SA 9:30-6, SU 12-5; STREET PARKING

Isis Maternity ★★★★★

"...*amazing, amazing, amazing... in addition being a fabulous parent resource, Isis has the unusual and well-made toys that get everyone excited at showers... the staff really knows about their products and are so friendly... they gave me several demonstrations when I bought our sling there... not the cheapest prices, but I gladly pay a little extra for the service... store is small, but what they do carry is all very useful stuff... convenient for after-class shopping and very baby-friendly...* **"**

Furniture, Bedding & Decor .... ✗ $$$ .... Prices
Gear & Equipment .... ✓   ❹ .... Product availability
Nursing & Feeding .... ✓   ❺ .... Staff knowledge
Safety & Babycare .... ✗   ❺ .... Customer service
Clothing, Shoes & Accessories....... ✓   ❹ .... Decor
Books, Toys & Entertainment .... ✓
WWW.ISISMATERNITY.COM

BROOKLINE —2 BROOKLINE PL (AT BROOKLINE AVE); 781.429.1500; M W-TH 9-9, T F-SA 9-5; GARAGE AT BROOKLINE PLACE

Jacadi ★★★★☆

"...*beautiful French clothes, baby bumpers and quilts... elegant and perfect for special occasions... quite expensive, but the clothing is hip and the quality really good... many handmade clothing and bedding items... take advantage of their sales... more of a store to buy gifts than practical, everyday clothes... beautiful, special clothing—especially for newborns and toddlers... velvet pajamas, coordinated nursery items... stores are as pretty as the clothes... they have a huge (half-off everything) sale twice a year that makes it very affordable...* **"**

Furniture, Bedding & Decor .... ✓ $$$$ .... Prices
Gear & Equipment .... ✗   ❹ .... Product availability
Nursing & Feeding .... ✗   ❹ .... Staff knowledge
Safety & Babycare .... ✗   ❹ .... Customer service
Clothing, Shoes & Accessories....... ✓   ❹ .... Decor
Books, Toys & Entertainment .... ✓
WWW.JACADIUSA.COM

WELLESLEY—571 WASHINGTON ST (AT GROVE ST); 781.239.9999; M-SA 10-6 SU 12-5; STREET PARKING

Janie And Jack ★★★★½

"...gorgeous clothing and some accessories (shoes, socks, etc.)... fun to look at, somewhat pricey, but absolutely adorable clothes for little ones... boutique-like clothes at non-boutique prices—especially on sale... high-quality infant and toddler clothes anyone would love—always good for a baby gift... I always check the clearance racks in the back of the store... their decor is darling—a really fun shopping experience..."

Furniture, Bedding & Decor	✗	$$$$	Prices
Gear & Equipment	✓	❹	Product availability
Nursing & Feeding	✗	❹	Staff knowledge
Safety & Babycare	✗	❹	Customer service
Clothing, Shoes & Accessories	✓	❹	Decor
Books, Toys & Entertainment	✗		

WWW.JANIEANDJACK.COM

CHESTNUT HILL—300 BOYLSTON ST (AT FLORENCE ST); 617.527.0456; M-SA 10-9:30, SU 11-6; FREE GARAGE

NATICK—1245 WORCESTER ST (AT NATICK MALL); 508.647.0146; M-SA 10-10, SU 11-6; MALL PARKING

Jordan's Furniture ★★★★☆

"...you can't beat Jordan's when shopping for quality furniture you want to last... reasonable prices and great selection... perfect for 'big kid' beds and furniture sets... my son loves the taxi-car strollers... customer service shines at Jordan's... all kinds of furniture for all budgets... they stand behind all of their products... their displays are amazing and they have fun events to keep the kids entertained while shopping... more than a furniture store it's an adventure for the kids..."

Furniture, Bedding & Decor	✓	$$$	Prices
Gear & Equipment	✗	❹	Product availability
Nursing & Feeding	✗	❹	Staff knowledge
Safety & Babycare	✗	❹	Customer service
Clothing, Shoes & Accessories	✗	❹	Decor
Books, Toys & Entertainment	✗		

WWW.JORDANS.COM

NATICK—1 UNDER PRICE WY (AT RT 9); 508.424.0088; M-SA 10-10, SU 11-7; PARKING LOT

KB Toys ★★★☆☆

"...hectic and always buzzing... wall-to-wall plastic and blinking lights... more Fisher-Price, Elmo and Sponge Bob than the eye can handle... a toy super store with discounted prices... they always have some kind of special sale going on... if you're looking for the latest and greatest popular toy, then look no further—not the place for unique or unusual toys... perfect for bulk toy shopping—especially around the holidays..."

Furniture, Bedding & Decor	✗	$$	Prices
Gear & Equipment	✗	❸	Product availability
Nursing & Feeding	✗	❸	Staff knowledge
Safety & Babycare	✗	❸	Customer service
Clothing, Shoes & Accessories	✗	❸	Decor
Books, Toys & Entertainment	✓		

WWW.KBTOYS.COM

MARLBOROUGH—580 DONALD LYNCH BLVD (AT SOLOMON POND MALL); 508.303.0813; M-SA 10-9:30 SU 11-7; MALL PARKING

NATICK—1245 WORCESTOR RD (AT NATICK MALL); 508.651.0093; M-SA 10-10 SU 11-6; MALL PARKING

NEWTON—241 NEEDHAM ST (AT MARSHALLS S/C); 617.630.5613; M-SA 9:30-9 SU 9:30-6 ; PARKING LOT

Kenzie Kids ★★★★☆

"...a kid's clothing store with style... Burberry, Jean Bourget, Lili Gaufrette, Tartine Et Chocolat, Petit Bateau... plus baby gifts and toys... the perfect place to find a present for the new addition... good return policy... pretty high-end and you probably won't find a lot of the stuff anywhere else... I wish they would add more clothing for boys..."

Furniture, Bedding & Decor .... ✗	$$$$ .... Prices
Gear & Equipment .... ✗	❹ .... Product availability
Nursing & Feeding .... ✗	❹ .... Staff knowledge
Safety & Babycare .... ✗	❹ .... Customer service
Clothing, Shoes & Accessories .... ✓	❹ .... Decor
Books, Toys & Entertainment .... ✓	

WWW.KENZIEKIDS.COM

CHESTNUT HILL—199 BOYLSTON ST (AT RT 9); 617.965.5566; M-F 10-9:30, SA 10-8, SU 12-6; PARKING LOT

Kid To Kid ★★★★⯨☆

"...best selection and best finds of all the secondhand children's stores that I have been to... wonderful resale outlet for high-end children's clothing, furniture, and toys... I make out really well there with books... beautifully arranged, the stock and the prices are great... the place to go for used equipment... they only accept items in excellent condition, many of them look brand new... finally I can actually fit my double stroller in the aisle of a children's clothing store..."

Furniture, Bedding & Decor .... ✗	$$ .... Prices
Gear & Equipment .... ✗	❹ .... Product availability
Nursing & Feeding .... ✗	❹ .... Staff knowledge
Safety & Babycare .... ✗	❹ .... Customer service
Clothing, Shoes & Accessories .... ✓	❸ .... Decor
Books, Toys & Entertainment .... ✓	

NATICK.KIDTOKID.COM

NATICK—42 WORCESTER ST (AT OAK ST); 508.650.4001; M-W 10-6, TH-SA 10-8, SU 12-5; PARKING LOT

Kid's Foot Locker ★★★⯨☆

"...Nike, Reebok and Adidas for your little ones... hip, trendy and quite pricey... perfect for the sports addict dad who wants his kid sporting the latest NFL duds... shoes cost close to what the adult variety costs... generally good quality... they carry infant and toddler sizes..."

Furniture, Bedding & Decor .... ✗	$$$ .... Prices
Gear & Equipment .... ✗	❸ .... Product availability
Nursing & Feeding .... ✗	❸ .... Staff knowledge
Safety & Babycare .... ✗	❸ .... Customer service
Clothing, Shoes & Accessories .... ✓	❸ .... Decor
Books, Toys & Entertainment .... ✗	

WWW.KIDSFOOTLOCKER.COM

WATERTOWN—485 ARSENAL ST (AT ARSENAL COURT DR); 617.923.1856; M-SA 10-9:30, SU 11-6

Kohl's ★★★★☆

"...nice one-stop shopping for the whole family—everything from clothing to baby gear... great sales on clothing and a good selection of higher-end brands... stylish, inexpensive clothes for babies through 24 months... very easy shopping experience... dirt-cheap sales and

clearance prices... nothing super fancy, but just right for those everyday romper outfits... Graco, Eddie Bauer and other well-known brands... **"**

Furniture, Bedding & Decor ✓	$$ .... Prices
Gear & Equipment ✓	❹ .... Product availability
Nursing & Feeding ✓	❸ .... Staff knowledge
Safety & Babycare ✓	❸ .... Customer service
Clothing, Shoes & Accessories ✓	❸ .... Decor
Books, Toys & Entertainment ✓	

WWW.KOHLS.COM

FRAMINGHAM—1 WORCESTER RD (AT SHOPPERS WORLD); 508.879.9103; M-SA 8-10, SU 10-8; PARKING IN FRONT OF BLDG

Macy's ★★★★☆

"...*Macy's has it all and I never leave empty-handed... if you time your visit right you can find some great deals... go during the week so you don't get overwhelmed with the weekend crowd... good for staples as well as beautiful party dresses for girls... lots of brand-names like Carter's, Guess, and Ralph Lauren... not much in terms of assistance... newspaper coupons and sales help keep the cost down... some stores are better organized and maintained than others... if you're going to shop at a department store for your baby, then Macy's is a safe bet...* **"**

Furniture, Bedding & Decor ✓	$$$ .... Prices
Gear & Equipment ✗	❸ .... Product availability
Nursing & Feeding ✗	❸ .... Staff knowledge
Safety & Babycare ✗	❸ .... Customer service
Clothing, Shoes & Accessories ✓	❸ .... Decor
Books, Toys & Entertainment ✓	

WWW.MACYS.COM

FRAMINGHAM—1 WORCESTER RD (AT SHOPPERS WORLD); 508.650.6000; M-SA 10-9:30, SU 11-7; PARKING LOT

NATICK—1245 WORCESTER RD (AT NATICK MALL); 508.650.6400; M-SA 10-10, SU 10-7; MALL PARKING

Magic Beans ★★★★★

"...*everything you would want or need for baby... clothes to books to high-end strollers... the kind of toy store you want right around the corner... delightful mix of toys and other kids' gear... wonderful owners who are approachable and helpful as are their staff... magical play area which lends itself to a very pleasant experience with your kids... items are all 'hot off the press'...* **"**

Furniture, Bedding & Decor ✓	$$$ .... Prices
Gear & Equipment ✓	❹ .... Product availability
Nursing & Feeding ✓	❹ .... Staff knowledge
Safety & Babycare ✓	❹ .... Customer service
Clothing, Shoes & Accessories ✓	❹ .... Decor
Books, Toys & Entertainment ✓	

WWW.MBEANS.COM

BROOKLINE—312 HARVARD ST (AT BABCOCK ST); 617.264.2326; M-W 10-7, TH-SA 10-8, SU 11-5; PARKING LOT AT CENTRE ST

Maxima Art Center ★★★★☆

"...*unique gifts and toys for all ages—including some hard-to-find items... great Dr. Seuss collection... plenty of new baby gifts like fun onesies and bibs... recently expanded to include a large children's selection... a great shop to get an artistic gift... lots of great books as well as Manhattan toys and Lizzy Bee toys... good ideas for making your own gifts...* **"**

Furniture, Bedding & Decor ✗	$$ .... Prices
Gear & Equipment ✗	❺ .... Product availability
Nursing & Feeding ✗	❹ .... Staff knowledge

Safety & Babycare ✗	❹ Customer service
Clothing, Shoes & Accessories ✗	❹ Decor
Books, Toys & Entertainment ✓	

WWW.MAXIMACENTER.COM

WALTHAM—284 MOODY ST (AT MAIN ST); 781.647.2228; M-T 10-7, W-TH 10-8, F-SA 10-10, SU 12-6; PARKING LOT

Michelson's Shoes ★★★★½

"...a great assortment of puddle boots... terrific staff that knows how to measure and fit a baby foot... an essential store for any parent of young children... great place to buy good-quality shoes for children... old school shoe store that really knows shoes... my kids both have wide feet and they always have wide widths in stock... so helpful and patient with kids that it's almost scary..."

Furniture, Bedding & Decor ✗	$$$ Prices
Gear & Equipment ✗	❹ Product availability
Nursing & Feeding ✗	❺ Staff knowledge
Safety & Babycare ✗	❺ Customer service
Clothing, Shoes & Accessories ✓	❸ Decor
Books, Toys & Entertainment ✗	

WWW.MICHELSONSHOES.COM

LEXINGTON—1780 MASSACHUSETTS AVE (AT WALTHAM ST); 781.862.1034; M-TH 8-6, F 8-9, SA 8-6; PARKING LOT

Old Navy ★★★★☆

"...hip and 'in' clothes for infants and tots... plenty of steals on clearance items... T-shirts and pants for $10 or less... busy, busy, busy—long lines, especially on weekends... nothing fancy and you won't mind when your kids get down and dirty in these clothes... easy to wash, decent quality... you can shop for your baby, your toddler, your teen and yourself all at the same time... clothes are especially affordable when you hit their sales (post-holiday sales are amazing!)..."

Furniture, Bedding & Decor ✗	$$ Prices
Gear & Equipment ✗	❹ Product availability
Nursing & Feeding ✗	❸ Staff knowledge
Safety & Babycare ✗	❸ Customer service
Clothing, Shoes & Accessories ✓	❸ Decor
Books, Toys & Entertainment ✗	

WWW.OLDNAVY.COM

BELLINGHAM—253 HARTFORD AVE (AT HWY 495); 508.966.3799; M-SA 9-9, SU 10-6; PARKING LOT

FRAMINGHAM—1 WORCESTER RD (AT SHOPPERS WORLD); 508.370.3888; M-SA 9-9, SU 10-6; PARKING LOT

WATERTOWN—485 ARSENAL ST (AT ARSENAL MALL); 617.926.0072; M-SA 10-9, SU 11-6; MALL PARKING

Periwinkles ★★★★☆

"...custom, hand-painted furniture and bedding... unique clothing... lovely store to browse or buy... costly, but you can design exactly what you are looking for... gorgeous gifts... an oasis in the desert of ready made, cookie cutter nursery items..."

Furniture, Bedding & Decor ✓	$$$$ Prices
Gear & Equipment ✗	❹ Product availability
Nursing & Feeding ✗	❹ Staff knowledge
Safety & Babycare ✗	❹ Customer service
Clothing, Shoes & Accessories ✓	❺ Decor
Books, Toys & Entertainment ✓	

WWW.PERIWINKLESBABY.COM

WELLESLEY—200 LINDEN ST; 781.237.8844; M-SA 10-6, SU 12-5; PARKING LOT

Pottery Barn Kids ★★★★½

"...stylish furniture, rugs, rockers and much more... they've found the right mix between quality and price... finally a company that stands behind what they sell—their customer service is great... gorgeous baby decor and furniture that will make your nursery to-die-for... the play area is so much fun—my daughter never wants to leave... a beautiful store with tons of ideas for setting up your nursery or kid's room... bright colors and cute patterns with basics to mix and match... if you see something in the catalog, but not in the store, just ask because they often have it in the back..."

Furniture, Bedding & Decor	✓	$$$$ .... Prices
Gear & Equipment	✗	❹ .... Product availability
Nursing & Feeding	✗	❹ .... Staff knowledge
Safety & Babycare	✗	❹ .... Customer service
Clothing, Shoes & Accessories	✗	❺ .... Decor
Books, Toys & Entertainment	✓	

WWW.POTTERYBARNKIDS.COM

CHESTNUT HILL—300 BOYLSTON ST (RT 9) (AT FLORENCE ST); 617.928.0670; M-SA 10-9:30, SU 11-6; PARKING LOT

NATICK—1245 WORCESTER RD (AT NATICK MALL); 508.653.4675; M-SA 10-10 SU 12-6; MALL PARKING

Priceless Kids ★★★½☆

"...inexpensive clothes and shoes even with brand-name labels... especially helpful for the early months as babies grow quickly... great place for T-shirts, socks and accessories... affordable and cute clothes, but quality can vary... good when you're not looking for anything in particular... great bargains and interesting variety of clothing..."

Furniture, Bedding & Decor	✗	$$ .... Prices
Gear & Equipment	✗	❸ .... Product availability
Nursing & Feeding	✗	❸ .... Staff knowledge
Safety & Babycare	✗	❸ .... Customer service
Clothing, Shoes & Accessories	✓	❸ .... Decor
Books, Toys & Entertainment	✗	

WWW.PRICELESSKIDS.COM

ACTON—340 GREAT RD (AT SATURN ST); 978.263.9496; M-F 10-9 SA 10-6 SU 12-5 ; PARKING LOT

Right Start, The ★★★★☆

"...higher-end, well selected items... Britax, Maclaren, Combi, Mustela—all the cool brands under one roof... everything from bibs to bottles and even the Bugaboo stroller... prices seem a little high, but the selection is good and the staff knowledgeable and helpful... there are toys all over the store that kids can play with while you shop... I have a hard time getting my kids out of the store because they are having so much fun... a boutique-like shopping experience but they carry most of the key brands... their registry works well..."

Furniture, Bedding & Decor	✓	$$$ .... Prices
Gear & Equipment	✓	❹ .... Product availability
Nursing & Feeding	✓	❹ .... Staff knowledge
Safety & Babycare	✓	❹ .... Customer service
Clothing, Shoes & Accessories	✓	❹ .... Decor
Books, Toys & Entertainment	✓	

WWW.RIGHTSTART.COM

NATICK—104 WORCESTER ST (AT OAK ST); 508.650.1271; M-SA 10-10, SU 11-7; MALL PARKING

participate in our survey at

Rugged Bear ★★★★☆

baby basics

"...their merchandise is truly top quality... employees go above and beyond to help... a little pricey, but the the durability of the clothes and shoes are worth it... top brands as well as their own which we have had very good luck with... if they don't have the size/style you are looking for they are more than happy to call other stores and have it sent to you... go and get great outdoor wear for your kids... sales near the end of the season are the best times to go...**"**

Furniture, Bedding & Decor ✗	$$$ .... Prices
Gear & Equipment ✓	❹ .... Product availability
Nursing & Feeding ✗	❹ .... Staff knowledge
Safety & Babycare ✗	❹ .... Customer service
Clothing, Shoes & Accessories ✓	❹ .... Decor
Books, Toys & Entertainment ✗	

WWW.RUGGEDBEAR.COM

ACTON—401 NAGOG SQ (AT WESTFORD LN); 978.263.8580; M W F-SA 9:30-6, TH 9:30-8, SU 12-5; PARKING LOT

BEDFORD—297 GREAT RD UNIT 6 (AT GREAT RD SHOPPING CTR); 781.275.9199; M T-W F SA 9:30-5:30, TH 9:30-8 SU 12-5; PARKING LOT

CHESTNUT HILL—49 BOYLSTON ST (AT THE MALL AT CHESTNUT HILL); 617.739.3320; M-SA 9:30-8 SU 12-5; PARKING LOT

SUDBURY—410 BOSTON POST RD (AT UNION AVE); 978.443.7565; M-W F 9:30-6, TH 9:30-8, SA 9:30-5, SU 12-5; PARKING LOT

WELLESLEY—34 CENTRAL ST (AT ABBOTT ST); 781.431.1715; M-T-W-F-SA 9:30-6, TH 9:30-8, SU 12-5; PARKING LOT

Sears ★★★☆☆

"...a decent selection of clothes and basic baby equipment... check out the Kids Club program—it's a great way to save money... you go to Sears to save money, not to be pampered... the quality of their merchandise is better than Wal-Mart, but don't expect anything too special or different... not much in terms of gear, but tons of well-priced baby and toddler clothing...**"**

Furniture, Bedding & Decor ✓	$$ .... Prices
Gear & Equipment ✓	❸ .... Product availability
Nursing & Feeding ✓	❸ .... Staff knowledge
Safety & Babycare ✓	❸ .... Customer service
Clothing, Shoes & Accessories ✓	❸ .... Decor
Books, Toys & Entertainment ✓	

WWW.SEARS.COM

NATICK—1235 WORCESTER RD (AT NATICK MALL); 508.650.2823; M-F 10-10, SA 8-10, SU 11-7; MALL PARKING

Stride Rite Shoes ★★★½☆

"...wonderful selection of baby and toddler shoes... sandals, sneakers, and even special-occasion shoes... decent quality shoes that last... they know a lot about kids' shoes and take the time to get it right—they always measure my son's feet before fittings... store sizes vary, but they always have something in stock that works... they've even special ordered shoes for my daughter... a fun 'first shoe' buying experience...**"**

Furniture, Bedding & Decor ✗	$$$ .... Prices
Gear & Equipment ✗	❹ .... Product availability
Nursing & Feeding ✗	❹ .... Staff knowledge
Safety & Babycare ✗	❹ .... Customer service
Clothing, Shoes & Accessories ✓	❹ .... Decor
Books, Toys & Entertainment ✗	

WWW.STRIDERITE.COM

BROOKLINE—1349 BEACON ST (AT HARVARD ST); 617.739.0582; M-F 10-6:45, SA 9-5:45, SU 12-4:45 ; STREET PARKING

NATICK—1245 WORCESTER RD (AT NATICK MALL); 508.651.9800; M-SA 10-10, SU 11-6; MALL PARKING

NEWTON—199 BOYLSTON ST (AT CHESTNUT HILL MALL); 617.244.5251; M-SA 10-9:30, SU 12-6; MALL PARKING

Talbots Kids ★★★⯨☆

"...a nice alternative to the typical department store experience... expensive, but fantastic quality... great for holiday and special occasion outfits including christening outfits... well-priced, conservative children's clothing... cute selections for infants, toddlers and kids... sales are fantastic—up to half off at least a couple times a year... the best part is, you can also shop for yourself while shopping for baby..."

Furniture, Bedding & Decor	✘	$$$$ .... Prices
Gear & Equipment	✘	❹ ...... Product availability
Nursing & Feeding	✘	❹ ...... Staff knowledge
Safety & Babycare	✘	❹ ...... Customer service
Clothing, Shoes & Accessories	✓	❹ ...... Decor
Books, Toys & Entertainment	✘	

WWW.TALBOTS.COM

NATICK—1245 WORCESTER ST (AT NATICK MALL); 508.653.6563; M-SA 10-10, SU 12-6; MALL PARKING

WELLESLEY—50 CENTRAL ST (AT ABBOTT ST); 781.416.2911; M-F 9:30-7, SA 9:30-6, SU 12-6

Target ★★★★☆

"...our favorite place to shop for kids' stuff—good selection and very affordable... guilt-free shopping—kids grow so fast so I don't want to pay high department-store prices... everything from diapers and sippy cups to car seats and strollers... easy return policy... generally helpful staff, but you don't go for the service—you go for the prices... decent registry that won't freak your friends out with outrageous prices... easy, convenient shopping for well-priced items... all the big-box brands available—Graco, Evenflo, Eddie Bauer, etc...."

Furniture, Bedding & Decor	✓	$$ .... Prices
Gear & Equipment	✓	❹ ...... Product availability
Nursing & Feeding	✓	❸ ...... Staff knowledge
Safety & Babycare	✓	❸ ...... Customer service
Clothing, Shoes & Accessories	✓	❸ ...... Decor
Books, Toys & Entertainment	✓	

WWW.TARGET.COM

FRAMINGHAM—400 COCHITUATE RD (AT FRAMINGTON MALL); 508.628.3136; M-SA 8-10, SU 8-9; PARKING IN FRONT OF BLDG

MILFORD—250 FORTUNE BLVD (AT E MAIN ST); 508.478.5880; M-SA 8-10, SU 8-9; PARKING IN FRONT OF BLDG

WATERTOWN—550 ARSENAL ST (AT ARSENAL MALL); 617.924.6574; M-SA 8-10, SU 8-9; PARKING IN FRONT OF BLDG

Toys R Us ★★★⯨☆

"...not just toys, but also tons of gear and supplies including diapers and formula... a hectic shopping experience but the prices make it all worthwhile... I've experienced good and bad service at the same store on the same day... the stores are huge and can be overwhelming... most big brand-names available... leave the kids at home unless you want to end up with a cart full of toys..."

Furniture, Bedding & Decor	✓	$$$ .... Prices
Gear & Equipment	✓	❹ ...... Product availability
Nursing & Feeding	✓	❸ ...... Staff knowledge
Safety & Babycare	✓	❸ ...... Customer service

| Clothing, Shoes & Accessories | ✓ | ❸ | Decor |

Books, Toys & Entertainment .... ✓
WWW.TOYSRUS.COM

FRAMINGHAM—1 WORCESTER RD (AT SHOPPERS WORLD); 508.370.4445; M-SA 10-9, SU 11-6; PARKING LOT

Village Baby ★★★★★

"...the unique pieces make it worth the subway trip... adorable, one-of-a-kind clothes... even though it is a smallish store they still pack it with good merchandise... a bit pricey, but worth it for special occasion wear... very knowledgeable and friendly staff... perfect place to shop for a great baby outfit that's sure to draw oohs and aahs... a great store in a wonderful, kid-friendly neighborhood..."

Furniture, Bedding & Decor	✗	$$$$	Prices
Gear & Equipment	✓	❹	Product availability
Nursing & Feeding	✗	❹	Staff knowledge
Safety & Babycare	✓	❹	Customer service
Clothing, Shoes & Accessories	✓	❹	Decor
Books, Toys & Entertainment	✓		

BROOKLINE—23A HARVARD ST (AT DAVIS AVE); 617.232.4900; T-TH SA 10-6, F 10-5, SU 12-5; PARKING LOT

Whimsy ★★★★★

"...finally a place where creativity rules... just show up and start making stuff... my daughter went to a birthday party there and had a blast... we've become frequent customers... fun mosaic projects and build/paint projects... a great source for birthday gifts... it gets busy so be prepared for a nap afterwards..."

Furniture, Bedding & Decor	✗	$$	Prices
Gear & Equipment	✗	❸	Product availability
Nursing & Feeding	✗	❺	Staff knowledge
Safety & Babycare	✗	❹	Customer service
Clothing, Shoes & Accessories	✗	❹	Decor
Books, Toys & Entertainment	✓		

FRAMINGHAM—686 WORCESTER RD (AT PROSPECT ST); 508.626.8989; M-SA 10-5, SU 12-5

Southern Suburbs

★★★★★
"lila picks"

★ Babies R US ★ Isis Maternity
★ Boston Baby

April Cornell ★★★★☆

"...beautiful, classic dresses and accessories for special occasions... I love the matching 'mommy and me' outfits... lots of fun knickknacks for sale... great selection of baby wear on their web site... rest assured your baby won't look like every other child in these adorable outfits... very frilly and girlie—beautiful..."

Furniture, Bedding & Decor .... ✗	$$$ .... Prices
Gear & Equipment .... ✗	❸ .... Product availability
Nursing & Feeding .... ✗	❹ .... Staff knowledge
Safety & Babycare .... ✗	❹ .... Customer service
Clothing, Shoes & Accessories ...... ✓	❹ .... Decor
Books, Toys & Entertainment .... ✗	

WWW.APRILCORNELL.COM

WRENTHAM—1 PREMIUM OUTLETS BLVD (OFF RT 495); 508.384.9538; M-SA 10-9, SU 10-8

Babies R Us ★★★★★

"...everything baby under one roof... they have a wide selection and carry most 'mainstream' items such as Graco, Fisher-Price, Avent and Britax... great customer service—given how big the stores are, I was pleasantly surprised at how attentive the staff was... easy return policy... super busy on weekends so try to visit on a weekday for the best service... keep an eye out for great coupons, deals and frequent sales... easy and comprehensive registry... shopping here is so easy—you've got to check it out..."

Furniture, Bedding & Decor .... ✓	$$$ .... Prices
Gear & Equipment .... ✓	❹ .... Product availability
Nursing & Feeding .... ✓	❹ .... Staff knowledge
Safety & Babycare .... ✓	❹ .... Customer service
Clothing, Shoes & Accessories ...... ✓	❹ .... Decor
Books, Toys & Entertainment .... ✓	

WWW.BABIESRUS.COM

BRAINTREE—450 GROSSMAN DR (AT UNION ST); 781.356.0475; M-SA 9:30-9:30, SU 11-7; PARKING IN FRONT OF BLDG

NORTH ATTLEBORO—1255 S WASHINGTON ST (AT EMERALD SQ MALL); 508.699.8218; M-SA 9:30-9:30, SU 11-7; PARKING IN FRONT OF BLDG

Baby Depot At Burlington Coat Factory ★★★★☆

"...a large, 'super store' layout with a ton of baby gear... wide aisles, packed shelves, barely existent customer service and awesome prices...

everything from bottles, car seats and strollers to gliders, cribs and clothes... I always find something worth getting... a little disorganized and hard to locate items you're looking for... the staff is not always knowledgeable about their merchandise... return policy is store credit only...

Furniture, Bedding & Decor	✓	$$ .... Prices
Gear & Equipment	✓	❸ .... Product availability
Nursing & Feeding	✓	❸ .... Staff knowledge
Safety & Babycare	✓	❸ .... Customer service
Clothing, Shoes & Accessories	✓	❸ .... Decor
Books, Toys & Entertainment	✓	

WWW.BABYDEPOT.COM

BRAINTREE—705 GRANITE ST (AT TOWN ST); 781.848.3200; M-SA 10-9, SU 11-6; PARKING LOT

Baby Furniture Warehouse Store ★★★★☆

...great selection of cribs and furniture... everything you could need under one roof... very helpful staff and the owner himself is on the floor to assist shoppers... warehouse atmosphere, but the selection is what it's all about... worth a drive for the prices and variety of items... some items are pricey, but you get what you pay for in quality... they can order what they don't have on display...

Furniture, Bedding & Decor	✓	$$$ .... Prices
Gear & Equipment	✓	❹ .... Product availability
Nursing & Feeding	✗	❹ .... Staff knowledge
Safety & Babycare	✗	❹ .... Customer service
Clothing, Shoes & Accessories	✗	❸ .... Decor
Books, Toys & Entertainment	✗	

WWW.BABYFURNITUREWAREHOUSE.COM

BRAINTREE—240 WOOD RD (AT SOUTH SHORE PLAZA SHOPPING MALL); 781.843.5353; M 10-3, TH 10-8, F-SA 10-5:30, SU 12-5; MALL PARKING

BabyGap/GapKids ★★★★☆

...colorful baby and toddler clothing in clean, well-lit stores... great return policy... it's the Gap, so you know what you're getting—colorful, cute and well-made clothing... best place for baby hats... prices are reasonable especially since there's always a sale of some sort going on... sales, sales, sales—frequent and fantastic... everything I'm looking for in infant clothing—snap crotches, snaps up the front, all natural fabrics and great styling... fun seasonal selections—a great place to shop for gifts as well as for your own kids... although it can get busy, staff generally seem accommodating and helpful...

Furniture, Bedding & Decor	✗	$$$ .... Prices
Gear & Equipment	✗	❹ .... Product availability
Nursing & Feeding	✗	❹ .... Staff knowledge
Safety & Babycare	✗	❹ .... Customer service
Clothing, Shoes & Accessories	✓	❹ .... Decor
Books, Toys & Entertainment	✗	

WWW.GAP.COM

BRAINTREE—250 GRANITE ST (AT NORTH ST); 781.849.1981; M-SA 10-10, SU 11-7; PARKING LOT

KINGSTON—101 INDEPENDENCE MALL WY (AT WILLIAM GOULD JR WAY); 781.585.9353; M-SA 10-9:30, SU 11-6; MALL PARKING

Beanstalk Consignment ★★★★½

...usually some nice bargains on gently worn or used items... everything from clothes to cribs... a great way to get high-quality clothing at reasonable prices... they even carry new kids' shoes and used maternity clothing... great selection of kids and baby clothing that

have often rarely been worn... some high-quality cribs at great prices... **"**

Furniture, Bedding & Decor	✓	$$$	Prices
Gear & Equipment	✓	❹	Product availability
Nursing & Feeding	✗	❹	Staff knowledge
Safety & Babycare	✗	❹	Customer service
Clothing, Shoes & Accessories	✓	❸	Decor
Books, Toys & Entertainment	✗		

WWW.BEANSTALKCONSIGNMENT.COM

HINGHAM—78 S ST (AT CENTRAL ST); 781.740.8135; M-SA 10-5; PARKING LOT

Bombay Kids   ★★★★☆

"*...the kids' section of this furniture store carries out-of-the-ordinary items... whimsical, pastel grandfather clocks... zebra bean bags... perfect for my eclectic taste... I now prefer my daughter's room to my own... clean bathroom with changing area and wipes... they have a little table with crayons and coloring books for the kids... easy and relaxed shopping destination...* **"**

Furniture, Bedding & Decor	✓	$$$	Prices
Gear & Equipment	✗	❹	Product availability
Nursing & Feeding	✗	❹	Staff knowledge
Safety & Babycare	✗	❹	Customer service
Clothing, Shoes & Accessories	✗	❹	Decor
Books, Toys & Entertainment	✗		

WWW.BOMBAYKIDS.COM

HINGHAM—94 DERBY ST (AT CUSHING ST); 781.740.0370; M-SA 10-9, SU 12-6

Boston Baby   ★★★★★

"*...a great place for first-time parents... an amazing array of baby furniture... they used to carry lots of gear too, but don't anymore... the staff was always available to answer any questions... great selection of cribs and other items for the nursery... good variety of high-end stuff which is hard to find elsewhere... wonderful displays and prices are reasonable given the quality... a great place to see lots of baby furniture under one roof...* **"**

Furniture, Bedding & Decor	✓	$$$$	Prices
Gear & Equipment	✓	❹	Product availability
Nursing & Feeding	✗	❹	Staff knowledge
Safety & Babycare	✗	❹	Customer service
Clothing, Shoes & Accessories	✗	❹	Decor
Books, Toys & Entertainment	✓		

WWW.BOSTONBABY.COM

BRAINTREE—250 GRANITE ST (AT COMMON ST); 781.843.0095; M-T F-SA 10-6, W-TH 10-8, SU 12-5

Carol Ann's   ★★★★⯪

"*...well-stocked infant to kid store... clothing, shoes, books and toys... they have old standards like 'Make Way for Ducklings' as well as new favorites... great shoe selection—includes trendy and traditional... a good place for holiday and christening outfits... good prices on most items... staff knows their stuff... they offer a slight discount on most items...* **"**

Furniture, Bedding & Decor	✗	$$$	Prices
Gear & Equipment	✗	❹	Product availability
Nursing & Feeding	✗	❹	Staff knowledge
Safety & Babycare	✗	❹	Customer service
Clothing, Shoes & Accessories	✓	❸	Decor
Books, Toys & Entertainment	✓		

WWW.CAROLANNSONLINE.COM

HINGHAM—31-35 MAIN ST (AT SOUTH ST); 781.749.8060; M-SA 9:30-5:30 ; PARKING IN FRONT OF BLDG

Carter's ★★★★☆

"...always a great selection of inexpensive baby basics—everything from clothing to linens... I always find something at 'giveaway prices' during one of their frequent sales... busy and crowded—it can be a chaotic shopping experience... 30 to 50 percent less than what you would pay at other boutiques... I bought five pieces of baby clothing for less than $40... durable, adorable and affordable... most stores have a small play area for kids in center of store so you can get your shopping done..."

Furniture, Bedding & Decor	✓	$$	Prices
Gear & Equipment	✗	❹	Product availability
Nursing & Feeding	✗	❹	Staff knowledge
Safety & Babycare	✗	❹	Customer service
Clothing, Shoes & Accessories	✓	❹	Decor
Books, Toys & Entertainment	✓		

WWW.CARTERS.COM

WRENTHAM—1 PREMIUM OUTLET BLVD (AT SOUTH ST); 508.384.0700; M-SA 10-9, SU 10-6; MALL PARKING

Children's Orchard ★★★½☆

"...a friendly resale boutique... the clothes and gear are super clean and sold at amazing prices... amazing prices on clothing that is hardly used and practically brand new... shoes, toys, furniture, hair pretties, crib sets, etc... fantastic deals on well-selected used items... prices are great and you can pretty much always find something useful... a great place to buy those everyday play outfits... a lot of name brands at steeply discounted prices..."

Furniture, Bedding & Decor	✓	$$	Prices
Gear & Equipment	✓	❸	Product availability
Nursing & Feeding	✓	❹	Staff knowledge
Safety & Babycare	✓	❹	Customer service
Clothing, Shoes & Accessories	✓	❸	Decor
Books, Toys & Entertainment	✓		

WWW.CHILDRENSORCHARD.COM

NORWOOD—1001 PROVIDENCE HWY (AT DEAN ST); 781.769.4388; M-W 9:30-5:30, TH-F 9-8, SA 9:30-5:30, SU 12-5; PARKING LOT

QUINCY—15 SCAMMELL ST (AT QUINCY AVE); 617.770.4979; M-F 9-5, SA 10-5; PARKING LOT

Children's Place, The ★★★½☆

"...great bargains on cute clothing... shoes, socks, swimsuits, sunglasses and everything in between... lots of '3 for $20' type deals on sleepers, pants and mix-and-match separates... so much more affordable than the other 'big chains'... don't expect the most unique stuff here, but it wears and washes well... cheap clothing for cheap prices... you can leave the store with bags full of clothes without putting a huge dent in your wallet..."

Furniture, Bedding & Decor	✗	$$	Prices
Gear & Equipment	✗	❹	Product availability
Nursing & Feeding	✗	❹	Staff knowledge
Safety & Babycare	✗	❹	Customer service
Clothing, Shoes & Accessories	✓	❹	Decor
Books, Toys & Entertainment	✓		

WWW.CHILDRENSPLACE.COM

BRAINTREE—250 GRANITE ST (AT NORTH ST); 781.848.1270; M-SA 10-10, SU 11-7; PARKING LOT

BROCKTON—200 WESTGATE DR (AT WESTGATE MALL AND PLAZA); 508.897.6500; M-SA 10-9, SU 11-7; MALL PARKING

HANOVER—1775 WASHINGTON ST (AT HANOVER MALL); 781.826.5718; M-SA 10-9:30, SU 11-6; PARKING LOT

NORTH ATTLEBORO—236 EMERALD SQ (AT S WASHINGTON ST); 508.643.0902; M-SA 10-9:30, SU 11-6; PARKING LOT

WRENTHAM—1 PREMIUM OUTLETS BLVD (AT SOUTH ST); 508.384.8740; M-SA 10-9, SU 10-6; PARKING LOT

Costco ★★★½☆

"...dependable place for bulk diapers, wipes and formula at discount prices... clothing selection is very hit-or-miss... avoid shopping there during nights and weekends if possible, because parking and checkout lines are brutal... they don't have a huge selection of brands, but the brands they do have are almost always in stock and at a great price... lowest prices around for diapers and formula... kid's clothing tends to be picked through, but it's worth looking for great deals on name-brand items like Carter's..."

Furniture, Bedding & Decor	✓	$$ .... Prices
Gear & Equipment	✓	❸ .... Product availability
Nursing & Feeding	✓	❸ .... Staff knowledge
Safety & Babycare	✓	❸ .... Customer service
Clothing, Shoes & Accessories	✓	❷ .... Decor
Books, Toys & Entertainment	✓	

WWW.COSTCO.COM

AVON—120 STOCKWELL DR; 508.232.4000; M-F 11-8:30, SA 9:30-6, SU 10-6

DEDHAM—400 COMMERCIAL CRL; 781.251.9975; M-F 11-8:30, SA 9:30-6, SU 10-6

Gymboree ★★★★☆

"...beautiful clothing and great quality... colorful and stylish baby and kids wear... lots of fun birthday gift ideas... easy exchange and return policy... items usually go on sale pretty quickly... save money with Gymbucks... many stores have a play area which makes shopping with my kids fun (let alone feasible)..."

Furniture, Bedding & Decor	✗	$$$ .... Prices
Gear & Equipment	✗	❹ .... Product availability
Nursing & Feeding	✗	❹ .... Staff knowledge
Safety & Babycare	✗	❹ .... Customer service
Clothing, Shoes & Accessories	✓	❹ .... Decor
Books, Toys & Entertainment	✓	

WWW.GYMBOREE.COM

BRAINTREE—250 GRANITE ST (AT BRAINTREE HILL PARK); 781.848.6113; M-SA 10-10, SU 11-7; PARKING LOT

NORTH ATTLEBORO—999 S WASHINGTON ST (AT EMERALD SQUARE MALL); 508.695.2122; M-SA 10-9:30, SU 11-6; MALL PARKING

Isis Maternity ★★★★★

"...amazing, amazing, amazing... in addition being a fabulous parent resource, Isis has the unusual and well-made toys that get everyone excited at showers... the staff really knows about their products and are so friendly... they gave me several demonstrations when I bought our sling there... not the cheapest prices, but I gladly pay a little extra for the service... store is small, but what they do carry is all very useful stuff... convenient for after-class shopping and very baby-friendly..."

Furniture, Bedding & Decor	✗	$$$ .... Prices
Gear & Equipment	✓	❹ .... Product availability
Nursing & Feeding	✓	❺ .... Staff knowledge
Safety & Babycare	✗	❺ .... Customer service
Clothing, Shoes & Accessories	✓	❹ .... Decor

Books, Toys & Entertainment .... ✓
WWW.ISISMATERNITY.COM

NEEDHAM —110 2ND AVE (AT HIGHLAND AVE); 781.429.1500; M-TU 9-9, W 9-5, TH 9-9, F-SU 9-5; PARKING LOT

JCPenney ★★★★½☆

❝...always a good place to find clothes and other baby basics... the registry process was seamless... staff is generally friendly but the lines always seem long and slow... they don't have the greatest selection of toddler clothes, but their baby section is great... we had some damaged furniture delivered but customer service was easy and accommodating... a pretty limited selection of gear, but what they have is priced right...❞

Furniture, Bedding & Decor	✓	$$ .... Prices
Gear & Equipment	✓	❸ ...... Product availability
Nursing & Feeding	✓	❸ ...... Staff knowledge
Safety & Babycare	✓	❸ ...... Customer service
Clothing, Shoes & Accessories	✓	❸ ...... Decor
Books, Toys & Entertainment	✓	

WWW.JCPENNEY.COM

NORTH ATTLEBORO—1019 S WASHINGTON ST (AT EMERALD SQUARE MALL); 508.699.6700; M-F 10-9:30, SA 9-9:30, SU 11-6; MALL PARKING

Jordan's Furniture ★★★★☆

❝...you can't beat Jordan's when shopping for quality furniture you want to last... reasonable prices and great selection... perfect for 'big kid' beds and furniture sets... my son loves the taxi-car strollers... customer service shines at Jordan's... all kinds of furniture for all budgets... they stand behind all of their products... their displays are amazing and they have fun events to keep the kids entertained while shopping... more than a furniture store it's an adventure for the kids...❞

Furniture, Bedding & Decor	✓	$$$ .... Prices
Gear & Equipment	✗	❹ ...... Product availability
Nursing & Feeding	✗	❹ ...... Staff knowledge
Safety & Babycare	✗	❹ ...... Customer service
Clothing, Shoes & Accessories	✗	❹ ...... Decor
Books, Toys & Entertainment	✗	

WWW.JORDANS.COM

AVON—100 STOCKWELL DR (AT DYKEMAN WY); 508.580.4900; M-SA 10-10, SU 11-6; PARKING LOT

KB Toys ★★★☆☆

❝...hectic and always buzzing... wall-to-wall plastic and blinking lights... more Fisher-Price, Elmo and Sponge Bob than the eye can handle... a toy super store with discounted prices... they always have some kind of special sale going on... if you're looking for the latest and greatest popular toy, then look no further—not the place for unique or unusual toys... perfect for bulk toy shopping—especially around the holidays...❞

Furniture, Bedding & Decor	✗	$$ .... Prices
Gear & Equipment	✗	❸ ...... Product availability
Nursing & Feeding	✗	❸ ...... Staff knowledge
Safety & Babycare	✗	❸ ...... Customer service
Clothing, Shoes & Accessories	✗	❸ ...... Decor
Books, Toys & Entertainment	✓	

WWW.KBTOYS.COM

BRAINTREE—250 GRANITE ST (AT SOUTH SHORE PLAZA); 781.843.1184; M-SA 10-10 SU 11-7; PARKING LOT

BRAINTREE—300 GROVE ST (AT TEDESCHI PLAZA); 781.848.9374; M-SA 9-9, SU 10-6; PARKING LOT

BROCKTON—200 WESTGATE DR (AT WESTGATE MALL (MA)); 508.583.5883; M-SA 10-9:30, SU 11-6; MALL PARKING

EAST WALPOLE—90 BOSTON-PROVIDENCE HWY (AT WALPOLE MALL); 508.668.8169; M-SA 10-9:30, SU 12-6; MALL PARKING

HANOVER—1775 WASHINGTON ST (AT HANOVER MALL); 781.829.8840; M-SA 10-9:30, SU 11-6; MALL PARKING

NORTH ATTLEBORO—999 SO WASHINGTON ST (AT EMERALD SQUARE); 508.643.0490; M-SA 10-9, SU 11-6; PARKING LOT

WRENTHAM—I-495 & RTE 1A (AT WRENTHAM VILLAGE); 508.384.1930; M-SA 10-9, SU 10-6; PARKING LOT

Kid's Foot Locker ★★★★½☆

"...Nike, Reebok and Adidas for your little ones... hip, trendy and quite pricey... perfect for the sports addict dad who wants his kid sporting the latest NFL duds... shoes cost close to what the adult variety costs... generally good quality... they carry infant and toddler sizes..."

Furniture, Bedding & Decor	✗	$$$	Prices
Gear & Equipment	✗	❸	Product availability
Nursing & Feeding	✗	❸	Staff knowledge
Safety & Babycare	✗	❸	Customer service
Clothing, Shoes & Accessories	✓	❸	Decor
Books, Toys & Entertainment	✗		

WWW.KIDSFOOTLOCKER.COM

BRAINTREE—250 GRANITE ST (AT COMMON ST); 781.843.7791; M-SA 10-9, SU 11-7

HANOVER—1775 WASHINGTON ST (AT HANOVER MALL); 781.829.6521; M-SA 9-9:30, SU 11-6

KINGSTON—101 INDEPENDENCE MALL WY (AT ENTERPRISE DR); 781.585.0264; M-SA 10-9:30, SU 11-6

Kohl's ★★★★☆

"...nice one-stop shopping for the whole family—everything from clothing to baby gear... great sales on clothing and a good selection of higher-end brands... stylish, inexpensive clothes for babies through 24 months... very easy shopping experience... dirt-cheap sales and clearance prices... nothing super fancy, but just right for those everyday romper outfits... Graco, Eddie Bauer and other well-known brands..."

Furniture, Bedding & Decor	✓	$$	Prices
Gear & Equipment	✓	❹	Product availability
Nursing & Feeding	✓	❸	Staff knowledge
Safety & Babycare	✓	❸	Customer service
Clothing, Shoes & Accessories	✓	❸	Decor
Books, Toys & Entertainment	✓		

WWW.KOHLS.COM

EAST WALPOLE—100 BOSTON-PROVIDENCE HWY (AT THE MALL AT WALPOLE); 508.660.9921; M-SA 8-10, SU 10-8; FREE PARKING

HINGHAM—100 DERBY ST (AT HINGHAM PLAZA); 781.749.0763; M-SA 8-10, SU 10-8; FREE PARKING

STOUGHTON—501 TECHNOLOGY CENTER DR (OFF RT 139); 781.341.5980; M-SA 8-10, SU 10-8; FREE PARKING

Macy's ★★★★½☆

"...Macy's has it all and I never leave empty-handed... if you time your visit right you can find some great deals... go during the week so you don't get overwhelmed with the weekend crowd... good for staples as well as beautiful party dresses for girls... lots of brand-names like Carter's, Guess, and Ralph Lauren... not much in terms of assistance...

newspaper coupons and sales help keep the cost down... some stores are better organized and maintained than others... if you're going to shop at a department store for your baby, then Macy's is a safe bet... **"**

Furniture, Bedding & Decor ✓	$$$ .... Prices
Gear & Equipment ✗	❸ .... Product availability
Nursing & Feeding ✗	❸ .... Staff knowledge
Safety & Babycare ✗	❸ .... Customer service
Clothing, Shoes & Accessories ✓	❸ .... Decor
Books, Toys & Entertainment ✓	

WWW.MACYS.COM

BRAINTREE—250 GRANITE ST (AT SOUTH SHORE PLAZA); 781.848.1500; M-SA 10-10, SU 11-7; PARKING LOT

BROCKTON—200 WESTGATE DR (AT WESTGATE MALL AND PLAZA); 508.588.7400; M-SA 10-9:30, SU 11-6; MALL PARKING

Michelson's Shoes ★★★★☆

" *...a great assortment of puddle boots... terrific staff that knows how to measure and fit a baby foot... an essential store for any parent of young children... great place to buy good quality shoe's for children... old school shoe store that really knows shoes... my kids both have wide feet and they always have wide widths in stock... so helpful and patient with kids that it's almost scary...* **"**

Furniture, Bedding & Decor ✗	$$$ .... Prices
Gear & Equipment ✗	❹ .... Product availability
Nursing & Feeding ✗	❺ .... Staff knowledge
Safety & Babycare ✗	❺ .... Customer service
Clothing, Shoes & Accessories ✓	❸ .... Decor
Books, Toys & Entertainment ✗	

WWW.MICHELSONSHOES.COM

NEEDHAM—1082 GREAT PLAIN AVE (AT CHESTNUT ST); 781.449.2753; M-TH 9-6, F 9-8, SA 9-5:30; PARKING LOT

Nutshell

Furniture, Bedding & Decor ✗	✗ .... Gear & Equipment
Nursing & Feeding ✗	✗ .... Safety & Babycare
Clothing, Shoes & Accessories ✓	✗ .... Books, Toys & Entertainment

WWW.THENUTSHELLMILTON.COM

MILTON—10 BASSETT ST (AT GRANITE); 617.698.7273; M-TU 9:30-6, W-TH 9:30-7, F-SA 9:30-6, SU 11-5; PARKING LOT

Old Navy ★★★★☆

" *...hip and 'in' clothes for infants and tots... plenty of steals on clearance items... T-shirts and pants for $10 or less... busy, busy, busy—long lines, especially on weekends... nothing fancy and you won't mind when your kids get down and dirty in these clothes... easy to wash, decent quality... you can shop for your baby, your toddler, your teen and yourself all at the same time... clothes are especially affordable when you hit their sales (post-holiday sales are amazing!)...* **"**

Furniture, Bedding & Decor ✗	$$ .... Prices
Gear & Equipment ✗	❹ .... Product availability
Nursing & Feeding ✗	❸ .... Staff knowledge
Safety & Babycare ✗	❸ .... Customer service
Clothing, Shoes & Accessories ✓	❸ .... Decor
Books, Toys & Entertainment ✗	

WWW.OLDNAVY.COM

BROCKTON—200 WESTGATE DR (AT WESTGATE MALL AND PLAZA); 508.587.6700; M-SA 9-9:30, SU 10-6; PARKING LOT

DEDHAM—300 PROVIDENCE HWY (AT DEDHAM MALL); 781.461.1350; M-SA 9-9, SU 10-6; PARKING LOT

HANOVER—1775 WASHINGTON ST (AT HANOVER MALL); 781.829.9332; M-SA 9-9, SU 11-6; MALL PARKING

HINGHAM—225 LINCOLN ST (AT LINCOLN ST); 781.740.1022; M-SA 9-9, SU 11-6; PARKING LOT

KINGSTON—101 INDEPENDENCE MALL WY (AT RABOTH RD); 781.582.0007; M-SA 10-9:30, SU 10-6; MALL PARKING

NORTH ATTLEBORO—1250 S WASHINGTON ST (AT EMERALD SQUARE MALL); 508.643.4664; M-SA 9-9, SU 11-6

WALPOLE—90 PROVIDENCE HWY (AT THE MALL AT WALPOLE); 508.668.2365; M-SA 9-9, SU 11-6; MALL PARKING

OshKosh B'Gosh ★★★★☆

"...cute, sturdy clothes for infants and toddlers... frequent sales make their high-quality merchandise a lot more affordable... doesn't every American kid have to get a pair of their overalls?.. great selection of cute clothes for boys... you can't go wrong here—their clothing is fun and worth the price... customer service is pretty hit-or-miss from store to store... we always walk out of here with something fun and colorful..."

Furniture, Bedding & Decor	✗	$$$ .... Prices
Gear & Equipment	✗	❹ .... Product availability
Nursing & Feeding	✗	❹ .... Staff knowledge
Safety & Babycare	✗	❹ .... Customer service
Clothing, Shoes & Accessories	✓	❹ .... Decor
Books, Toys & Entertainment	✗	

WWW.OSHKOSHBGOSH.COM

WRENTHAM—1 PREMIUM OUTLETS BLVD (AT SOUTH ST); 508.384.0271; M-SA 10-9, SU 10-6; PARKING LOT

Parents' Pride ★★★★½☆

"...if you are looking for kid stuff with an Irish twist, this is your store... from wool hats, mittens and sweaters to tartans and kilts... they even have little tiny claddagh rings... I have found a better boys selection here than in most stores, even boutiques... easy with kids because they have a great train set in the back..."

Furniture, Bedding & Decor	✗	$$$ .... Prices
Gear & Equipment	✗	❺ .... Product availability
Nursing & Feeding	✗	❺ .... Staff knowledge
Safety & Babycare	✗	❺ .... Customer service
Clothing, Shoes & Accessories	✓	❹ .... Decor
Books, Toys & Entertainment	✓	

WWW.PARENTSPRIDE.COM

NORWOOD—710 WASHINGTON ST (AT DAY ST); 781.551.8989; DAILY 10-5; PARKING LOT

Priceless Kids ★★★★½☆

"...inexpensive clothes and shoes even with brand-name labels... especially helpful for the early months as babies grow quickly... great place for T-shirts, socks and accessories... affordable and cute clothes, but quality can vary... good when you're not looking for anything in particular... great bargains and interesting variety of clothing..."

Furniture, Bedding & Decor	✗	$$ .... Prices
Gear & Equipment	✗	❸ .... Product availability
Nursing & Feeding	✗	❸ .... Staff knowledge
Safety & Babycare	✗	❸ .... Customer service
Clothing, Shoes & Accessories	✓	❸ .... Decor
Books, Toys & Entertainment	✗	

WWW.PRICELESSKIDS.COM

SOUTH ATTLEBORO—265 WASHINGTON ST (AT SOUTH ATTLEBORO SQ); 508.399.5300; M-F 9-9, SA 10-9, SU 12-5; PARKING LOT

STOUGHTON—1334 PARK PLAZA (AT NORTH POINT ST); 781.344.6818; M-SA 10-9, SU 12-5; PARKING LOT

Rainbow Kids ★★⯪☆☆

"...fun clothing styles for infants and tots at low prices... the quality isn't the same as the more expensive brands, but the sleepers and play outfits always hold up well... great place for basics... cute trendy shoe selection for your little walker... we love the prices... up-to-date selection..."

Furniture, Bedding & Decor	✗	$$ .... Prices
Gear & Equipment	✓	❸ .... Product availability
Nursing & Feeding	✗	❸ .... Staff knowledge
Safety & Babycare	✗	❸ .... Customer service
Clothing, Shoes & Accessories	✓	❸ .... Decor
Books, Toys & Entertainment	✓	

WWW.RAINBOWSHOPS.COM

BROCKTON—200 WESTGATE DR (AT REYNOLDS MEMORIAL HWY); 508.588.7978; M-SA 10-9:30; PARKING LOT

Roseann's ★★★★⯪

"...the children's area is tucked into a bigger store full of all kinds of beautiful trinkets—from jewelry to flowers... the kid's section has crocheted baby hats and sweaters... dolls, wooden rockers, toys, picture frames... the baby dresses are so sweet they could be for a doll... preppy accessories for little girls... inexpensive, check it out... all handmade and affordable..."

Furniture, Bedding & Decor	✗	$ .... Prices
Gear & Equipment	✗	❺ .... Product availability
Nursing & Feeding	✗	❺ .... Staff knowledge
Safety & Babycare	✗	❺ .... Customer service
Clothing, Shoes & Accessories	✓	❹ .... Decor
Books, Toys & Entertainment	✓	

WWW.ROSEANNSHOPE.COM

QUINCY—1089 HANCOCK ST (AT NEXT TOTHOMAS S BURGIN PKWY); 617.773.4353; T 9:30-5:30, W-TH 9:30-7, F-SA 9:30-5:30; STREET

Rugged Bear ★★★★☆

"...their merchandise is truly top quality... employees go above and beyond to help... a little pricey, but the the durability of the clothes and shoes are worth it... top brands as well as their own which we have had very good luck with... if they don't have the size/style you are looking for they are more than happy to call other stores and have it sent to you... go and get great outdoor wear for your kids... sales near the end of the season are the best times to go..."

Furniture, Bedding & Decor	✗	$$$ .... Prices
Gear & Equipment	✓	❹ .... Product availability
Nursing & Feeding	✗	❹ .... Staff knowledge
Safety & Babycare	✗	❹ .... Customer service
Clothing, Shoes & Accessories	✓	❹ .... Decor
Books, Toys & Entertainment	✗	

WWW.RUGGEDBEAR.COM

HANOVER—2053 WASHINGTON ST (AT MERCHANT ROW); 781.982.1828; M-SA 10-6, TH 10-8; PARKING IN FRONT OF BLDG

NORWOOD—111 LENOX ST (AT NAHATAN ST); 781.762.4847; M-SA 10-5:30 SU 12-5; PARKING LOT

Sears ★★★☆☆

"...a decent selection of clothes and basic baby equipment... check out the Kids Club program—it's a great way to save money... you go to Sears to save money, not to be pampered... the quality of their

merchandise is better than Wal-Mart, but don't expect anything too special or different... not much in terms of gear, but tons of well-priced baby and toddler clothing... **"**

Furniture, Bedding & Decor ✓	$$ .... Prices
Gear & Equipment ✓	❸ .... Product availability
Nursing & Feeding ✓	❸ .... Staff knowledge
Safety & Babycare ✓	❸ ....Customer service
Clothing, Shoes & Accessories ✓	❸ .... Decor
Books, Toys & Entertainment ✓	

WWW.SEARS.COM

BRAINTREE—250 GRANITE ST (AT SOUTH SHORE PLAZA); 781.356.6000; M-SA 9:30-10, SU 11-7

BROCKTON—200 WESTGATE DR (AT WESTGATE MALL AND PLAZA); 508.897.4200; M-F 9:30-9:30, SA 8-9:30, SU 11-6

DEDHAM—300 PRIVIDENCE HWY (AT DEDHAM MALL); 781.320.5125; M-SA 9-9:30, SU 11-5

KINGSTON—101 INDEPENDENCE MALL WY (AT INDEPENDENCE MALL); 781.582.3600; M-SA 9:30-9:30, SU 11-6; MALL PARKING

Shoe Market Kids ★★★★½

"*...a customer-oriented shoe store... Stride Rite, Primigi, Merrell... clogs... excellent selection of footwear... I go here so that I can have fun buying shoes for the kids... fabulous shoe selection, especially of the European brands... nice range of prices so that you can definitely find a shoe in your budget... train table makes the shopping easy—but the leaving hard...* **"**

Furniture, Bedding & Decor ✗	$$$$ .... Prices
Gear & Equipment ✗	❹ .... Product availability
Nursing & Feeding ✗	❹ .... Staff knowledge
Safety & Babycare ✗	❹ ....Customer service
Clothing, Shoes & Accessories ✓	❹ .... Decor
Books, Toys & Entertainment ✗	

WWW.SHOEMARKETKIDS.COM

COHASSET—390 CHIEF JUSTICE CUSHING HWY (AT BREWSTER RD); 781.383.8637; M-SA 10-6, SU 12-5; PARKING LOT

Strasburg Children ★★★★☆

"*...totally adorable special occasion outfits for babies and kids... classic baby, toddler, and kids clothes... dress-up clothes for kids... if you are looking for a flower girl or ring bearer outfit, look no further... handmade clothes that will last through multiple kids or generations... it's not cheap, but you can find great sales if you are patient...* **"**

Furniture, Bedding & Decor ✗	$$$$ .... Prices
Gear & Equipment ✗	❹ .... Product availability
Nursing & Feeding ✗	❹ .... Staff knowledge
Safety & Babycare ✗	❹ ....Customer service
Clothing, Shoes & Accessories ✓	❹ .... Decor
Books, Toys & Entertainment ✗	

WWW.STRASBURGCHILDREN.COM

WRENTHAM—WRENTHAM PREMIUM STORES; 508.384.0158; M-SA 10-9, SU 10-8

Stride Rite Shoes ★★★½☆

"*...wonderful selection of baby and toddler shoes... sandals, sneakers, and even special-occasion shoes... decent quality shoes that last... they know a lot about kids' shoes and take the time to get it right—they always measure my son's feet before fittings... store sizes vary, but they always have something in stock that works... they've even special ordered shoes for my daughter... a fun 'first shoe' buying experience...* **"**

baby basics

Furniture, Bedding & Decor .... ✗	$$$ .... Prices
Gear & Equipment .... ✗	❹ .... Product availability
Nursing & Feeding .... ✗	❹ .... Staff knowledge
Safety & Babycare .... ✗	❹ .... Customer service
Clothing, Shoes & Accessories .... ✓	❹ .... Decor
Books, Toys & Entertainment .... ✗	

WWW.STRIDERITE.COM

BRAINTREE—250 GRANITE ST (AT FORBES RD); 781.843.8651; M-SA 10-10, SU 11-7; PARKING LOT

Sweet William ★★★★½

"...beautiful, but will cost you an arm and a leg... fine baby linens for your princess or prince... high thread counts... everything you could ever need for your nursery... our nursery is my favorite room in the house..."

Furniture, Bedding & Decor .... ✓	$$$ .... Prices
Gear & Equipment .... ✗	❹ .... Product availability
Nursing & Feeding .... ✗	❺ .... Staff knowledge
Safety & Babycare .... ✗	❺ .... Customer service
Clothing, Shoes & Accessories .... ✗	❺ .... Decor
Books, Toys & Entertainment .... ✗	

WWW.SWEETWILLIAM.COM

HINGHAM—5 POND PARK RD (AT INDUSTRIAL PARK RD); 781.749.9103; M-F 9-5; PARKING LOT

Talbots Kids ★★★★½☆

"...a nice alternative to the typical department store experience... expensive, but fantastic quality... great for holiday and special occasion outfits including christening outfits... well-priced, conservative children's clothing... cute selections for infants, toddlers and kids... sales are fantastic—up to half off at least a couple times a year... the best part is, you can also shop for yourself while shopping for baby..."

Furniture, Bedding & Decor .... ✗	$$$$ .... Prices
Gear & Equipment .... ✗	❹ .... Product availability
Nursing & Feeding .... ✗	❹ .... Staff knowledge
Safety & Babycare .... ✗	❹ .... Customer service
Clothing, Shoes & Accessories .... ✓	❹ .... Decor
Books, Toys & Entertainment .... ✗	

WWW.TALBOTS.COM

BRAINTREE—250 GRANITE ST (AT HWY 1 JUNCTION); 781.849.6751; M-SA 10-10, SU 11-7; PARKING LOT

HINGHAM—96 DERBY ST (AT HINGHAM PLAZA); 781.740.9234; M-SA 10-9, SU 11-6

Target ★★★★☆

"...our favorite place to shop for kids' stuff—good selection and very affordable... guilt-free shopping—kids grow so fast so I don't want to pay high department-store prices... everything from diapers and sippy cups to car seats and strollers... easy return policy... generally helpful staff, but you don't go for the service—you go for the prices... decent registry that won't freak your friends out with outrageous prices... easy, convenient shopping for well-priced items... all the big-box brands available—Graco, Evenflo, Eddie Bauer, etc...."

Furniture, Bedding & Decor .... ✓	$$ .... Prices
Gear & Equipment .... ✓	❹ .... Product availability
Nursing & Feeding .... ✓	❸ .... Staff knowledge
Safety & Babycare .... ✓	❸ .... Customer service
Clothing, Shoes & Accessories .... ✓	❸ .... Decor
Books, Toys & Entertainment .... ✓	

WWW.TARGET.COM

KINGSTON—101 INDEPENDENCE MALL WAY (AT INDEPENDENCE MALL); 781.585.5825; M-SA 8-10, SU 8-9; PARKING IN FRONT OF BLDG

NORTH ATTLEBORO—1205 S WASHINGTON ST (AT EMERALD SQUARE MALL); 508.699.9118; M-SA 8-10, SU 8-9; PARKING IN FRONT OF BLDG

Toy Box ★★★★☆

"...toys, toys, toys... from infants to big kids... salespeople are willing and able to guide your gift buying... they will even gift wrap for free... loose toys to occupy your kids while you shop is a bonus... indoor and outdoor games and toys..."

Furniture, Bedding & Decor	✗	$$$	Prices
Gear & Equipment	✗	❺	Product availability
Nursing & Feeding	✗	❺	Staff knowledge
Safety & Babycare	✗	❺	Customer service
Clothing, Shoes & Accessories	✗	❹	Decor
Books, Toys & Entertainment	✓		

WWW.THETOYBOXHANOVER.COM

HANOVER—2053 WASHINGTON ST (AT RT 53); 781.871.3650; M-F 9:30-8, SA 9:30-6, SU 12-5; PARKING LOT

Toys R Us ★★★★☆

"...not just toys, but also tons of gear and supplies including diapers and formula... a hectic shopping experience but the prices make it all worthwhile... I've experienced good and bad service at the same store on the same day... the stores are huge and can be overwhelming... most big brand-names available... leave the kids at home unless you want to end up with a cart full of toys..."

Furniture, Bedding & Decor	✓	$$$	Prices
Gear & Equipment	✓	❹	Product availability
Nursing & Feeding	✓	❸	Staff knowledge
Safety & Babycare	✓	❸	Customer service
Clothing, Shoes & Accessories	✓	❸	Decor
Books, Toys & Entertainment	✓		

WWW.TOYSRUS.COM

BROCKTON—105 CAMPENELLI INDUSTRIAL (AT WESTGATE MALL); 508.584.8697; M-SA 10-9, SU 11-6; MALL PARKING

DEDHAM—100 PROVIDENCE HWY (AT DEDHAM MALL); 781.329.4924; M-SA 10-9, SU 11-6; MALL PARKING

Village Toy Shop ★★★★★

"...family-friendly atmosphere... from stuffed animals to science projects... all ages, you might even find something for your parents... nice clean bathroom with lots of room for diaper changing... free gift wrapping... don't miss the story reading and craft classes..."

Furniture, Bedding & Decor	✗	$$	Prices
Gear & Equipment	✗	❺	Product availability
Nursing & Feeding	✗	❺	Staff knowledge
Safety & Babycare	✗	❺	Customer service
Clothing, Shoes & Accessories	✗	❺	Decor
Books, Toys & Entertainment	✓		

WWW.VILLAGETOY.COM

NORTH EASTON—285 WASHINGTON ST (AT RT 138/MAIN ST); 508.238.8697; M-T 10-6, W-F 10-8, SA 10-6, SU 12-5; PARKING LOT

Online

"lila picks" ★★★★★

- ★ babycenter.com
- ★ babyuniverse.com
- ★ babystyle.com
- ★ joggingstroller.com

ababy.com
Furniture, Bedding & Decor ✓	✓ Gear & Equipment
Nursing & Feeding ✗	✓ Safety & Babycare
Clothing, Shoes & Accessories ✓	✗ Books, Toys & Entertainment

aikobaby.com ★★★☆☆
"...high end clothes that are so cute...everything from Catamini to Jack and Lily... you can find super expensive infant and baby clothes at discounted prices... amazing selection of diaper bags so you don't have to look like a frumpy mom (or dad)..."

Furniture, Bedding & Decor ✗	✓ Gear & Equipment
Nursing & Feeding ✗	✗ Safety & Babycare
Clothing, Shoes & Accessories ✓	✗ Books, Toys & Entertainment

albeebaby.com ★★★★☆
"...they offer a really comprehensive selection of baby gear... their prices are some of the best online... great discounts on Maclarens before the new models come out... good product availability—fast shipping and easy transactions... the site is pretty easy to use... the prices are surprisingly great..."

Furniture, Bedding & Decor ✓	✓ Gear & Equipment
Nursing & Feeding ✓	✓ Safety & Babycare
Clothing, Shoes & Accessories ✓	✓ Books, Toys & Entertainment

amazon.com ★★★★½
"...unless you've been living under a rock, you know that in addition to books, Amazon carries an amazing amount of baby stuff too... they have the best prices and offer free shipping on bigger purchases... you can even buy used items for dirt cheap... I always read the comments written by others—they're very useful in helping make my decisions... I love Amazon for just about everything, but their baby selection only carries the big box standards..."

Furniture, Bedding & Decor ✗	✓ Gear & Equipment
Nursing & Feeding ✓	✓ Safety & Babycare
Clothing, Shoes & Accessories ✓	✓ Books, Toys & Entertainment

arunningstroller.com ★★★★½
"...the prices are very competitive and the customer service is great... I talked to them on the phone for a while and they totally hooked me up with the right model... if you're looking for a new stroller, look no further... talk to Marilyn—she's the best... shipping costs are reasonable and their prices overall are good..."

Furniture, Bedding & Decor ✓	✓ Gear & Equipment
Nursing & Feeding ✗	✗ Safety & Babycare
Clothing, Shoes & Accessories ✗	✗ Books, Toys & Entertainment

babiesinthesun.com ★★★★☆

"...one-stop shopping for cloth diapers... run by a fantastic woman who had 3 cloth diapered babies herself and is a wealth of knowledge... if you live in South Florida, the owner will let you into her home to see the merchandise and ask questions... great selection and the customer service is the best..."

Furniture, Bedding & Decor ✗	✓ Gear & Equipment
Nursing & Feeding ✗	✓ Safety & Babycare
Clothing, Shoes & Accessories ✗	✗ Books, Toys & Entertainment

babiesrus.com ★★★★☆

"...terrific web site with all the baby gear you'll need... registering online made it easy for my family and friends... getting the registry activated was a bit tricky... super convenient and ideal for the moms-to-be who are on bedrest... web site prices are comparable to in-store prices... shipping is usually free... a very efficient way to buy and send baby gifts... our local Babies R Us said they will accept returns if they carry the same item... not all online items are available in your local store..."

Furniture, Bedding & Decor ✓	✓ Gear & Equipment
Nursing & Feeding ✓	✓ Safety & Babycare
Clothing, Shoes & Accessories ✓	✓ Books, Toys & Entertainment

babiestravellite.com ★★★★½

"...caters to traveling families... they deliver baby items to your hotel room anywhere in the country... all of the different baby supplies you will need when you travel with a baby or a toddler... they sell almost every major brand for each product and their prices are sometimes cheaper than you would find at your local store..."

Furniture, Bedding & Decor ✗	✗ Gear & Equipment
Nursing & Feeding ✓	✓ Safety & Babycare
Clothing, Shoes & Accessories ✗	✓ Books, Toys & Entertainment

babyage.com ★★★★☆

"...fast shipping and the best prices around... flat rate shipping is great after the baby has arrived and you don't have time to go to the store... very attentive customer service... clearance items are a great deal (regular items are very competitive too)... ordering and delivery were super smooth... I usually check this web site before I purchase any baby gear... sign up for their newsletter and they'll notify you when they are having a sale..."

Furniture, Bedding & Decor ✓	✓ Gear & Equipment
Nursing & Feeding ✓	✓ Safety & Babycare
Clothing, Shoes & Accessories ✓	✓ Books, Toys & Entertainment

babyant.com ★★★★☆

"...wide variety of brands and products available through their site... super easy to navigate... fun, whimsical ideas... nice people and helpful... easy to return items and you can call them with questions... often has the best prices and low shipping costs..."

Furniture, Bedding & Decor ✓	✓ Gear & Equipment
Nursing & Feeding ✓	✓ Safety & Babycare
Clothing, Shoes & Accessories ✓	✓ Books, Toys & Entertainment

babybazaar.com

"...high-end baby stuff available on an easy-to-use web site... lots of European styles... quick processing and shipping... mom's tips, educational toys, exclusive favorites Bugaboo and Stokke..."

Furniture, Bedding & Decor ✓	✓ Gear & Equipment
Nursing & Feeding ✓	✓ Safety & Babycare
Clothing, Shoes & Accessories ✓	✓ Books, Toys & Entertainment

babybestbuy.com

Furniture, Bedding & Decor ✓	✓ Gear & Equipment
Nursing & Feeding ✓	✓ Safety & Babycare
Clothing, Shoes & Accessories ✓	✓ Books, Toys & Entertainment

babycatalog.com ★★★★☆

"...great deals on many essentials... wide selection of rockers but fewer options in other categories... the web site could be more user-friendly... customer service and delivery was fast and efficient... check out their seasonal specials... the baby club is a great way to save additional money... sign up for their wonderful pregnancy/new baby email newsletter... check this web site before you buy anywhere else..."

Furniture, Bedding & Decor ✓	✓ Gear & Equipment
Nursing & Feeding ✓	✓ Safety & Babycare
Clothing, Shoes & Accessories ✓	✓ Books, Toys & Entertainment

babycenter.com ★★★★★

"...a terrific selection of all things baby, plus quick shipping... free shipping on big orders... makes shopping convenient for new parents... web site is very user friendly... they always email you about sale items and special offers... lots of useful information for parents... carries everything you may need... online registry is simple, easy and a great way to get what you need... includes helpful products ratings by parents... they've created a nice online community in addition to their online store..."

Furniture, Bedding & Decor ✓	✓ Gear & Equipment
Nursing & Feeding ✓	✓ Safety & Babycare
Clothing, Shoes & Accessories ✓	✓ Books, Toys & Entertainment

babydepot.com ★★★☆☆

"...carries everything you'll find in a big department store but at cheaper prices and with everything all in one place... be certain you know what you want because returns can be difficult... site could be more user-friendly... online selection can differ from instore selection... love the online registry..."

Furniture, Bedding & Decor ✓	✓ Gear & Equipment
Nursing & Feeding ✓	✓ Safety & Babycare
Clothing, Shoes & Accessories ✓	✓ Books, Toys & Entertainment

babygeared.com

Furniture, Bedding & Decor ✓	✓ Gear & Equipment
Nursing & Feeding ✓	✓ Safety & Babycare
Clothing, Shoes & Accessories ✓	✓ Books, Toys & Entertainment

babyphd.com

Furniture, Bedding & Decor ✓	✗ Gear & Equipment
Nursing & Feeding ✗	✗ Safety & Babycare
Clothing, Shoes & Accessories ✓	✓ Books, Toys & Entertainment

babystyle.com ★★★★★

"...their web site is just like their stores—terrific... an excellent source for everything a parent needs... fantastic maternity and baby clothes...

they always respond quickly by email... their site seems to have even more merchandise than their stores... I started shopping on their site after receiving a gift card—very easy and convenient... wonderful selection... **"**

Furniture, Bedding & Decor ✓	✓ Gear & Equipment
Nursing & Feeding ✓	✓ Safety & Babycare
Clothing, Shoes & Accessories ✓	✓ Books, Toys & Entertainment

babysupermall.com

Furniture, Bedding & Decor ✓	✓ Gear & Equipment
Nursing & Feeding ✓	✓ Safety & Babycare
Clothing, Shoes & Accessories ✓	✓ Books, Toys & Entertainment

babyuniverse.com ★★★★★

" *...nice large selection of specialty and basic items... easy-to-use web site with decent prices... carries Carter's clothes and many other popular brands... great bedding selection - they're one of the few places with the Kidsline bedding I wanted... adorable backpacks for toddlers and preschoolers... check out the site for strollers and car seats... this was my first online shopping experience and they made it so easy, convenient and fast, I was hooked... fine customer service... flat rate (if not free) shipping takes the 'ouch' factor out of those big ticket purchases...* **"**

Furniture, Bedding & Decor ✓	✓ Gear & Equipment
Nursing & Feeding ✓	✓ Safety & Babycare
Clothing, Shoes & Accessories ✓	✓ Books, Toys & Entertainment

barebabies.com

Furniture, Bedding & Decor ✓	✓ Gear & Equipment
Nursing & Feeding ✓	✓ Safety & Babycare
Clothing, Shoes & Accessories ✓	✓ Books, Toys & Entertainment

birthandbaby.com ★★★★☆

" *...incredible site for buying a nursing bra... there is more information about different manufacturers than you can imagine... I've even received a phone call from the owner after placing an order to clarify something... free shipping, so it's easy to buy multiple sizes and send back the ones that don't fit... their selection of nursing bras is better than any other place I've found... if you are a hard to fit size, this is the place to go...* **"**

Furniture, Bedding & Decor ✗	✓ Gear & Equipment
Nursing & Feeding ✓	✓ Safety & Babycare
Clothing, Shoes & Accessories ✗	✓ Books, Toys & Entertainment

blueberrybabies.com

Furniture, Bedding & Decor ✓	✓ Gear & Equipment
Nursing & Feeding ✓	✓ Safety & Babycare
Clothing, Shoes & Accessories ✓	✓ Books, Toys & Entertainment

buybuybaby.com ★★★★½

" *...this is the web site for the popular New York-based baby retailer... you name it, they've got it... all the items in their store can also be found on their web site... prices are fair - especially since things get shipped right to your door... we had some items that were damaged and their online customer service took care of it without any problems...* **"**

Furniture, Bedding & Decor ✓	✓ Gear & Equipment
Nursing & Feeding ✓	✓ Safety & Babycare
Clothing, Shoes & Accessories ✓	✓ Books, Toys & Entertainment

childcarriers.com

Furniture, Bedding & Decor ✗	✓ Gear & Equipment

participate in our survey at

| Nursing & Feeding | ✗ | ✗ | Safety & Babycare |
| Clothing, Shoes & Accessories | ✗ | ✗ | Books, Toys & Entertainment |

clothdiaper.com
Furniture, Bedding & Decor	✗	✓	Gear & Equipment
Nursing & Feeding	✓	✓	Safety & Babycare
Clothing, Shoes & Accessories	✗	✗	Books, Toys & Entertainment

cocoacrayon.com
Furniture, Bedding & Decor	✓	✓	Gear & Equipment
Nursing & Feeding	✓	✓	Safety & Babycare
Clothing, Shoes & Accessories	✓	✓	Books, Toys & Entertainment

cvs.com ★★★★☆

"...super convenient web site for any 'drug store' items... items are delivered in a reasonable amount of time... decent selection of baby products... prices are competitive and ordering online definitely beats making the trip out to the drugstore... order a bunch of stuff at a time so shipping is free... I used them for my baby announcements and everyone loved them... super easy to refill prescriptions... it was a real relief to order all my formula, baby wipes and diapers online..."

Furniture, Bedding & Decor	✗	✗	Gear & Equipment
Nursing & Feeding	✓	✓	Safety & Babycare
Clothing, Shoes & Accessories	✗	✗	Books, Toys & Entertainment

dreamtimebaby.com
Furniture, Bedding & Decor	✓	✓	Gear & Equipment
Nursing & Feeding	✓	✓	Safety & Babycare
Clothing, Shoes & Accessories	✓	✓	Books, Toys & Entertainment

drugstore.com ★★★★☆
Furniture, Bedding & Decor	✗	✗	Gear & Equipment
Nursing & Feeding	✓	✓	Safety & Babycare
Clothing, Shoes & Accessories	✗	✗	Books, Toys & Entertainment

ebay.com ★★★★☆

"...great way to save money on everything from maternity clothes to breast pumps... be careful with whom you do business... it's always worth checking out what's available... I picked up a brand new jogger for dirt cheap... great deals to be had if you have patience to browse and be willing to resell or exchange what you don't like... baby stuff is easily found and often reasonably priced... keep an eye on shipping costs when you're bidding..."

Furniture, Bedding & Decor	✓	✓	Gear & Equipment
Nursing & Feeding	✓	✓	Safety & Babycare
Clothing, Shoes & Accessories	✓	✓	Books, Toys & Entertainment

egiggle.com ★★★★☆

"...nice selection—not overwhelming... don't expect the big box store brands here—they carry higher-end, specialty items that you won't find elsewhere... smooth shopping experience... nice site—convenient and easy to use..."

Furniture, Bedding & Decor	✓	✓	Gear & Equipment
Nursing & Feeding	✓	✓	Safety & Babycare
Clothing, Shoes & Accessories	✓	✓	Books, Toys & Entertainment

gagagifts.com ★★★★☆

"...great online store that carries fun clothes and unique gifts and toys for kids and adults... unique and special gifts like designer diaper bags, Whoozit learning toys and handmade quilts... this site makes gift buying incredibly easy—I'm done in less than 5 minutes... prices are high but products are special..."

www.lilaguide.com

Furniture, Bedding & Decor .... ✓	✓ .... Gear & Equipment
Nursing & Feeding .... ✓	✓ .... Safety & Babycare
Clothing, Shoes & Accessories ...... ✓	✓ .... Books, Toys & Entertainment

gap.com ★★★★☆

"...I love the Gap's online store—all the cool things in their stores available via my computer... terrific selection of boys and girls clothes plus cute shoes... you can find awesome deals and return online purchases to Gap stores... their clothes are very durable... it's easy to purchase items online and delivery is prompt... a very practical and affordable way to shop... site makes it easy to quickly find what you need... sign up for the weekly newsletter and you'll find out about online sales..."

Furniture, Bedding & Decor .... ✓	✓ .... Gear & Equipment
Nursing & Feeding .... ✗	✗ .... Safety & Babycare
Clothing, Shoes & Accessories ...... ✓	✓ .... Books, Toys & Entertainment

geniusbabies.com ★★★½☆

"...the best selection available of developmental toys and gifts... the only place to order real puppets from the Baby Einstein video series... cool place for unique baby shower and birthday gifts... their site navigation could use an upgrade..."

Furniture, Bedding & Decor .... ✗	✗ .... Gear & Equipment
Nursing & Feeding .... ✗	✗ .... Safety & Babycare
Clothing, Shoes & Accessories ...... ✗	✓ .... Books, Toys & Entertainment

gymboree.com ★★★★☆

"...beautiful clothing and great quality... colorful and stylish baby and kids wear... lots of fun birthday gift ideas... easy exchange and return policy... items usually go on sale pretty quickly... save money with gymbucks... many stores have a play area which makes shopping with my kids fun (let alone feasible)..."

Furniture, Bedding & Decor .... ✗	✗ .... Gear & Equipment
Nursing & Feeding .... ✗	✗ .... Safety & Babycare
Clothing, Shoes & Accessories ...... ✓	✓ .... Books, Toys & Entertainment

hannaandersson.com

Furniture, Bedding & Decor .... ✓	✗ .... Gear & Equipment
Nursing & Feeding .... ✓	✗ .... Safety & Babycare
Clothing, Shoes & Accessories ...... ✓	✓ .... Books, Toys & Entertainment

jcpenney.com

Furniture, Bedding & Decor .... ✓	✗ .... Gear & Equipment
Nursing & Feeding .... ✗	✓ .... Safety & Babycare
Clothing, Shoes & Accessories ...... ✓	✗ .... Books, Toys & Entertainment

joggingstroller.com ★★★★★

"...an excellent resource when you're choosing a jogging stroller... the entire site is devoted to joggers... very helpful information that's worth checking whether you plan to buy from them or not... the best online guide for researching jogging strollers... includes helpful comparisons and parent reviews on the top strollers..."

Furniture, Bedding & Decor .... ✗	✓ .... Gear & Equipment
Nursing & Feeding .... ✗	✗ .... Safety & Babycare
Clothing, Shoes & Accessories ...... ✗	✗ .... Books, Toys & Entertainment

kidsurplus.com

Furniture, Bedding & Decor .... ✓	✗ .... Gear & Equipment
Nursing & Feeding .... ✓	✗ .... Safety & Babycare
Clothing, Shoes & Accessories ...... ✓	✓ .... Books, Toys & Entertainment

landofnod.com ★★★★☆

baby basics

"...cool site with adorable and unique furnishings... hip kid style art work... fabulous furniture and bedding... the catalog is amusing and nicely laid out... lots of sweet selections for both boys and girls... good customer service... fun but small selection of music, books, toys and more... a great way to get ideas for putting rooms together..."

Furniture, Bedding & Decor .... ✓	✗ .... Gear & Equipment
Nursing & Feeding .... ✗	✗ .... Safety & Babycare
Clothing, Shoes & Accessories .... ✗	✓ .... Books, Toys & Entertainment

landsend.com ★★★★☆

"...carries the best quality in children's wear—their stuff lasts forever... durable and adorable clothing, shoes and bedding... they offer a huge variety of casual clothing and awesome pajamas... not as inexpensive as other sites, but you can't beat the quality... the very best diaper bags... site is easy to navigate and has great finds for the entire family... love the flannel sheets, maternity clothes and shoes for mom..."

Furniture, Bedding & Decor .... ✓	✗ .... Gear & Equipment
Nursing & Feeding .... ✗	✗ .... Safety & Babycare
Clothing, Shoes & Accessories .... ✓	✗ .... Books, Toys & Entertainment

letsgostrolling.com

Furniture, Bedding & Decor .... ✓	✓ .... Gear & Equipment
Nursing & Feeding .... ✓	✗ .... Safety & Babycare
Clothing, Shoes & Accessories .... ✓	✓ .... Books, Toys & Entertainment

llbean.com ★★★★☆

"...high quality clothing for babies, toddlers and kids at reasonable prices... the clothes are extremely durable and stand up to wear and tear very well... a great site for winter clothing and gear shopping... wonderful selection for older kids, too... fewer options for infants... an awesome way to shop for clothing basics... you can't beat the diaper bags..."

Furniture, Bedding & Decor .... ✗	✗ .... Gear & Equipment
Nursing & Feeding .... ✗	✗ .... Safety & Babycare
Clothing, Shoes & Accessories .... ✓	✗ .... Books, Toys & Entertainment

modernseed.com ★★★★½

"...it was fun finding many unique items for my son's nursery... I wanted a contemporary theme and they had lots of wonderful items including crib linens, wall art and lighting... the place to find super cool baby and kid stuff and the best place for modern nursery decor... they also carry children and adult clothing and furniture and toys... not cheap but one of my favorite places..."

Furniture, Bedding & Decor .... ✓	✓ .... Gear & Equipment
Nursing & Feeding .... ✓	✓ .... Safety & Babycare
Clothing, Shoes & Accessories .... ✓	✓ .... Books, Toys & Entertainment

naturalbaby-catalog.com ★★★½☆

"...all natural products—clothes, toys, herbal medicines, bathing, etc... fine quality and a great alternative to the usual products... site is fairly easy to navigate and has a good selection... dealing with returns is pretty painless... love the catalogue and the products... excellent customer service... lots of organic clothing made with natural materials... high quality shoes in a range of prices..."

Furniture, Bedding & Decor .... ✓	✓ .... Gear & Equipment
Nursing & Feeding .... ✓	✓ .... Safety & Babycare
Clothing, Shoes & Accessories .... ✓	✓ .... Books, Toys & Entertainment

www.lilaguide.com

netkidswear.com

Furniture, Bedding & Decor .... ✓	✓ .... Gear & Equipment
Nursing & Feeding .... ✓	✓ .... Safety & Babycare
Clothing, Shoes & Accessories ...... ✓	✓ .... Books, Toys & Entertainment

nordstrom.com ★★★★☆

"...just like their stores, the site carries a great selection of high-quality items... you can't go wrong with Nordstrom—even online... quick shipping and easy site navigation... a little pricey, but great quality items... I've purchased a bunch of baby stuff from their website and have never had a problem... a great shoe selection for all ages..."

Furniture, Bedding & Decor .... ✓	✓ .... Gear & Equipment
Nursing & Feeding .... ✗	✓ .... Safety & Babycare
Clothing, Shoes & Accessories ...... ✓	✓ .... Books, Toys & Entertainment

oldnavy.com ★★★★☆

"...shopping online with Old Navy makes it easy to find incredible bargains... site was easy to use and my products arrived quickly... site carries items that aren't necessarily available in their stores... an inexpensive way to get trendy baby clothes... you can return items directly to any store... check out the sale page of this web site for deep discounts on current season clothing... I signed up for the email savings and get free shipping several times a year..."

Furniture, Bedding & Decor .... ✗	✗ .... Gear & Equipment
Nursing & Feeding .... ✗	✗ .... Safety & Babycare
Clothing, Shoes & Accessories ...... ✓	✗ .... Books, Toys & Entertainment

oliebollen.com ★★★★½

"...perfect for the busy mom looking for a fun baby shower gift... this online-only store has all the best brands—Catamini and Tea Collection to name a couple... great for gifts and home stuff, too... lots of style... very easy to use... 30 days full refund, 60 days store credit..."

Furniture, Bedding & Decor .... ✓	✗ .... Gear & Equipment
Nursing & Feeding .... ✓	✗ .... Safety & Babycare
Clothing, Shoes & Accessories ...... ✓	✓ .... Books, Toys & Entertainment

onestepahead.com ★★★★½

"...one stop shopping site with everything parents are looking for... huge variety of items to choose from... I bought everything from a crib to a nursery bottle... high quality items, many of which are developmental in nature... great line of safety equipment... easy to order and fast delivery but you will pay for shipping... web site has helpful reviews... great site for hard to find items..."

Furniture, Bedding & Decor .... ✓	✓ .... Gear & Equipment
Nursing & Feeding .... ✓	✓ .... Safety & Babycare
Clothing, Shoes & Accessories ...... ✓	✓ .... Books, Toys & Entertainment

peapods.com

Furniture, Bedding & Decor .... ✓	✓ .... Gear & Equipment
Nursing & Feeding .... ✗	✓ .... Safety & Babycare
Clothing, Shoes & Accessories ...... ✓	✓ .... Books, Toys & Entertainment

pokkadots.com

Furniture, Bedding & Decor .... ✓	✓ .... Gear & Equipment
Nursing & Feeding .... ✓	✗ .... Safety & Babycare
Clothing, Shoes & Accessories ...... ✓	✓ .... Books, Toys & Entertainment

poshtots.com ★★★★☆

"...incredible selection of whimsical and out-of-the-ordinary nursery decor... beautiful, unique designer room sets in multiple styles... they do boys and girls bedrooms... great for the baby that has everything—

including parents with an unlimited cash account... you can get great ideas about decor just from browsing the site, even if you don't buy... "

Furniture, Bedding & Decor .... ✓   ✓ .... Gear & Equipment
Nursing & Feeding .... ✓   ✗ .... Safety & Babycare
Clothing, Shoes & Accessories .... ✓   ✓ .... Books, Toys & Entertainment

potterybarnkids.com ★★★★⯨

"*...beautiful high end furniture and bedding... they have a way with matching everything perfectly and I am always a sucker for that look... adorable merchandise of great quality... you will get what you pay for: high quality furniture at high prices... web site is easy to navigate... items like hooded towels and plush blankets make this place special... if I could afford it I would buy everything in the store...*"

Furniture, Bedding & Decor .... ✓   ✓ .... Gear & Equipment
Nursing & Feeding .... ✗   ✗ .... Safety & Babycare
Clothing, Shoes & Accessories .... ✗   ✓ .... Books, Toys & Entertainment

preemie.com

Furniture, Bedding & Decor .... ✗   ✓ .... Gear & Equipment
Nursing & Feeding .... ✓   ✓ .... Safety & Babycare
Clothing, Shoes & Accessories .... ✓   ✓ .... Books, Toys & Entertainment

rei.com

Furniture, Bedding & Decor .... ✗   ✓ .... Gear & Equipment
Nursing & Feeding .... ✗   ✗ .... Safety & Babycare
Clothing, Shoes & Accessories .... ✓   ✓ .... Books, Toys & Entertainment

royalnursery.com ★★★⯨☆

"*...this used to be a store in San Diego and now it is only online... if you need a silver rattle, luxury baby blanket or shower gift—this is the place... a beautiful site with elegant baby clothes, jewelry, and gifts...love the hand print kits—they are my current favorite gift... high end baby wear and gear... be sure to check out the sale items...*"

Furniture, Bedding & Decor .... ✓   ✗ .... Gear & Equipment
Nursing & Feeding .... ✗   ✓ .... Safety & Babycare
Clothing, Shoes & Accessories .... ✓   ✓ .... Books, Toys & Entertainment

showeryourbaby.com

Furniture, Bedding & Decor .... ✓   ✓ .... Gear & Equipment
Nursing & Feeding .... ✓   ✓ .... Safety & Babycare
Clothing, Shoes & Accessories .... ✓   ✓ .... Books, Toys & Entertainment

snipsnsnails.com ★★★★⯨

"*...a great boys clothing store for infants to 14 years old... clothes for every occasion, from casual to special occasion... pajamas and swimsuits, too... pricey, but upscale and fun... items on the web site are not always in stock ...*"

Furniture, Bedding & Decor .... ✓   ✗ .... Gear & Equipment
Nursing & Feeding .... ✗   ✗ .... Safety & Babycare
Clothing, Shoes & Accessories .... ✓   ✗ .... Books, Toys & Entertainment

strollerdepot.com

Furniture, Bedding & Decor .... ✗   ✓ .... Gear & Equipment
Nursing & Feeding .... ✗   ✗ .... Safety & Babycare
Clothing, Shoes & Accessories .... ✗   ✓ .... Books, Toys & Entertainment

strollers4less.com ★★★⯨☆

"*...some of the best prices on strollers... I love this site... we purchased our stroller online for a lot less than it costs locally... online ordering went smoothly—from ordering through receiving... wide* *selection and some incredible deals... shipping is relatively fast... free shipping if you spend $100, which isn't hard to do...* 🙶

Furniture, Bedding & Decor .... ✗	✓ .... Gear & Equipment
Nursing & Feeding .... ✗	✗ .... Safety & Babycare
Clothing, Shoes & Accessories .... ✗	✓ .... Books, Toys & Entertainment

target.com ★★★★☆

🙷*...our favorite place to shop for kids stuff—good selection and very affordable... guilt free shopping—kids grow so fast so I don't want to pay high department store prices... everything from diapers and sippy cups to car seats and strollers... easy return policy... generally helpful staff, but you don't go for the service—you go for the prices... decent registry that won't freak your friends out with outrageous prices... easy, convenient shopping for well-priced items... all the big box brands available—Graco, Evenflo, Eddie Bauer, etc....* 🙶

Furniture, Bedding & Decor .... ✓	✓ .... Gear & Equipment
Nursing & Feeding .... ✓	✓ .... Safety & Babycare
Clothing, Shoes & Accessories ...... ✓	✓ .... Books, Toys & Entertainment

teddylux.com

Furniture, Bedding & Decor .... ✗	✗ .... Gear & Equipment
Nursing & Feeding .... ✗	✗ .... Safety & Babycare
Clothing, Shoes & Accessories .... ✗	✓ .... Books, Toys & Entertainment

thebabyhammock.com ★★★★☆

🙷*...a family owned business selling parent-tested products from morning sickness relief products to baby carriers, natural skincare, gift sets and more... fast friendly service... natural products and waldorf influenced toys...* 🙶

Furniture, Bedding & Decor .... ✓	✓ .... Gear & Equipment
Nursing & Feeding .... ✓	✓ .... Safety & Babycare
Clothing, Shoes & Accessories ...... ✓	✗ .... Books, Toys & Entertainment

thebabyoutlet.com

Furniture, Bedding & Decor .... ✗	✓ .... Gear & Equipment
Nursing & Feeding .... ✓	✓ .... Safety & Babycare
Clothing, Shoes & Accessories .... ✗	✓ .... Books, Toys & Entertainment

tinyride.com

Furniture, Bedding & Decor .... ✗	✓ .... Gear & Equipment
Nursing & Feeding .... ✓	✗ .... Safety & Babycare
Clothing, Shoes & Accessories .... ✗	✗ .... Books, Toys & Entertainment

toadsandtulips.com

Furniture, Bedding & Decor .... ✗	✗ .... Gear & Equipment
Nursing & Feeding .... ✗	✗ .... Safety & Babycare
Clothing, Shoes & Accessories .... ✗	✗ .... Books, Toys & Entertainment

toysrus.com ★★★★☆

🙷*...makes shopping incredibly easy... well organized site with discount prices... makes registering for gifts super simple... even more products are online than in the actual stores... check out the outlet section and coupon codes for even more discounts... I did most of my Christmas shopping here, paid no shipping and had my gifts delivered in 3 days... web site includes helpful toy reviews... use this to send your wish lists to relatives...* 🙶

Furniture, Bedding & Decor .... ✓	✓ .... Gear & Equipment
Nursing & Feeding .... ✓	✓ .... Safety & Babycare
Clothing, Shoes & Accessories ...... ✓	✓ .... Books, Toys & Entertainment

tuttibella.com
★★★★☆

"...well-designed web site with beautiful, original clothing, toys, bedding and accessories... cute vintage stuff for babies and kids... stylish designer goods from here and abroad... your child will stand out among the Baby Gap-clothed masses... gorgeous fabrics... a great place to find that perfect gift for someone special and stylish..."

Furniture, Bedding & Decor ....✓
Nursing & Feeding ....✗
Clothing, Shoes & Accessories.......✓
✓ .... Gear & Equipment
✗ .... Safety & Babycare
✗ .... Books, Toys & Entertainment

usillygoose.com
Furniture, Bedding & Decor ....✓
Nursing & Feeding ....✗
Clothing, Shoes & Accessories.......✗
✗ .... Gear & Equipment
✗ .... Safety & Babycare
✓ .... Books, Toys & Entertainment

walmart.com
★★★☆☆

"...the site is packed with information, which can be a little difficult to navigate... anything and everything you need at a huge discount... good idea to browse the site and research prices before you visit a store... my order was delivered well before the estimated delivery date... I've found cheaper deals online than in the store..."

Furniture, Bedding & Decor ....✓
Nursing & Feeding ....✓
Clothing, Shoes & Accessories.......✓
✓ .... Gear & Equipment
✓ .... Safety & Babycare
✓ .... Books, Toys & Entertainment

baby basics

maternity clothing

City of Boston

★★★★★

"lila picks"

★ 9 Months   ★ Motherhood Maternity

9 Months ★★★★★

"...before and after the big day, this shop is the source for fashion-conscious consumers... the selection is small but the buyer has great taste... the Japanese Weekend pants are amazing... I was able to dress like myself all 9 months, even at work... the best selection of stylish nursing tops to be found in Boston and a couch there where you can nurse your little one..."

Casual wear	✓	$$$$	Prices
Business wear	✓	❹	Product availability
Intimate apparel	✓	❹	Customer service
Nursing wear	✓	❹	Decor

WWW.9MONTHSINC.COM

BACK BAY—286 NEWBURY ST (AT GLOUSTER ST); 617.236.5523; M-W 10-6, TH 10-7, F-SA 10-6, SU 12-5; STREET PARKING

A Pea In The Pod ★★★★☆

"...excellent if you are looking for stylish maternity clothes and don't mind paying for them... start here for special occasions and business wear... the decor is lovely and most of the clothes are beautiful... stylish fashion solutions, but expect to pay more than at department stores... keep your eyes open for the sale rack—the markdowns can be terrific... an upscale shop that carries everything from intimates to fancy dresses... stylish, fun and non-maternity-like..."

Casual wear	✓	$$$$	Prices
Business wear	✓	❹	Product availability
Intimate apparel	✓	❹	Customer service
Nursing wear	✓	❹	Decor

WWW.APEAINTHEPOD.COM

BACK BAY—10 NEWBURY ST (AT ARLINGTON ST); 617.262.8012; M-T 10-6, W-TH 10-8, F-SA 10-6, SU 12-5

H & M ★★★½☆

"...hip, cute and cheap maternity clothes... wonderful stretch pants without the cutout for tummy... great style... lots of cool clothes, but need to visit often, as selection changes frequently... you can find some hip business type clothes on sale... not the place to go for personalized service..."

Casual wear	✓	$$	Prices
Business wear	✓	❸	Product availability
Intimate apparel	✓	❸	Customer service
Nursing wear	✗	❸	Decor

WWW.HM.COM

DOWNTOWN—350 WASHINGTON ST (AT FRANKLIN ST); 617.482.7001; M-SA 10-8, SU 11-7; PAID GARAGES

Macy's ★★★½☆

"...if your local Macy's has a maternity section, you're in luck... I bought my entire pregnancy work wardrobe at Macy's... the styles are all relatively recent and the brands are well known... you can generally find some attractive dresses at very reasonable prices on their sales rack... like other large department stores, you're bound to find something that works if you dig enough... very convenient because you can get your other shopping done at the same time... the selection isn't huge, but what they have is nice..."

Casual wear	✓	$$$	Prices
Business wear	✓	❸	Product availability
Intimate apparel	✓	❸	Customer service
Nursing wear	✗	❸	Decor

WWW.MACYS.COM

DOWNTOWN—450 WASHINGTON ST (AT STORES AT 500 WASHINGTON); 617.357.3000; M-SA 9:30-8, SU 10-7; PARKING LOT

Motherhood Maternity ★★★★★

"...a wide variety of styles, from business to weekend wear, all at a good price... affordable and cute... everything from bras and swimsuits to work outfits... highly recommended for those who don't want to spend a fortune on maternity clothes... less fancy and pricey than their sister stores—A Pea in the Pod and Mimi Maternity... they have frequent sales, so you just need to keep dropping in—you're bound to find something good..."

Casual wear	✓	$$$	Prices
Business wear	✓	❹	Product availability
Intimate apparel	✓	❹	Customer service
Nursing wear	✓	❸	Decor

WWW.MOTHERHOOD.COM

DOWNTOWN—450 WASHINGTON ST (AT MACY'S AT 500 WASHINGTON); 617.426.6201; M-SA 10-9, SU 11-8

Old Navy ★★★½☆

"...the best for casual maternity clothing like stretchy T-shirts with Lycra and comfy jeans... prices are so reasonable it's ridiculous... not much for the workplace, but you can't beat the prices on casual clothes... not all Old Navy locations carry their maternity line... don't expect a huge or diverse selection... the staff is not always knowledgeable about maternity clothing and can't really help with questions about sizing... they have the best return policy—order online and return to the nearest store location... perfect for inexpensive maternity duds..."

Casual wear	✓	$$	Prices
Business wear	✗	❹	Product availability
Intimate apparel	✗	❸	Customer service
Nursing wear	✗	❸	Decor

WWW.OLDNAVY.COM

DORCHESTER—8 ALLSTATE RD (AT MASSACHUSETTS AVE); 617.989.9950; M-SA 9-9:30, SU 10-7; PARKING LOT

Target ★★★★☆

"...I was surprised at how fashionable their selection is—they carry Liz Lange and other really cute selections... the price is right—especially since you'll only be wearing these clothes for a few months... great for maternity basics—T-shirts, skirts, sweaters, even maternity bras... best of all, you can do some maternity shopping while you're shopping for other household basics... shirts for $10—you can't beat that... not the *most exciting or romantic maternity shopping, but once you see the prices you'll get over it... as always, Target provides the perfectly priced solution...* **"**

Casual wear	✓	$$	Prices
Business wear	✓	❸	Product availability
Intimate apparel	✓	❸	Customer service
Nursing wear	✓	❸	Decor

WWW.TARGET.COM

DORCHESTER—7 ALLSTATE RD (AT MASSACHUSETTS AVE); 617.602.1921; M-SA 8-10, SU 8-9; PARKING IN FRONT OF BLDG

Northern Suburbs

★★★★★
"lila picks"

★ Babystyle ★ Gap Maternity

maternity

Baby Depot At Burlington Coat Factory ★★★☆☆

❝...a surprisingly good selection of maternity clothes at great prices... staff can be hard to find so be prepared to dig... cute pants, skirts and sets... I wouldn't have thought that their selection would be as good as it is... not much other than casual items, but what they have is pretty good... ❞

Casual wear	✓	$$	Prices
Business wear	✗	❸	Product availability
Intimate apparel	✗	❸	Customer service
Nursing wear	✗	❸	Decor

WWW.BABYDEPOT.COM

BILLERICA—480 BOSTON RD (AT TOWER FARM RD); 978.663.0405; M-SA 10-9, SU 11-6; PARKING LOT

PEABODY—310 ANDOVER ST (AT MACARTHUR BLVD); 978.531.8822; M-SA 9:30-9:30, SU 11-6; PARKING LOT

Babystyle ★★★★★

❝...compared to their web site their in-store maternity selection is more limited, but still worth checking out... the staff are really sweet and helpful... great maternity basics like pants, tops and casual wear... very fashionable stuff... an awesome range of casual and dressy maternity wear... ❞

Casual wear	✓	$$$	Prices
Business wear	✓	❹	Product availability
Intimate apparel	✓	❹	Customer service
Nursing wear	✓	❹	Decor

WWW.BABYSTYLE.COM

BURLINGTON—75 MIDDLESEX TURNPIKE (AT BURLINGTON MALL); 781.653.0004; M-SA 10-9, SU 11-6

Gap Maternity ★★★★★

❝...the styles are very modern and attractive... the clothes are reasonably priced and wash well... comfy yet stylish basics... they have a great online resource and you can return online purchases at the store... average everyday prices, but catch a sale and you're golden... sizes run big so buy small... always a sale going on where you'll find hip items for a steal... ❞

Casual wear	✓	$$$	Prices
Business wear	✓	❸	Product availability
Intimate apparel	✓	❹	Customer service
Nursing wear	✓	❸	Decor

WWW.GAP.COM

CAMBRIDGE—100 CAMBRIDGESIDE PL (AT CHARLES ST); 617.494.9181; M-SA 10-9:30, SU 11-7

Kohl's ★★★☆☆

"...a small maternity selection but I always manage to find several items I like... our favorite shopping destination—clean, wide open aisles... not a huge amount of maternity, but if you find something the price is always right... the selection is very inconsistent but sometimes you can find nice casuals... best for the bare-bone basics like T-shirts, shorts or casual pants..."

Casual wear	✓	$$	Prices
Business wear	✗	❸	Product availability
Intimate apparel	✗	❸	Customer service
Nursing wear	✗	❸	Decor

WWW.KOHLS.COM

BURLINGTON—150 LEXINGTON ST (AT BURLINGTON MALL RD); 781.229.6494; M-SA 8-10, SU 10-8; MALL PARKING

CHELMSFORD—265-10 CHELMSFORD ST (AT MANAHAN ST); 978.250.0054; M-SA 8-10, SU 10-8; FREE PARKING

DANVERS—50 INDEPENDENCE WY (AT LIBERTY TREE MALL); 978.774.6199; M-SA 8-10, SU 10-8; MALL PARKING

MEDFORD—3850 MYSTIC VALLEY PKWY (AT MEADOW GLEN MALL); 781.395.6001; M-SA 8-10, SU 10-8; MALL PARKING

SAUGUS—333 BROADWAY (AT NEWBURYPORT TPKE); 781.941.8145; M-SA 8-10, SU 10-8; FREE PARKING

WOBURN—425 WASHINGTON ST (AT MISHAWUM RD); 781.376.1222; M-SA 8-10, SU 10-8; PARKING LOT

Lady Grace ★★★★☆

"...best place in town for pregnancy and post-pregnancy bras... they don't really have much maternity beyond intimates... they were so helpful in finding the right bra for all stages of pregnancy and breastfeeding... they are true professionals and always get it just right... salespeople range from extremely polite to unfriendly..."

Casual wear	✗	$$$	Prices
Business wear	✗	❹	Product availability
Intimate apparel	✓	❹	Customer service
Nursing wear	✓	❸	Decor

WWW.LADYGRACE.COM

MALDEN—61 EXCHANGE ST (AT DARTMOUTH ST); 781.322.1721; M-SA 9:30-5:30

Macy's ★★★½☆

"...if your local Macy's has a maternity section, you're in luck... I bought my entire pregnancy work wardrobe at Macy's... the styles are all relatively recent and the brands are well known... you can generally find some attractive dresses at very reasonable prices on their sales rack... like other large department stores, you're bound to find something that works if you dig enough... very convenient because you can get your other shopping done at the same time... the selection isn't huge, but what they have is nice..."

Casual wear	✓	$$$	Prices
Business wear	✓	❸	Product availability
Intimate apparel	✓	❸	Customer service
Nursing wear	✗	❸	Decor

WWW.MACYS.COM

BURLINGTON—1300 MIDDLESEX TURNPIKE (AT THE MITRE); 781.272.6000; M-SA 10-10, SU 11-7; PARKING LOT

participate in our survey at

PEABODY—NORTH SHORE PEABODY MALL (AT NORTH SHORE PEABODY MALL); 978.531.9000; M-SA 10-10, SU 11-7; MALL PARKING

Mimi Maternity ★★★★☆

"...it's definitely worth stopping here if you're still working and need some good-looking outfits... not cheap, but the quality is fantastic... not as expensive as A Pea In The Pod, but better quality than Motherhood Maternity... nice for basics that will last you through multiple pregnancies... perfect for work clothes, but pricey for the everyday stuff... good deals to be found on their sales racks... a good mix of high-end fancy clothes and items you can wear every day..."

Casual wear .... ✓	$$$	Prices
Business wear .... ✓	❹	Product availability
Intimate apparel .... ✓	❹	Customer service
Nursing wear .... ✓	❹	Decor

WWW.MIMIMATERNITY.COM

BURLINGTON—75 MIDDLESEX TPKE (AT OLD CONCORD RD); 781.273.4994; M-SA 10-10, SU 11-7

Motherhood Maternity ★★★★☆

"...a wide variety of styles, from business to weekend wear, all at a good price... affordable and cute... everything from bras and swimsuits to work outfits... highly recommended for those who don't want to spend a fortune on maternity clothes... less fancy and pricey than their sister stores—A Pea in the Pod and Mimi Maternity... they have frequent sales, so you just need to keep dropping in—you're bound to find something good..."

Casual wear .... ✓	$$$	Prices
Business wear .... ✓	❹	Product availability
Intimate apparel .... ✓	❹	Customer service
Nursing wear .... ✓	❸	Decor

WWW.MOTHERHOOD.COM

BURLINGTON—75 MIDDLESEX TPKE (AT WOODS CORNER); 781.273.4447; M-SA 10-10, SU 11-7

CAMBRIDGE—100 CAMBRIDESIDE PL (AT CAMBRIDESIDE GALLERIA); 617.621.1460; M-SA 10-9:30, SU 12-7:30; MALL PARKING

PEABODY—210 ANDOVER ST (AT CROSS ST); 978.531.9620; M-SA 10-10, SU 11-6; MALL PARKING

SAUGUS—1277 BROADWAY (AT SQUARE ONE MALL); 781.233.8271; M-SA 10-10, SU 11-6

Old Navy ★★★★☆

"...the best for casual maternity clothing like stretchy T-shirts with Lycra and comfy jeans... prices are so reasonable it's ridiculous... not much for the workplace, but you can't beat the prices on casual clothes... not all Old Navy locations carry their maternity line... don't expect a huge or diverse selection... the staff is not always knowledgeable about maternity clothing and can't really help with questions about sizing... they have the best return policy—order online and return to the nearest store location... perfect for inexpensive maternity duds..."

Casual wear .... ✓	$$	Prices
Business wear .... ✗	❹	Product availability
Intimate apparel .... ✗	❸	Customer service
Nursing wear .... ✗	❸	Decor

WWW.OLDNAVY.COM

CAMBRIDGE—100 CAMBRIDESIDE PL (AT CAMBRIDESIDE GALLERIA); 617.577.0070; M-SA 10-9:30, SU 11-7; PARKING LOT

EVERETT—9 MYSTIC VIEW RD (AT REVERE BEACH PKWY); 617.387.1422; M-SA 9-9, SU 10-6; PARKING LOT

METHUEN—90 PLEASANT VALLEY ST (AT MILK ST); 978.689.9066; M-SA 10-9, SU 11-7; PARKING LOT

Pink Dolly

Casual wear	✓	✗	Nursing wear
Business wear	✓	✗	Intimate apparel

ARLINGTON—8 MEDFORD ST (AT MASSACHUSETTS AVE); 781.646.7811; M-W F-SA 10-6, TH 10-7

Sears ★★★☆☆

"...good place to get maternity clothes for a low price... the clearance rack always has good deals and their sales are quite frequent... not necessarily super high-quality, but if you just need them for nine months, who cares... good selection of nursing bras... I love the fact that they carry maternity wear in larger sizes—I got so tired of looking in those cutesy boutiques and then being disappointed because they didn't have my size... the only place I found maternity for plus-sized women..."

Casual wear	✓	$$	Prices
Business wear	✗	❸	Product availability
Intimate apparel	✓	❸	Customer service
Nursing wear	✓	❸	Decor

WWW.SEARS.COM

BURLINGTON—1100 MIDDLESEX TPKE (AT BULINGTON MALL); 781.221.4900; M-SA 9:30-10, SU 11-5; MALL PARKING

CAMBRIDGE—100 CAMBRIDGESIDE PL (AT CAMBRIDGESIDE GALLERIA); 617.252.9001; M-SA 10-9, SU 10-6 ; MALL PARKING

PEABODY—HWYS 114 & 128 (AT HWY 128); 978.977.7500; M-SA 9-10, SU 11-7

SAUGUS—1325 BROADWAY (AT SQUARE ONE MALL); 781.231.4500; M-SA 9:30-10, SU 11-7; MALL PARKING

Target ★★★★☆

"...I was surprised at how fashionable their selection is—they carry Liz Lange and other really cute selections... the price is right—especially since you'll only be wearing these clothes for a few months... great for maternity basics—T-shirts, skirts, sweaters, even maternity bras... best of all, you can do some maternity shopping while you're shopping for other household basics... shirts for $10—you can't beat that... not the most exciting or romantic maternity shopping, but once you see the prices you'll get over it... as always, Target provides the perfectly priced solution..."

Casual wear	✓	$$	Prices
Business wear	✓	❸	Product availability
Intimate apparel	✓	❸	Customer service
Nursing wear	✓	❸	Decor

WWW.TARGET.COM

DANVERS—240 INDEPENDENCE WY (AT LIBERTY TREE MALL); 978.762.4439; M-SA 8-10, SU 8-9; PARKING IN FRONT OF BLDG

EVERETT—1 MYSTIC VIEW RD (AT REVERE BEACH PKWY); 617.420.0000; M-SA 8-10, SU 8-9; PARKING IN FRONT OF BLDG

SALEM—227 HIGHLAND AVE (AT FARRELL CT); 978.224.4000; M-SA 8-10, SU 8-9; PARKING IN FRONT OF BLDG

SAUGUS—400 LYNN FELLS PKWY (AT FOREST ST); 781.307.0000; M-SA 8-10, SU 8-9; PARKING IN FRONT OF BLDG

SOMERVILLE—180 SOMERVILLE AVE (AT NANSFIELD ST); 617.776.4036; M-SA 8-10, SU 8-9; PARKING IN FRONT OF BLDG

WOBURN—101 COMMERCE WY (AT ATLANTIC AVE); 781.904.0002; M-SA 8-10, SU 8-9; PARKING IN FRONT OF BLDG

Western Suburbs

★★★★★ "lila picks"

- ★ Babystyle
- ★ Destination Maternity
- ★ Gap Maternity
- ★ Isis Maternity
- ★ Mommy Chic Maternity

Baby Depot ★★★☆☆

"...a surprisingly good selection of maternity clothes at great prices... staff can be hard to find so be prepared to dig... cute pants, skirts and sets... I wouldn't have thought that their selection would be as good as it is... not much other than casual items, but what they have is pretty good..."

Casual wear	✓	$$	Prices
Business wear	✗	❸	Product availability
Intimate apparel	✗	❸	Customer service
Nursing wear	✗	❸	Decor

WWW.BABYDEPOT.COM

NATICK—321 SPEEN ST (AT MARLBORO PIKE); 508.651.2526; M-SA 9:30-9, SU 11-6; LOT

Babystyle ★★★★★

"...compared to their web site their in-store maternity selection is more limited, but still worth checking out... the staff are really sweet and helpful... great maternity basics like pants, tops and casual wear... very fashionable stuff... an awesome range of casual and dressy maternity wear..."

Casual wear	✓	$$$	Prices
Business wear	✓	❹	Product availability
Intimate apparel	✓	❹	Customer service
Nursing wear	✓	❹	Decor

WWW.BABYSTYLE.COM

CHESTNUT HILL—300 BOYLSTON ST (AT FLORENCE ST); 617.796.8982; M-F 10-9:30, SA 10-9:30, SU 11-6

Destination Maternity ★★★★★

"...Motherhood, Mimi, and A Pea in the Pod all under one roof... fantastic maternity Superstore... much better than having to run to three different shops... helpful concept... it's big, with a generous selection... great if you have another child with you—the play area is enclosed and close to the dressing rooms... nursing-wear, casuals and formal wear too..."

Casual wear	✓	$$$	Prices
Business wear	✓	❹	Product availability
Intimate apparel	✓	❹	Customer service
Nursing wear	✓	❺	Decor

WWW.DESTINATIONMATERNITY.COM

NATICK—104 WORCESTER RD (AT COOPER RD); 508.653.1605; M-SA 10-9, SU 11-6

Gap Maternity ★★★★★

"*...the styles are very modern and attractive... the clothes are reasonably priced and wash well... comfy yet stylish basics... they have a great online resource and you can return online purchases at the store... average every day prices but catch a sale and you're golden... sizes run big so buy small... always a sale going on where you'll find hip items for a steal...*"

Casual wear	✓	$$$	Prices
Business wear	✓	❸	Product availability
Intimate apparel	✓	❹	Customer service
Nursing wear	✓	❸	Decor

WWW.GAP.COM

WATERTOWN—550 ARSENAL ST (AT ARSENAL COURT DR); 617.923.1966; M-SA 9:30-9, SU 11-6

Isis Maternity ★★★★★

"*...they have a small but good selection of maternity clothes and bras... the items are unique and just what a new mom needs... a great selection of maternity bras and lots of knowledgeable people on staff to help fit them... nice and comfortable exercise clothing as well... a nice shopping environment...*"

Casual wear	✓	$$$	Prices
Business wear	✗	❹	Product availability
Intimate apparel	✓	❹	Customer service
Nursing wear	✓	❹	Decor

WWW.ISISMATERNITY.COM

BROOKLINE —2 BROOKLINE PL (AT BROOKLINE AVE); 781.429.1500; M W-TH 9-9, T F-SA 9-5; GARAGE AT BROOKLINE PLACE

Kohl's ★★★☆☆

"*...a small maternity selection but I always manage to find several items I like... our favorite shopping destination—clean, wide open aisles... not a huge amount of maternity, but if you find something the price is always right... the selection is very inconsistent but sometimes you can find nice casuals... best for the bare bone basics like T-shirts, shorts or casual pants...*"

Casual wear	✓	$$	Prices
Business wear	✗	❸	Product availability
Intimate apparel	✗	❸	Customer service
Nursing wear	✗	❸	Decor

WWW.KOHLS.COM

FRAMINGHAM—1 WORCESTER RD (AT SHOPPERS WORLD); 508.879.9103; M-SA 8-10, SU 10-8; PARKING LOT IN FRONT OF STORE

Lady Grace ★★★★☆

"*...best place in town for pregnancy and post-pregnancy bra's... they don't really have much maternity beyond intimates... they were so helpful in finding the right bra for all stages of pregnancy and breastfeeding... they are true professionals and always get it just right... sales people range from extremely polite to unfriendly...*"

Casual wear	✗	$$$	Prices
Business wear	✗	❹	Product availability
Intimate apparel	✓	❹	Customer service
Nursing wear	✓	❸	Decor

WWW.LADYGRACE.COM

BROOKLINE—1364 BEACON ST (AT CENTRE ST); 617.566.8194; M-SA 9:30-5:30

WATERTOWN—485 ARSENAL ST (AT ARSENAL MALL); 617.923.0923; M-SA 10-9:30, SU 11-6; LOT IN FRONT OF STORE

Macy's ★★★½☆

"...if your local Macy's has a maternity section, you're in luck—call ahead!.. I bought my entire pregnancy work wardrobe at Macy's... the styles are all relatively recent and the brands are well known... you can generally find some attractive dresses at very reasonable prices on their sales rack... like other large department stores, you're bound to find something that works if you dig enough... very convenient because you can get your other shopping done at the same time... the selection isn't huge, but what they have is nice..."

Casual wear	✓	$$$	Prices
Business wear	✓	❸	Product availability
Intimate apparel	✓	❸	Customer service
Nursing wear	✗	❸	Decor

WWW.MACYS.COM

FRAMINGHAM—1 WORCESTER RD (AT SHOPPERS WORLD); 508.650.6000; M-SA 10-9:30, SU 11-7; LOT

NATICK—1245 WORCESTER RD (AT NATICK MALL); 508.650.6400; M-SA 10-10, SU 10-7; PARKING LOT AT MALL

Mimi Maternity ★★★★☆

"...it's definitely worth stopping here if you're still working and need some good looking outfits... not cheap, but the quality is fantastic... not as expensive as A Pea In The Pod, but better quality than Motherhood Maternity... nice for basics that will last you through multiple pregnancies... perfect for work clothes, but pricey for the everyday stuff... good deals to be found on their sales racks... a good mix of high-end fancy clothes and items you can wear every day..."

Casual wear	✓	$$$	Prices
Business wear	✓	❹	Product availability
Intimate apparel	✓	❹	Customer service
Nursing wear	✓	❹	Decor

WWW.MIMIMATERNITY.COM

NATICK—104 WORCESTER RD (AT THE MALL AT CHESTNUT HILL); 508.653.1605; M-F 10-9:30, SA 10-8, SU 12-6; PARKING LOT AT MALL

NATICK—1245 WORCESTER RD (AT NATICK MALL); 508.651.8811; M-SA 10-10, SU 11-6; PARKING LOT AT MALL

Mommy Chic Maternity ★★★★★

"...smart selection but clothes are trendy but wearable... nice selection of jeans and business maternity wear... super chic—expect to pay a little extra for the style... good place to buy a special occasion outfit... the service was good and I enjoyed shopping here... check out the discount section..."

Casual wear	✓	$$$$	Prices
Business wear	✓	❸	Product availability
Intimate apparel	✓	❹	Customer service
Nursing wear	✓	❹	Decor

WWW.MOMMYCHIC.COM

CHESTNUT HILL—HAMMOND POND PKWY (AT THE MALL AT CHESTNUT HILL); 617.244.6204; M-F 10-9:30, SA 10-8, SU 12-6

NEWTON—199 BOYLSTON ST (AT THE MALL AT CHESTNUT HILL); 617.244.6204; M-F 10-9:30, SA 10-8, SU 12-6; PARKING LOT AT MALL

Motherhood Maternity ★★★★☆

"...a wide variety of styles, from business to weekend wear—all at a good price... affordable and cute... everything from bras and swimsuits to work outfits... highly recommended for those who don't want to

spend a fortune on maternity clothes... less fancy and pricey than their sister stores—A Pea in the Pod and Mimi Maternity... they have frequent sales, so you just need to keep dropping in—you're bound to find something good..."

Casual wear	✓	$$$	Prices
Business wear	✓	❹	Product availability
Intimate apparel	✓	❹	Customer service
Nursing wear	✓	❸	Decor

WWW.MOTHERHOOD.COM

MARLBOROUGH—DONALD LYNCH BLVD (AT SOLOMON POND MALL); 508.303.6277; M-SA 10-9:30, SU 11-7; PARKING LOT AT MALL

NATICK—1245 WORCESTER RD (AT NATICK MALL); 508.647.1688; M-SA 9-10, SU 10-7; PARKING LOT AT MALL

WATERTOWN—485 ARSENAL ST (AT ARSENAL COURT DR); 617.924.5827; M-SA 10-9:30, SU 11-6

Sears ★★★☆☆

"*...good place to get maternity clothes for a low price... the clearance rack always has good deals and their sales are quite frequent... not necessarily super high quality but if you just need them for 9 months, who cares... good selection of nursing bras... I love the fact that they carry maternity wear in larger sizes—I got so tired of looking in those cutesy boutiques and then being disappointed because they didn't have my size... the only place I found maternity for plus-sized women...*"

Casual wear	✓	$$	Prices
Business wear	✗	❸	Product availability
Intimate apparel	✓	❸	Customer service
Nursing wear	✓	❸	Decor

WWW.SEARS.COM

NATICK—1235 WORCESTER RD (AT NATICK MALL); 508.650.2823; M-F 10-10, SA 8-10, SU 11-7; PARKING LOT AT MALL

Target ★★★★☆

"*...I was surprised at how fashionable their selection is—they carry Liz Lange and other really cute selections... the price is right—especially since you'll only be wearing these clothes for a few months... great for maternity basics—T-shirts, skirts, sweaters, even maternity bras... best of all, you can do some maternity shopping while you're shopping for other household basics... shirts for $10—you can't beat that... not the most exciting or romantic maternity shopping, but once you see the prices you'll get over it... as always, Target provides the perfectly priced solution...*"

Casual wear	✓	$$	Prices
Business wear	✓	❸	Product availability
Intimate apparel	✓	❸	Customer service
Nursing wear	✓	❸	Decor

WWW.TARGET.COM

FRAMINGHAM—400 COCHITUATE RD (AT FRAMINGTON MALL); 508.628.3136; M-SA 8-10, SU 8-9; PARKING LOT IN FRONT OF STORE

MILFORD—250 FORTUNE BLVD (AT E MAIN ST); 508.478.5880; M-SA 8-10, SU 8-9; PARKING LOT IN FRONT OF STORE

WATERTOWN—550 ARSENAL ST (AT ARSENAL MALL); 617.924.6574; M-SA 8-10, SU 8-9; PARKING LOT IN FRONT OF STORE

Southern Suburbs

★★★★★
"lila picks"

★ Gap Maternity ★ Isis Maternity

Baby Depot At Burlington Coat Factory ★★★☆☆

"...a surprisingly good selection of maternity clothes at great prices... staff can be hard to find so be prepared to dig... cute pants, skirts and sets... I wouldn't have thought that their selection would be as good as it is... not much other than casual items, but what they have is pretty good..."

Casual wear	✓	$$	Prices
Business wear	✗	❸	Product availability
Intimate apparel	✗	❸	Customer service
Nursing wear	✗	❸	Decor

WWW.BABYDEPOT.COM

BRAINTREE—705 GRANITE ST (AT TOWN ST); 781.848.3200; M-SA 10-9, SU 11-6; PARKING LOT

Gap Maternity ★★★★★

"...the styles are very modern and attractive... the clothes are reasonably priced and wash well... comfy yet stylish basics... they have a great online resource and you can return online purchases at the store... average everyday prices, but catch a sale and you're golden... sizes run big so buy small... always a sale going on where you'll find hip items for a steal..."

Casual wear	✓	$$$	Prices
Business wear	✓	❸	Product availability
Intimate apparel	✓	❹	Customer service
Nursing wear	✓	❸	Decor

WWW.GAP.COM

BRAINTREE—250 GRANITE ST (AT NORTH ST); 781.849.1981; M-SA 10-10, SU 11-7

Isis Maternity ★★★★★

"...they have a small, but good selection of maternity clothes and bras... the items are unique and just what a new mom needs... a great selection of maternity bras and lots of knowledgeable people on staff to help fit them... nice and comfortable exercise clothing as well... a nice shopping environment..."

Casual wear	✓	$$$	Prices
Business wear	✗	❹	Product availability
Intimate apparel	✓	❹	Customer service
Nursing wear	✓	❹	Decor

WWW.ISISMATERNITY.COM

NEEDHAM —110 2ND AVE (AT HIGHLAND AVE); 781.429.1500; M-TU 9-9, W 9-5, TH 9-9, F-SU 9-5; PARKING LOT

JCPenney ★★★☆☆

"...competitive prices and a surprisingly cute selection... they carry bigger sizes that are very hard to find at other stores... much cheaper than most maternity boutiques and they always seem to have some sort of sale going on... an especially large selection of maternity jeans for plus sizes... a more conservative collection than the smaller, hipper boutiques... good for casual basics, but not much for special occasions..."

Casual wear	✓	$$	Prices
Business wear	✓	❸	Product availability
Intimate apparel	✓	❸	Customer service
Nursing wear	✗	❸	Decor

WWW.JCPENNEY.COM

NORTH ATTLEBORO—1019 S WASHINGTON ST (AT EMERALD SQUARE MALL); 508.699.6700; M-F 10-9:30, SA 9-9:30, SU 11-6; MALL PARKING

Kohl's ★★★☆☆

"...a small maternity selection but I always manage to find several items I like... our favorite shopping destination—clean, wide open aisles... not a huge amount of maternity, but if you find something the price is always right... the selection is very inconsistent but sometimes you can find nice casuals... best for the bare-bone basics like T-shirts, shorts or casual pants..."

Casual wear	✓	$$	Prices
Business wear	✗	❸	Product availability
Intimate apparel	✗	❸	Customer service
Nursing wear	✗	❸	Decor

WWW.KOHLS.COM

EAST WALPOLE—100 BOSTON-PROVIDENCE HWY (AT THE MALL AT WALPOLE); 508.660.9921; M-SA 8-10, SU 10-8; FREE PARKING

HINGHAM—100 DERBY ST (AT HINGHAM PLAZA); 781.749.0763; M-SA 8-10, SU 10-8; FREE PARKING

STOUGHTON—501 TECHNOLOGY CENTER DR (OFF RT 139); 781.341.5980; M-SA 8-10, SU 10-8; FREE PARKING

Lady Grace ★★★★☆

"...best place in town for pregnancy and post-pregnancy bras... they don't really have much maternity beyond intimates... they were so helpful in finding the right bra for all stages of pregnancy and breastfeeding... they are true professionals and always get it just right... salespeople range from extremely polite to unfriendly..."

Casual wear	✗	$$$	Prices
Business wear	✗	❹	Product availability
Intimate apparel	✓	❹	Customer service
Nursing wear	✓	❸	Decor

WWW.LADYGRACE.COM

BRAINTREE—250 GRANITE ST (AT NORTH ST); 781.848.6188; M-SA 10-10, SU 11-7

Macy's ★★★½☆

"...if your local Macy's has a maternity section, you're in luck... I bought my entire pregnancy work wardrobe at Macy's... the styles are all relatively recent and the brands are well known... you can generally find some attractive dresses at very reasonable prices on their sales rack... like other large department stores, you're bound to find something that works if you dig enough... very convenient because you

can get your other shopping done at the same time... the selection isn't huge, but what they have is nice... **"**

Casual wear	✓	$$$	Prices
Business wear	✓	❸	Product availability
Intimate apparel	✓	❸	Customer service
Nursing wear	✗	❸	Decor

WWW.MACYS.COM

BRAINTREE—250 GRANITE ST (AT SOUTH SHORE PLAZA); 781.848.1500; M-SA 10-10, SU 11-7; PARKING LOT

BROCKTON—200 WESTGATE DR (AT WESTGATE MALL AND PLAZA); 508.588.7400; M-SA 10-9:30, SU 11-6; MALL PARKING

Mimi Maternity ★★★★☆

...it's definitely worth stopping here if you're still working and need some good-looking outfits... not cheap, but the quality is fantastic... not as expensive as A Pea In The Pod, but better quality than Motherhood Maternity... nice for basics that will last you through multiple pregnancies... perfect for work clothes, but pricey for the everyday stuff... good deals to be found on their sales racks... a good mix of high-end fancy clothes and items you can wear every day... **"**

Casual wear	✓	$$$	Prices
Business wear	✓	❹	Product availability
Intimate apparel	✓	❹	Customer service
Nursing wear	✓	❹	Decor

WWW.MIMIMATERNITY.COM

BRAINTREE—250 GRANITE ST (AT NORTH ST); 781.356.2486; M-SA 10-10, SU 11-7

Motherhood Maternity ★★★★☆

...a wide variety of styles, from business to weekend wear, all at a good price... affordable and cute... everything from bras and swimsuits to work outfits... highly recommended for those who don't want to spend a fortune on maternity clothes... less fancy and pricey than their sister stores—A Pea in the Pod and Mimi Maternity... they have frequent sales, so you just need to keep dropping in—you're bound to find something good... **"**

Casual wear	✓	$$$	Prices
Business wear	✓	❹	Product availability
Intimate apparel	✓	❹	Customer service
Nursing wear	✓	❸	Decor

WWW.MOTHERHOOD.COM

HANOVER—1775 WASHINGTON ST (AT HANOVER MALL); 781.826.2030; M-SA 9-9:30, SU 11-6; MALL PARKING

KINGSTON—101 INDEPENDENCE MALL WY (AT RABOTH RD); 781.585.7048; M-SA 10-9:30, SU 11-6; MALL PARKING

NORTH ATTLEBORO—999 S WASHINGTON ST (AT EMERALD SQUARE MALL); 508.695.8511; M-SA 10-9:30, SU 11-6; MALL PARKING

WRENTHAM—1 PREMIUM OUTLET BLVD (AT SOUTH ST); 508.384.5378; M-SA 10-9, SU 10-6

Old Navy ★★★★☆

...the best for casual maternity clothing like stretchy T-shirts with Lycra and comfy jeans... prices are so reasonable it's ridiculous... not much for the workplace, but you can't beat the prices on casual clothes... not all Old Navy locations carry their maternity line... don't expect a huge or diverse selection... the staff is not always knowledgeable about maternity clothing and can't really help with questions about sizing... they have the best return policy—order online and return to the nearest store location... perfect for inexpensive maternity duds... **"**

Casual wear	✓	$$	Prices
Business wear	✗	❹	Product availability
Intimate apparel	✗	❸	Customer service
Nursing wear	✗	❸	Decor

WWW.OLDNAVY.COM

BROCKTON—200 WESTGATE DR (AT WESTGATE MALL AND PLAZA); 508.587.6700; M-SA 9-9:30, SU 10-6; PARKING LOT

DEDHAM—300 PROVIDENCE HWY (AT DEDHAM MALL); 781.461.1350; M-SA 9-9, SU 10-6; PARKING LOT

KINGSTON—101 INDEPENDENCE MALL WY (AT RABOTH RD); 781.582.0007; M-SA 10-9:30, SU 10-6; MALL PARKING

NORTH ATTLEBORO—1250 S WASHINGTON ST (AT EMERALD SQUARE MALL); 508.643.4664; M-SA 9-9, SU 11-6

Sears   ★★★☆☆

❝...good place to get maternity clothes for a low price... the clearance rack always has good deals and their sales are quite frequent... not necessarily super high-quality, but if you just need them for nine months, who cares... good selection of nursing bras... I love the fact that they carry maternity wear in larger sizes—I got so tired of looking in those cutesy boutiques and then being disappointed because they didn't have my size... the only place I found maternity for plus-sized women...❞

Casual wear	✓	$$	Prices
Business wear	✗	❸	Product availability
Intimate apparel	✓	❸	Customer service
Nursing wear	✓	❸	Decor

WWW.SEARS.COM

BRAINTREE—250 GRANITE ST (AT SOUTH SHORE PLAZA); 781.356.6000; M-SA 9:30-10, SU 11-7

BROCKTON—200 WESTGATE DR (AT WESTGATE MALL AND PLAZA); 508.897.4200; M-F 9:30-9:30, SA 8-9:30, SU 11-6

DEDHAM—300 PRIVIDENCE HWY (AT DEDHAM MALL); 781.320.5125; M-SA 9-9:30, SU 11-5

KINGSTON—101 INDEPENDENCE MALL WY (AT INDEPENDENCE MALL); 781.582.3600; M-SA 9:30-9:30, SU 11-6; MALL PARKING

Target   ★★★★☆

❝...I was surprised at how fashionable their selection is—they carry Liz Lange and other really cute selections... the price is right—especially since you'll only be wearing these clothes for a few months... great for maternity basics—T-shirts, skirts, sweaters, even maternity bras... best of all, you can do some maternity shopping while you're shopping for other household basics... shirts for $10—you can't beat that... not the most exciting or romantic maternity shopping, but once you see the prices you'll get over it... as always, Target provides the perfectly priced solution...❞

Casual wear	✓	$$	Prices
Business wear	✓	❸	Product availability
Intimate apparel	✓	❸	Customer service
Nursing wear	✓	❸	Decor

WWW.TARGET.COM

KINGSTON—101 INDEPENDENCE MALL WAY (AT INDEPENDENCE MALL); 781.585.5825; M-SA 8-10, SU 8-9; PARKING IN FRONT OF BLDG

NORTH ATTLEBORO—1205 S WASHINGTON ST (AT EMERALD SQUARE MALL); 508.699.9118; M-SA 8-10, SU 8-9; PARKING IN FRONT OF BLDG

Online

> ★★★★★
> **"lila picks"**
>
> ★ breastisbest.com   ★ gap.com
> ★ maternitymall.com ★ naissancematernity.com

babiesrus.com ★★★★☆
"...their online store is surprisingly plentiful for maternity wear in addition to all of the baby stuff... they carry everything from Mimi Maternity to Belly Basics... easy shopping and good return policy... the price is right and the selection is really good..."
Casual wear ....✓   ✓ ....Nursing wear
Business wear ....✓   ✓ .... Intimate apparel

babycenter.com ★★★★☆
"...it's babycenter.com—of course it's good... a small but well selected maternity section... I love being able to read other people's comments before purchasing... prices are reasonable and the convenience is priceless... great customer service and easy returns..."
Casual wear ....✓   ✓ ....Nursing wear
Business wear .... ✗   ✗ .... Intimate apparel

babystyle.com ★★★★☆
"...compared to their web site their in-store maternity selection is more limited, but still worth checking out... the staff are really sweet and helpful... great maternity basics like pants, tops and casual wear... very fashionable stuff... an awesome range of casual and dressy maternity wear..."
Casual wear ....✓   ✓ ....Nursing wear
Business wear ....✓   ✓ .... Intimate apparel

bellablumaternity.com
Casual wear ....✓   ✓ ....Nursing wear
Business wear ....✓   ✓ .... Intimate apparel

breakoutbras.com
Casual wear .... ✗   ✓ ....Nursing wear
Business wear .... ✗   ✓ .... Intimate apparel

breastisbest.com ★★★★★
"...by far the best resource for purchasing good quality nursing bras online... the site is easy to use and they have an extensive online fitting guide... returns are a breeze... since they are only online you may have to try a few before you get it exactly right..."
Casual wear ....✓   ✓ ....Nursing wear
Business wear .... ✗   ✓ .... Intimate apparel

childishclothing.com
Casual wear............................. ✓	✗ .... Nursing wear
Business wear............................. ✗	✗ ....Intimate apparel

duematernity.com ★★★★☆
"...refreshing styles... fun and hip clothing... the site is easy to navigate and use... I've ordered a bunch of clothes from them and never had a problem... everything from casual wear to fun, funky items for special occasions... prices are reasonable..."
Casual wear............................. ✓	✓ .... Nursing wear
Business wear............................. ✓	✓ ....Intimate apparel

evalillian.com
Casual wear............................. ✓	✓ .... Nursing wear
Business wear............................. ✓	✓ ....Intimate apparel

expressiva.com ★★★★⯨
"...the best site for nursing clothes... prices are good and their selection is terrific... lots of selection on dressy, casual, sleep, workout and even bathing suits... if you're going to shop for maternity online then be sure not to miss this cool site... good customer service—quite prompt in answering questions about my order..."
Casual wear............................. ✓	✓ .... Nursing wear
Business wear............................. ✗	✓ ....Intimate apparel

gap.com ★★★★★
"...stylish maternity clothes delivered right to your doorstep... always something worth buying... the best place for functional, comfortable and affordable maternity clothes... classic styles, not too trendy... more available online than in a store... no fancy dresses but lots of casual outfits that are cheap, look good and I don't mind parting with them after my baby is born... easy to use site and deliveries are generally prompt... you can return them to any Gap store..."
Casual wear............................. ✓	✓ .... Nursing wear
Business wear............................. ✓	✓ ....Intimate apparel

japaneseweekend.com ★★★★☆
"...pregnancy clothes that scream 'I am proud of my pregnant body'... a must for comfy, stylish stuff... they make the best maternity pants which cradle your belly as it grows... a little expensive but I lived in their pants my entire pregnancy—I definitely got my money's worth... really nice clothing that just doesn't look and feel like your traditional pregnancy wear—I still wear a couple of the outfits (my baby is now 6 months old)..."
Casual wear............................. ✓	✓ .... Nursing wear
Business wear............................. ✓	✓ ....Intimate apparel

jcpenney.com ★★★☆☆
"...competitive prices and a surprisingly cute selection... they carry bigger sizes that are very hard to find at other stores... much cheaper than most maternity boutiques and they always seem to have some sort of sale going on... an especially large selection of maternity jeans for plus sizes... a more conservative collection than the smaller, hipper boutiques... good for casual basics, but not much for special occasions..."
Casual wear............................. ✓	✓ .... Nursing wear
Business wear............................. ✓	✓ ....Intimate apparel

lizlange.com ★★★★⯨
"...well-designed and cute... the real buys on this site are definitely in the sale section... cute, hip selection of jeans, skirts, blouses and

bathing suits... their evening and dressy clothes are the best with wonderful fabrics and designs... easy and convenient online shopping... practical but not frumpy styles—their web site made my maternity shopping so easy... "

Casual wear	✓	✗	Nursing wear
Business wear	✓	✗	Intimate apparel

maternitymall.com ★★★★★

"*...I had great luck with maternitymall.com... a large selection of vendors in all price ranges... quick and easy without having to leave my house... found everything I needed... their merchandise tends to be true to size... site is a bit hard to navigate and cluttered with ads... sale and clearance prices are fantastic...* "

Casual wear	✓	✓	Nursing wear
Business wear	✓	✓	Intimate apparel

mommygear.com

Casual wear	✓	✓	Nursing wear
Business wear	✗	✓	Intimate apparel

momsnightout.com

"*...for that fashionable-not-frumpy fancy occasion dress... beautiful store with gorgeous selection of dresses from cocktail to bridal... one on one attention... expensive but worth it...* "

Casual wear	✗	✗	Nursing wear
Business wear	✓	✗	Intimate apparel

motherhood.com ★★★★☆

"*...a wide variety of styles, from business to weekend wear—all at a good price... affordable and cute... everything from bras and swimsuits to work outfits... highly recommended for those who don't want to spend a fortune on maternity clothes... less fancy and pricey than their sister stores—A Pea in the Pod and Mimi Maternity... they have frequent sales, so you just need to keep dropping in—you're bound to find something good...* "

Casual wear	✓	✓	Nursing wear
Business wear	✓	✓	Intimate apparel

motherwear.com ★★★★½

"*...excellent selection of cute and practical nursing clothes at reasonable prices... sign up for their e-mail newsletter for great offers, including free shipping... top quality clothes... decent selection of hard to find plus sizes... golden return policy, you can return any item (even used!) you aren't 100% happy with... they sell the only nursing tops I could actually wear outside the house... cute styles that aren't frumpy... so easy... pricey but worth it for the quality... top notch customer service...* "

Casual wear	✗	✓	Nursing wear
Business wear	✗	✓	Intimate apparel

naissancematernity.com ★★★★★

"*...the cutest maternity clothes around... hip and funky clothes for the artsy, well-dressed mom to be... their site is easy to navigate... if you can't make it down to the actual store in LA, just go online... clothes that make you look and feel sexy... it ain't cheap but you will look marvelous and the clothes will grow with you... web site is great and their phone order service was incredible...* "

Casual wear	✓	✗	Nursing wear
Business wear	✓	✗	Intimate apparel

nordstrom.com ★★★☆☆

"*...now that they don't carry maternity in stores anymore, this is the only way to get any maternity from Nordstrom... overpriced but nice... makes returns harder, since you have to ship everything instead of just going back to a store... they carry Cadeau, Liz Lange, Belly Basics, etc... nice stuff, not so nice prices...*"

Casual wear ✓	✓ Nursing wear
Business wear ✓	✓ Intimate apparel

oldnavy.com ★★★★☆

"*...since not all Old Navy stores carry maternity clothes, this is the easiest way to go... just like their regular clothes, the maternity selection is great for casual wear... cheap, cheap, cheap... the quality is good and the price is definitely right... frequent sales make great prices even better...*"

Casual wear ✓	✓ Nursing wear
Business wear ✗	✗ Intimate apparel

onehotmama.com ★★★★½☆

"*...you'll find many things you must have... cool and very nice clothing... they carry everything from underwear and tights to formal dresses... you can find some real bargains online... super fast shipping... also, lots of choices for nursing and get-back-in-shape wear...*"

Casual wear ✓	✓ Nursing wear
Business wear ✓	✓ Intimate apparel

showeryourbaby.com

Casual wear ✓	✓ Nursing wear
Business wear ✗	✓ Intimate apparel

target.com ★★★★☆

"*...lots of Liz Lange at very fair prices... the selection is great and it's so easy to shop online—we bought most of our baby gear here and I managed to slip in a couple of orders for some maternity wear too... maternity shirts for $10—where else can you find deals like that...*"

Casual wear ✓	✓ Nursing wear
Business wear ✓	✓ Intimate apparel

activities & outings

City of Boston

★★★★★

"lila picks"

★ Boston Children's Museum
★ Family Music Makers
★ New England Aquarium

Barnes & Noble ★★★★½

❝...wonderful weekly story times for all ages and frequent author visits for older kids... lovely selection of books and the story times are fun and very well done... they have evening story times—we put our kids in their pjs and come here as a treat before bedtime... they read a story, and then usually have a little craft or coloring project related to the story... times vary by location so give them a call...❞

Customer service..........................❹ $$...Prices
Age range................. 6 mths to 5 yrs
WWW.BARNESANDNOBLE.COM
BACK BAY—800 BOYLSTON ST (AT THE PRUDENTIAL CTR); 617.247.6959; CALL FOR SCHEDULE
DOWNTOWN—395 WASHINGTON ST (AT WINTER ST); 617.426.5184; CALL FOR SCHEDULE

Borders Books ★★★★☆

❝...very popular weekly story time held in most branches (check the web site for locations and times)... call before you go since they are very popular and get extremely crowded... kids love the unique blend of songs, stories, and dancing... Mr. Hatbox's appearances are a delight to everyone... large children's section is well categorized and well priced... they make it fun for young tots to browse through the board book section by hanging toys around the shelves... the low-key cafe is a great place to have coffee with your baby and leaf through some magazines...❞

Customer service..........................❹ $$...Prices
Age range................. 6 mths to 6 yrs
WWW.BORDERSSTORES.COM
BOSTON—10 SCHOOL ST (AT WASHINGTON ST); 617.557.7188; CALL FOR SCHEDULE

Boston Athenaeum ★★★★★

❝...fine programs for young children and a thoughtfully arranged library with a dedicated children's librarian... a special place to take your children... great children's library and terrific staff... story hours with snacks are Tuesday and Saturday mornings... low-price membership for those under 40... family memberships are reasonable and well worth it...❞

Customer service..........................❺ $$$$......................................Prices
Age range.................... 2 yrs and up

participate in our survey at

WWW.BOSTONATHENAEUM.ORG

DOWNTOWN—10 1/2 BEACON ST (AT TREMONT ST); 617.227.0270; M 8:30-8 T-F 8:30- 5:30 SA 9-4; PARKING GARAGES NEARBY

Boston Children's Museum ★★★★★

"...one of the best children's museums we've ever been to... many interactive exhibits and activities for enthralled little minds... clean and spacious... dedicated space for the little ones... free passes available from your local library... it's definitely worth the money to buy a membership—that way you can also take advantage of members-only time... plenty of hands-on activities... the play space is great in the winter... bring food with you, because the restaurant choices are limited..."

Customer service .... ❹ $$ .... Prices
Age range .... 3 yrs and up
WWW.BOSTONCHILDRENSMUSEUM.ORG

DOWNTOWN—300 CONGRESS ST (AT DORCHESTER AVE); 617.426.8855; SA-TH 10-5, F 10-9; GARAGE ON FARNSWORTH ST

Clayroom ★★★☆☆

"...arts and crafts that go beyond just glue and paper... not specifically geared towards kids, but the staff is great and will help make it fun... better for older kids who have better coordination and can be independent... you can make things from scratch, or simply paint what they have in stock... a fun birthday party outing..."

Customer service .... ❸ $$$ .... Prices
Age range .... 3 yrs and up
WWW.CLAYROOM.COM

JAMAICA PLAIN—172 SOUTH STREET (ROSEMARY AND SPALDING STS.); 617.522.7474; M-TH 10-8, F-SA 10-9

Family Music Makers ★★★★★

"...fun classes with lots of music, clapping and singing... many locations... variety of instruments and activities... parents have to be willing to sing and dance, too... the class price includes a free music book and CD for the session... we've been going since my son was three months old, and it has been terrific fun..."

Customer service .... ❺ $$$ .... Prices
Age range .... 3.5 yrs to 6 yrs
WWW.FAMILYMUSICMAKERS.COM

BACK BAY—66 MARLBOROUGH ST (AT BERKELEY ST); 617.783.9818; CALL FOR SCHEDULE; STREET PARKING

Franklin Park Zoo ★★★★☆

"...a small, but fun zoo... I've been to bigger and better zoos, but this 'neighborhood' zoo is perfect for quick trips... we had a nice time and didn't like we had to rush to see everything... definitely buy the family pass—it's well worth it so you can go more frequently... wonderful place and everyone there is very courteous and helpful... something for kids of all ages... admission is $9.50 for adults, free for children under 2..."

Customer service .... ❸ $$ .... Prices
Age range .... 12 mths and up
WWW.ZOONEWENGLAND.COM

DORCHESTER—1 FRANKLIN PARK RD (AT PEABODY CIR); 617.541.5466; M-F 10-5, SA-SU 10-6; FREE PARKING

Hill House ★★☆☆☆

"...facility hosts Music Together, Kindermusik and other music classes, 'Coffee Talk" for new parents, arts and crafts, creative movement and

activities & outings

www.lilaguide.com

gymnastics for young tots ages six months to five years... you can rent the space for birthday parties... "
Customer service.......................... ❶ $$$$$ .... Prices
Age range.................. 6 mths and up
WWW.HILLHOUSEBOSTON.ORG

BOSTON—127 MT VERNON ST (AT CHARLES ST); 617.227.5838; CHECK ONLINE FOR SCHEDULE

Mary Baker Eddy Library ★★★☆☆

"*...a very neat library... the Mapparium (a huge stained-glass globe that you can walk through) is definitely worth checking out... it stimulated lots of questions about the oceans, world, etc... one of a kind and very fun...* "
Customer service.......................... ❹ $$.. Prices
Age range.................. 3 mths to 6 yrs
WWW.MARYBAKEREDDYLIBRARY.ORG

BACK BAY—200 MASSACHUSETTS AVE (AT CLEARWAY ST); 617.450.7000; TU-SU 10-4

Museum Of Science ★★★★☆

"*...cool exhibits for older kids—very little ones should head to the Children's Museum instead... I especially like the changing themes...the museum's IMAX theater is the highlight for us... I highly recommend getting a membership... I have three kids, and we go there all the time... nice to go for short visits more frequently with the little ones... wonderful huge food court, good bathroom facilities... attached garage makes parking easy...* "
Customer service.......................... ❹ $$.. Prices
Age range..................... 3 yrs and up
WWW.MOS.ORG

BEACON HILL/WEST END—SCIENCE PARK (AT MUSEUM WY); 617.723.2500; SA-TH 9-5, F 9-9

Music For Aardvarks And Other Mammals ★★★★☆

"*...fun, energetic, lively music classes... take one—you won't be sorry... unique songs for kids that my daughter still sings years later (I sometimes sing them too)... incredible introduction to music, especially good for toddlers... teachers are charming, energetic and talented... the songs are different and appeal to grownups too... $115 for a 5 week program...* "
Customer service.......................... ❹ $$.. Prices
Age range.................. 3 mths to 5 yrs
WWW.MUSICFORAARDVARKS.COM

BOSTON—199 LAFAYETTE ST (AT THE SANDRA CAMERON DANCE CTR); 617.797.5562; CHECK SCHEDULE ONLINE

Music Together ★★★★⯪

"*...the best mom and baby classes out there... music, singing, dancing—even instruments for tots to play with... liberal make-up policy, great venues, take home books, CDs and tapes which are different each semester... it's a national franchise so instructors vary and have their own style... different age groups get mixed up which makes it a good learning experience for all involved... the highlight of our week—grandma always comes along... be prepared to have your tot sing the songs at home, in the car—everywhere...* "
Customer service.......................... ❹ $$$... Prices
Age range.................. 2 mths to 5 yrs
WWW.MUSICTOGETHER.COM

JAMAICA PLAIN—617.696.5200; CALL FOR SCHEDULE
ROSLINDALE—617.524 1784; CALL FOR SCHEDULE
WEST ROXBURY—617.532.4401; CALL FOR SCHEDULE

New England Aquarium ★★★★★

"...a fabulous trip for all ages, including babies and toddlers... penguins, penguins, penguins—we could spend hours and hours watching the penguins... even our five month-old enjoyed it... my 22-month old daughter also loved the fish and it was so hard to get her to leave... my kids love the big tank in the middle... general admission is expensive—$16 for adults and $14 for children 3 to 11 years, it may be worth getting a family membership... try getting free passes to the aquarium through your local library... parking can be a challenge... go during the week, avoid the crowds!... always something spectacular to see at the IMAX theater, can be overwhelming for the young ones though..."

Customer service .... ❹ $$$ .... Prices
Age range .... 12 mths and up
WWW.NEAQ.ORG
DOWNTOWN—CENTRAL WHARF (AT ATLANTIC AVE); 617.973.5200; CALL FOR HOURS; FREE PARKING

Reel Moms (Loews Theatres) ★★★★☆

"...not really an activity for kids, but rather something you can easily do with your baby... first-run movies for people with babies... the sound is low, the lights turned up and no one cares if your baby cries... packed with moms changing diapers all over the place... so nice to be able to go see current movies... don't have to worry about baby noise... relaxed environment with moms, dads and babies wandering all over... the staff is very friendly and there is a real community feel... a great idea and very well done..."

Customer service .... ❹ $$ .... Prices
Age range .... 3 mths to 2 yrs
WWW.ENJOYTHESHOW.COM/REELMOMS
DOWNTOWN—175 TREMONT ST (AT HEAD ST); 617.423.5801; CHECK SCHEDULE ONLINE

Swan Boats at the Public Garden ★★★★☆

"...a timeless classic—a must-do on a nice day in Boston... a little touristy, but fun even for us locals... quick ride, cute boats and beautiful setting... a wonderful inexpensive outing... make sure to read 'Make Way For Ducklings' aloud before you go or when you get home... even if you don't go on a boat ride, you can just sit and watch the swans, ducks and other people... $2.50 for adults; under 2 is free..."

Customer service .... ❹ $ .... Prices
Age range .... 2 yrs and up
WWW.SWANBOATS.COM
BACK BAY—BOSTON PUBLIC GARDEN (AT CHARLES ST); 617.552.1966; CHECK WEBSITE; FREE PARKING

Northern Suburbs

★★★★★
"lila picks"

- ★ Bonkers Fun House
- ★ Family Music Makers
- ★ North Shore Children's Museum

Artbeat ★★★★☆

❝...great classes in a small store... there was paint everywhere—it was so much fun... their hands-on art studio caters to 4 years and up... our Artbeat party was the easiest and best birthday party we've had so far... more than a store—an arts and crafts studio for all ages... a great place to nurture my budding Picasso... they charge on a per-project basis, so no need to rush... ❞

Customer service.........................❹ $ .... Prices
Age range......................4 yrs and up
WWW.ARTBEATONLINE.COM
ARLINGTON—212A MASSACHUSETTS AVE (AT LAKE ST); 781.646.2200; M-W 10-6, TH-SA 10-8, SU 12-6; STREET PARKING

Barnes & Noble ★★★★☆

❝...wonderful weekly story times for all ages and frequent author visits for older kids... lovely selection of books and the story times are fun and very well done... they have evening story times—we put our kids in their pjs and come here as a treat before bedtime... they read a story, and then usually have a little craft or coloring project related to the story... times vary by location so give them a call... ❞

Customer service.........................❹ $$..Prices
Age range................. 6 mths to 5 yrs
WWW.BARNESANDNOBLE.COM
BURLINGTON—98 MIDDLESEX PKWY (OFF RT 128); 781.273.3871; CALL FOR SCHEDULE
PEABODY—210 ANDOVER ST (AT CROSS ST); 978.573.3261; CALL FOR SCHEDULE
SAUGUS—444A BROADWAY (AT LYNN FELLS PKY); 781.231.4711; CALL FOR SCHEDULE

Bonkers Fun House ★★★★★

❝...loud and buzzing with activity—great for birthday parties... arcade games, food, prizes and real rides for little kids like the frog hopper, carousel and Ferris wheel... a section for little kids and one for school-aged children... they also have a giant maze with tons of slides... if your little one has special needs, you get in free and your child gets a free individual pizza... great place for a hassle-free party... the staff is engaged and interested in hanging with the kids... ❞

Customer service.........................❹ $$..Prices

Age range .... 3 yrs to 12 yrs
WWW.BONKERSFUNHOUSE.COM
PEABODY—535 LOWELL ST (AT BOURBON ST); 978.535.8355; SU-TH 10-9, F-SA 10-10; FREE PARKING

Borders Books ★★★★☆

"...very popular weekly storytime held in most branches (check the web site for locations and times)... call before you go since they are very popular and get extremely crowded... kids love the unique blend of songs, stories, and dancing... Mr. Hatbox's appearances are a delight to everyone... large children's section is well categorized and well priced... they make it fun for young tots to browse through the board book section by hanging toys around the shelves... the low-key cafe is a great place to have coffee with your baby and leaf through some magazines..."

Customer service .... ❹ $$ .... Prices
Age range .... 6 mths to 6 yrs
WWW.BORDERSSTORES.COM
CAMBRIDGE—CAMBRIDGE SIDE GALLERIA (AT CHARLES & 1ST STS); 617.679.0887; CALL FOR SCHEDULE
METHUEN—90 PLEASANT VALLEY ST (AT MILK ST); 978.689.1999; CALL FOR SCHEDULE
PEABODY—151 ANDOVER ST (AT NORTHSHORE SHOPPING CTR); 978.538.3003; CALL FOR SCHEDULE
SWAMPSCOTT—450 PARADISE RD (IN SWAMPSCOTT MALL); 781.592.1290; CALL FOR SCHEDULE

Brattle Theatre ★★★★½

"...if you missed a new release in the theaters, you can see it here—even better, you can bring your baby with you... they have free movies every Wednesday... although the movies are older, it's a perfect way to get out of the house... two hours out of the house, in Harvard Square, surrounded by new parents—you'll feel your IQ coming back... this place is just plain cool..."

Customer service .... ❹ $ .... Prices
Age range .... 2 mths and up
WWW.BRATTLEFILM.ORG
CAMBRIDGE—40 BRATTLE ST (AT STORY ST); 617.876.6837; VISIT WEBSITE FOR SHOWTIMES; FREE PARKING

Brujito's Play Cafe ★★★★☆

"...what a great idea—a play space and cafe... mom and dad can eat while the kids are entertained... it's clean and has enough room to maneuver a stroller without bumping other tables... two separate play areas for kids—the one for babies is gated... the layout allows you to sit and enjoy your food while you watch your kids play... a nice indoor play space..."

Customer service .... ❹ $$$ .... Prices
Age range .... 6 mths and up
WWW.BRUJITOS.COM
SALEM—89 MARGIN ST (AT PRESCOTT ST); 978.740.4444; M-TH 9-6, F-SA 9-7:30, SU 11-5; FREE PARKING

Build-A-Bear Workshop ★★★½☆

"...design and make your own bear—it's a dream come true... the most cherished toy my daughter owns... they even come with birth certificates... the staff is fun and knows how to play along with the kids' excitement... the basic stuffed animal is only about $15, but the extras add up quickly... great for field trips, birthdays and special

occasions... how darling—my nephew is 8 years old now, and still sleeps with his favorite bear... **"**

Customer service..........................❹ $$$...Prices

Age range.....................3 yrs and up

WWW.BUILDABEAR.COM

BURLINGTON—75 MIDDLESEX TURNPIKE (AT BURLINGTON MALL); 781.272.5155; CHECK SCHEDULE ONLINE; PARKING LOT AT MALL

PEABODY—210 ANDOVER ST (AT NORTHSHORE MALL); 978.532.6588; CHECK SCHEDULE ONLINE; PARKING LOT AT MALL

SAUGUS—1201 BROADWAY (AT SQUARE ONE SHOPPING CENTRE); 781.233.6855; M-SA 10-10, SU 11-6

Chuck E Cheese's ★★★☆☆

"...lots of games, rides, playrooms and very greasy food... the kids can play and eat and parents can unwind a little... a good rainy day activity... the kids love the food, but it's a bit greasy for adults... always crowded and crazy—but that's half the fun... can you ever go wrong with pizza, games and singing?.. although they do have a salad bar for adults, remember, you're not going for the food—you're going because your kids will love it... just about the easiest birthday party around—just pay money and show up... **"**

Customer service..........................❸ $$..Prices

Age range.................12 mths to 7 yrs

WWW.CHUCKECHEESE.COM

BURLINGTON—10 WALL ST (AT CAMBRIDGE ST); 781.229.2024; SU-TH 9-10, F-SA 9-11; FREE PARKING

DANVERS—139 ENDICOTT (AT ENDICOTT PLAZA); 978.777.6274; SU-TH 9-10, F-SA 9-11; FREE PARKING

EVERETT—29 MYSTIC VIEW RD (OFF REVERE BEACH PKWY); 617.387.4689; SU-TH 9-10, F-SA 9-11

LOWELL—209 PLAIN ST (AT TANNER ST); 978.970.3636; SU-TH 9-10, F-SA 9-11

METHUEN—90 PLEASANT VALLEY RD (AT THE LOOP); 978.557.9900; SU-TH 9-10, F-SA 9-11

Clayroom ★★★☆☆

"...arts and crafts that go beyond just glue and paper... not specifically geared towards kids, but the staff is great and will help make it fun... better for older kids who have better coordination and can be independent... you can make things from scratch, or simply paint what they have in stock... a fun birthday party outing... **"**

Customer service..........................❸ $$$...Prices

Age range.....................3 yrs and up

WWW.CLAYROOM.COM

MEDFORD—24 RIVERSIDE AVENUE (SALEM AND RIVER STS.); 781.393.7900; SU-TU 11-6, W-SA 10-8

WOBURN—428 MAIN STREET (EVERETT AND WALNUT STS.); 781.937.0100; SU-TU 11-6, W-SA 10-8

Family Music Makers ★★★★★

"...fun classes with lots of music, clapping and singing... many locations... variety of instruments and activities... parents have to be willing to sing and dance, too... the class price includes a free music book and CD for the session... we've been going since my son was 3 months old, and it has been terrific fun... **"**

Customer service..........................❺ $$$...Prices

Age range................. 3 mths to 3 yrs

WWW.FAMILYMUSICMAKERS.COM

CAMBRIDGE—3 CHURCH ST (AT MASSACHUSETTS AVE.); 617.783.9818; CALL FOR SCHEDULE

Gymboree Play & Music ★★★★½

"...we've done several rounds of classes with our kids and they absolutely love it... colorful, padded environment with tons of things to climb and play on... a good indoor place to meet other families and for kids to learn how to play with each other... the equipment and play areas are generally neat and clean... an easy birthday party spot... a guaranteed nap after class... costs vary, so call before showing up..."

Customer service ❹ $$$ Prices
Age range 3 mths to 5 yrs
WWW.GYMBOREE.COM

BURLINGTON—279 CAMBRIDGE ST (AT PONTOS AVE); 781.229.1886; CHECK SCHEDULE ONLINE; FREE PARKING

MELROSE—131 W EMERSON ST (AT LEBANON ST); 978.531.5420; CHECK SCHEDULE ONLINE; FREE PARKING

PEABODY—64 PULASKI ST (AT DOBBS RD); 978.531.5420; CHECK SCHEDULE ONLINE; FREE PARKING

Gymnastics Academy Of Boston ★★★★☆

"...a gymnastics center for serious gymnasts, but they also have classes for little ones... parent participation is required for very small kids... it's basically a guided, indoor play group... our son loved the class and the teachers... great for basic body coordination skills... lots of different, age-specific programs to choose from..."

Customer service ❸ $$$ Prices
Age range 18 mths to 6 yrs
WWW.GYMNASTICACADEMY.COM

CAMBRIDGE—128 SMITH PLACE (AT FAWCETT ST); 617.441.9700; CALL FOR SCHEDULE; FREE PARKING

Jewish Community Center ★★★★☆

"...programs vary from facility to facility, but most JCCs have outstanding early childhood programs... everything from mom and me music classes to arts and crafts for older kids... a wonderful place to meet other parents and make new friends... class fees are cheaper (if not free) for members, but still quite a good deal for nonmembers... a superb resource for new families looking for fun..."

Customer service ❹ $$$ Prices
Age range 3 mths and up
WWW.JCCNS.COM

MARBLEHEAD—4 COMMUNITY RD (AT ATLANTIC AVE); 781.631.8330; CALL FOR SCHEDULE

Kids Playground ★★★½☆

"...a fun place with a huge climbing structure, ball pits, mini golf and more... a nice spot to get out of the cold and rain... lots of activities for toddler-aged kids on up to about age 5... snack bar for lunch with limited selection (pizza, hot dogs, etc.), no outside food permitted... a decent place for a child's birthday party... some of the equipment is very worn..."

Customer service ❸ $$$ Prices
Age range 3 yrs and up
WWW.KIDSPLAYGROUND.COM

WOBURN—15 NORMAC RD (AT OLYMPIC AVE); 781.935.2300; M-W 10-6, TH 10-7, F 10-8, SA 9:30-8, SU 11-7

Little Gym, The ★★★★☆

"...a well thought-out program of gym and tumbling geared towards different age groups... a clean facility, excellent and knowledgeable staff... we love the small-sized gym equipment and their willingness to work with kids with special needs... activities are fun and personalized to match the kids' age... great place for birthday parties with a nice party room—they'll organize and do everything for you..."

Customer service.........................❹ $$$...Prices
Age range................4 mths to 12 yrs
WWW.THELITTLEGYM.COM

DANVERS—29 ANDOVER ST (AT BOW ST); 978.777.7977; CALL FOR SCHEDULE; FREE PARKING

Made By Me Paint Your Own Pottery ★★★★☆

"...you can decorate pottery and make prints of kids' hands and feet... great gifts for Father's Day and for grandparents... the best part is that you pay per piece rather than by time, so you don't have to rush... the memories and shared creative time with my daughter are exquisite..."

Customer service.........................❹ $$..Prices
Age range.....................2 yrs and up
WWW.MADE-BY-ME.COM

CAMBRIDGE—1685 MASSACHUSETTS AVE (AT ARROW ST); 617.354.8111; M 12-10, TU-SA 10-10, SU 12-6; STREET PARKING

Music Together ★★★★½

"...the best mom and baby classes out there... music, singing, dancing—even instruments for tots to play with... liberal make-up policy, great venues, take home books, CDs and tapes which are different each semester... it's a national franchise so instructors vary and have their own style... different age groups get mixed up which makes it a good learning experience for all involved... the highlight of our week—grandma always comes along... be prepared to have your tot sing the songs at home, in the car—everywhere..."

Customer service.........................❹ $$$...Prices
Age range................ 2 mths to 5 yrs
WWW.MUSICTOGETHER.COM

ANDOVER—978.688.3326; CALL FOR SCHEDULE
ARLINGTON—781.648.4084; CALL FOR SCHEDULE
CAMBRIDGE—800.728.2692; CALL FOR SCHEDULE
CAMBRIDGE—617.471.5779; CALL FOR SCHEDULE
CHELMSFORD—978.761.5143; CALL FOR SCHEDULE
DANVERS—978.688.3326; CALL FOR SCHEDULE
GROTON—978.897.0874; CALL FOR SCHEDULE
LOWELL—978.761.5143; CALL FOR SCHEDULE
MARBLEHEAD—781.639.0112; CALL FOR SCHEDULE
MEDFORD—617.513.1844; CALL FOR SCHEDULE
NEWBURYPORT—603.659.4798; CALL FOR SCHEDULE
NORTH ANDOVER—978.688.3326; CALL FOR SCHEDULE
PEPPERELL—978.897.0874; CALL FOR SCHEDULE
READING—978.688.3326; CALL FOR SCHEDULE
SOMERVILLE—617.471.5779; CALL FOR SCHEDULE
WAKEFIELD—781.674.9997; CALL FOR SCHEDULE

My Gym Children's Fitness Center ★★★★☆

"...a wonderful gym environment for babies with parents and older tots on their own... classes range from tiny tots to school-age children and the staff is great about making it fun for all ages... equipment and facilities are really neat—ropes, pulleys, swings, you name it... the kind of place your kids hate to leave... the staff's enthusiasm is contagious... great for memorable birthday parties... although it's a franchise, each gym seems to have its own individual feeling... awesome for meeting playmates and other parents..."

Customer service .... ❹ $$$ .... Prices
Age range .... 3 mths to 9 yrs
WWW.MY-GYM.COM
WOBURN—362 CAMBRIDGE RD (AT REHABILITATION WAY); 781.376.9102; CHECK SCHEDULE ONLINE

North Shore Children's Museum ★★★★★

"...a great interactive museum... it's relatively small, and you can spend an hour or two playing with your tot... it's geared towards imaginative play where children can be creative... play blocks, dress up, music and story time... the tide pool is fun, but your clothes will be soaked... $6 per person; free for children under 1..."

Customer service .... ❹ $$$ .... Prices
Age range .... 3 mths and up
WWW.NSCHILDRENSMUSEUM.ORG
SALEM—294 ESSEX ST (OFF WASHINGTON ST); 978.741.1811; M-TH 9-3, F-SU 9-5

Perpetual Motion

Age range .... 12 mths to 6 yrs
WWW.PERPETUALMOTIONINC.COM
LOWELL—345 CHELMSFORD ST; 978.452.0777; CALL FOR HOURS

Reel Moms (Loews Theatres) ★★★★☆

"...not really an activity for kids, but rather something you can easily do with your baby... first-run movies for people with babies... the sound is low, the lights turned up and no one cares if your baby cries... packed with moms changing diapers all over the place... so nice to be able to go see current movies... don't have to worry about baby noise... relaxed environment with moms, dads and babies wandering all over... the staff is very friendly and there is a real community feel... a great idea and very well done..."

Customer service .... ❹ $$ .... Prices
Age range .... 3 mths to 2 yrs
WWW.ENJOYTHESHOW.COM/REELMOMS
METHUEN—90 PLEASANT VALLEY ST (AT THE LOOP); 978.738.8942; CHECK SCHEDULE ONLINE

Salem Willows Park

Age range .... 2 yrs and up
WWW.SALEMWILLOWSPARK.COM
SALEM—171-185 FORT AVE (AT ESSEX ST); 978.745.0251; CALL FOR HOURS; FREE PARKING

Stone Zoo ★★★★⯪☆

"...not the biggest park, but they have some cougars, jaguars and wolves... the most wonderful Christmas display... I'd recommend wearing your child in a carrier or backpack, since it's hard to see the *animals from a stroller... mostly smaller, less exotic animals... they have a nice carousel and train ride... passes available at many local libraries...* **"**

Customer service..........................❸ $$..Prices
Age range......................2 yrs and up
WWW.ZOONEWENGLAND.COM
STONEHAM—149 POND ST (AT MAIN ST); 781.438.5100; M-SU 10-4

Tumble Kids USA ★★★★☆

"...*offers very active gymnastic classes for all ages... open gym a few times a week where tots can run, roll, tumble wherever they want... awesome inflatable and bouncy equipment for young tots... a bit serious for some 3-year-olds... class activities and intensity varies depending on the instructor... $10 per child for open gym (in addition to your class tuition)...* **"**

Customer service..........................❸ $$$$......................................Prices
Age range................15 mths to 6 yrs
WWW.TUMBLEKIDSUSA.COM
WINCHESTER—38 RIVER ST (AT VERPLAST AVE.); 781.721.1144; CHECK SCHEDULE ONLINE

YMCA ★★★★☆

"...*most of the Ys in the area have classes and activities for kids... swimming, gym classes, dance—even play groups for the really little ones...... some facilities are nicer than others, but in general their programs are worth checking out... prices are more than reasonable for what is offered... the best bang for your buck... they have it all—great programs that meet the needs of a diverse range of families... check out their camps during the summer and school breaks...* **"**

Customer service..........................❹ $$..Prices
Age range..................3 mths and up
WWW.CAMBRIDGEYMCA.ORG
CAMBRIDGE—820 MASSACHUSETTS AVE (AT BIGELOW ST); 617.661.9622; CHECK ONLINE FOR SCHEDULE

Western Suburbs

"lila picks"

★★★★★

- ★ Discovery Museums
- ★ Drumlin Farm Wildlife Sanctuary
- ★ Family Music Makers
- ★ Marcie & Me
- ★ My Gym Children's Fitness Center

activities & outings

Arena Farms ★★★★☆
"...fun for little ones to feed the ducks and see turtles and fish in the pond... moms and dads can pick up some fresh fruit and veggies... the staff is wonderful and takes the time to interact with kids... milk, eggs, pies, baked goods, ice cream and more... tractors to climb on... a small place, perfect for a fun outing..."

Customer service .... **5** $$ .... Prices
Age range ....6 mths and up

CONCORD—167 FAIRHAVEN RD (AT RTE 2); 978.369.4769; DAILY 9-7; FREE PARKING

Atkinson Pool ★★★⯨☆
"...affordable swim lessons with a really friendly staff... lots of different free swim and lesson programs available... my son and husband really enjoyed the parent-tot swim class... my boy loves jumping off the diving boards while I hold on to my baby in the shallow end..."

Customer service .... **4** $$ .... Prices
Age range ....3 mths and up

WWW.TOWN.SUDBURY.MA.US/SERVICES/DEPARTMENT_HOME.ASP?DEPT=POOL
SUDBURY—40 FAIRBANK RD (AT HUDSON RD); 978.443.1092; CHECK ONLINE; FREE PARKING

Barnes & Noble ★★★★⯨
"...wonderful weekly story times for all ages and frequent author visits for older kids... lovely selection of books and the story times are fun and very well done... they have evening story times—we put our kids in their pjs and come here as a treat before bedtime... they read a story, and then usually have a little craft or coloring project related to the story... times vary by location so give them a call..."

Customer service .... **4** $$ .... Prices
Age range ....6 mths to 5 yrs

WWW.BARNESANDNOBLE.COM
BELLINGHAM—270 HARTFORD AVE (OFF RT 495); 508.966.7600; CALL FOR SCHEDULE

BROOKLINE—325 HARVARD ST (OFF BEACON ST); 617.232.0594; CALL FOR SCHEDULE

CHESTNUT HILL—170 BOYLSTON ST (AT HAMMOND POND PKY); 617.965.7621; CALL FOR SCHEDULE

FRAMINGHAM—1 WORCESTER RD (AT SHOPPERS WORLD); 508.628.5567; CALL FOR SCHEDULE

Borders Books ★★★★☆

❝...very popular weekly story time held in most branches (check the web site for locations and times)... call before you go since they are very popular and get extremely crowded... kids love the unique blend of songs, stories and dancing... Mr. Hatbox's appearances are a delight to everyone... large children's section is well categorized and well priced... they make it fun for young tots to browse through the board book section by hanging toys around the shelves... the low-key cafe is a great place to have coffee with your baby and leaf through some magazines... ❞

Customer service.......................... ❹ $$..Prices
Age range................. 6 mths to 6 yrs
WWW.BORDERSSTORES.COM

CHESTNUT HILL—300 BOYLSTON ST (AT FLORENCE ST); 617.630.1120; CALL FOR SCHEDULE

FRAMINGHAM—85 WORCESTER RD (AT RING RD IN SHOPPERS WORLD); 508.875.2321; CALL FOR SCHEDULE

MARLBOROUGH—739 DONALD J LYNCH BLVD (AT SOLOMON POND MALL & RIVER RD); 508.490.8521; CALL FOR SCHEDULE

Boston Sports Clubs ★★★★☆

❝...you have to see it to believe it—one of the best-kept secrets outside of Boston... the pool is wonderful and provides hours of fun for your children... the lifeguards set up games for the kids, and there are slides and water animal fountains in only three feet of water... it tends to be crowded and isn't cheap... babysitting available if you want to workout... ❞

Customer service.......................... ❹ $$$$......................................Prices
Age range................. 12 mths and up
WWW.MYSPORTSCLUBS.COM

LEXINGTON—475 BEDFORD ST (AT HWY 225); 781.861.8600; M-F 5-11, SA-SU 5:30-11; FREE PARKING

Build-A-Bear Workshop ★★★½☆

❝...design and make your own bear—it's a dream come true... the most cherished toy my daughter owns... they even come with birth certificates... the staff is fun and knows how to play along with the kids' excitement... the basic stuffed animal is only about $15, but the extras add up quickly... great for field trips, birthdays and special occasions... how darling—my nephew is 8 years old now, and still sleeps with his favorite bear... ❞

Customer service.......................... ❹ $$$...Prices
Age range......................3 yrs and up
WWW.BUILDABEAR.COM

NATICK—1245 WORCESTER RD (AT NATICK MALL); 508.651.0241; CHECK SCHEDULE ONLINE; PARKING LOT AT MALL

Butterfly Place ★★★★☆

❝...a fun learning experience for kids and adults... knowledgeable staff... a wonderful hands-on experience with butterflies and moths of all types... some of the exhibits enable you to have the butterflies land on you... great for capturing some adorable pictures... bring a picnic to

round out the excursion... not very big—it only takes a few minutes to see...

Customer service .... ❹ $$$ .... Prices
Age range ....6 mths and up
WWW.BUTTERFLYPLACE-MA.COM
WESTFORD—120 TYNGSBORO RD (AT STONERIDGE RD); 978.392.0955; DAILY 10-5; FREE PARKING

Chuck E Cheese's ★★★☆☆

...lots of games, rides, playrooms and very greasy food... the kids can play and eat and parents can unwind a little... a good-rainy day activity... the kids love the food, but it's a bit greasy for adults... always crowded and crazy—but that's half the fun... can you ever go wrong with pizza, games and singing?.. although they do have a salad bar for adults, remember, you're not going for the food—you're going because your kids will love it... just about the easiest birthday party around—just pay money and show up...

Customer service .... ❸ $$ .... Prices
Age range .... 12 mths to 7 yrs
WWW.CHUCKECHEESE.COM
NATICK—801 WORCESTER (AT NATICK CTR); 508.650.9497; SU-TH 9-10, F-SA 9-11; FREE PARKING

Clayroom ★★★☆☆

...arts and crafts that go beyond just glue and paper... not specifically geared towards kids, but the staff is great and will help make it fun... better for older kids who have better coordination and can be independent... you can make things from scratch, or simply paint what they have in stock... a fun birthday party outing...

Customer service .... ❸ $$$ .... Prices
Age range .... 3 yrs and up
WWW.CLAYROOM.COM
AUBURNDALE—303 AUBURN STREET (LEXINGTON STREET); 617.965.6999; M-W 11-5, TH 11-9, F-SA 11-5, SU 12-5
BROOKLINE—1408 BEACON STREET (BETWEEN SUMMIT AVE AND WINCHESTER ST); 617.566.7575; TU-SA 10-10, SU-M 10-8
NATICK—29 MAIN STREET (UNION CT. AND SUMMER ST.); 508.651.2318; M-F 12-6, TH 12-9, SA-SU 11-6

Coolidge Corner Theatre ★★★★½

...a small, friendly theater that has wonderful film festivals for parents with infants... they focus primarily on indie flicks... the staff sets up a changing station in the back of the theater, so you don't have to miss a thing... it usually isn't packed, and the other moms are really friendly... hopefully more people will attend the 'baby' movies so they'll continue to have them... only $5...

Customer service .... ❹ $$ .... Prices
Age range ....2 mths and up
WWW.COOLIDGE..ORG
BROOKLINE—290 HARVARD ST (AT BEACON ST); 617.734.2500; CALL FOR SHOWTIMES; STREET PARKING

DeCordova Museum & Sculpture Park ★★★★½

...gorgeous outdoor setting for picnics... great sculptures for kids to run around and explore... the inside of the museum isn't specifically geared toward very young children, but there are exhibits they will enjoy... children can actually enjoy art and not have to be quiet... if you

only go to the garden, it's free; if you enter the museum, it's $9 for adults, free for children under 2 ... **"**

Customer service.......................... ❹ $$.. Prices
Age range................ 12 mths and up
WWW.DECORDOVA.ORG

LINCOLN—51 SANDY POND RD (AT BAKER BRIDGE RD); 781.259.8355; T-SU 11-5; LOT ON CAMPUS

Discovery Museums, The ★★★★★

"*...a phenomenal children's museum that's highly interactive... each room has a different theme... plenty to touch, crawl into and play with... a very creative, educational—but most importantly fun—space for toddlers... the water room is a blast—although you are going to get wet, even if you wear one of their plastic aprons... a great field trip for kids of all ages... always packed with screaming tots and their parents... an excellent place for toddlers—especially during the winter...* **"**

Customer service.......................... ❸ $$$.. Prices
Age range................ 12 mths and up
WWW.DISCOVERYMUSEUMS.ORG

ACTON—177 MAIN ST (AT CENTRAL ST); 978.264.4200; CHECK WEBSITE; PARKING LOT AVAILABLE

Drumlin Farm Wildlife Sanctuary ★★★★★

"*...an enchanting place to visit—farm animals to pet and feed... pigs, sheep, goats, cows and more... tasty fresh fruit and other produce to take home after your adventure... the hay ride is super fun and makes it easy to get around... enthusiastic teachers make classes interesting... a very relaxing setting... admission is free with purchase of an Audubon membership...* **"**

Customer service.......................... ❹ $$.. Prices
Age range............... 12 mths to 12 yrs
WWW.MASSAUDUBON.ORG

LINCOLN—208 S GREAT RD (AT LINCOLD RD); 781.259.2200; CALL FOR HOURS; PARKING LOT AT SANCTUARY

Family Music Makers ★★★★★

"*...fun classes with lots of music, clapping and singing... many locations... variety of instruments and activities... parents have to be willing to sing and dance, too... the class price includes a free music book and CD for the session... we've been going since my son was 3 months old, and it has been terrific fun...* **"**

Customer service.......................... ❺ $$$.. Prices
Age range................. 3 mths to 3 yrs
WWW.FAMILYMUSICMAKERS.COM

BROOKLINE—1773 BEACON ST (AT DEAN RD); 617.783.9818; CALL FOR SCHEDULE; STREET PARKING

WELLESLEY—309 WASHINGTON ST (AT MAUGUS AVE); 617.783.9818; CALL FOR SCHEDULE

Garden In The Woods ★★★★½

"*...beautiful trails through the woods... the Big Bug exhibit is pretty cool... unless you have a stroller with big wheels, it's best to have the kids walk... a wonderful change of scenery from the city... just the right size for young children... don't forget the bug repellent...* **"**

Customer service.......................... ❹ $$.. Prices
Age range................ 12 mths and up
WWW.NEWFS.ORG/GARDEN.HTM

FRAMINGHAM—180 HEMENWAY RD (AT CATHERINE RD); 508.877.7630; APRIL-OCTOBER DAILY 9-5; FREE PARKING

Green Planet
WWW.THEGREENPLANET.COM

NEWTON—22 LINCOLN ST (AT WALNUT ST); 617.332.7841; M-F 10-6, SA 10-5; STREET AND PARKING LOT

Gym Fit ★★★★☆
"...all the kids in my parents group love these fun gymnastic programs... the staff members are mellow and work really well with the tots... they always manage to make it fun, even when things get a little chaotic... a small but cozy facility... music, songs, games and an obstacle course that is slightly different each week... a wonderful activity during those long winter months..."

Customer service .... ❺ $$$ .... Prices
Age range .... 10 mths and up

NATICK—148 E CENTRAL ST (AT BRIGHAM CT); 508.651.3838; CALL FOR SCHEDULE; PARKING LOT

Gymboree Play & Music ★★★★½
"...we've done several rounds of classes with our kids and they absolutely love it... colorful, padded environment with tons of things to climb and play on... a good indoor place to meet other families and for kids to learn how to play with each other... the equipment and play areas are generally neat and clean... an easy birthday party spot... a guaranteed nap after class... costs vary, so call before showing up..."

Customer service .... ❹ $$$ .... Prices
Age range .... 3 mths to 5 yrs

WWW.GYMBOREE.COM

ACTON—102 NAGOG PARK (AT WESTFORD LN); 508.548.0737; CHECK SCHEDULE ONLINE; FREE PARKING

FRAMINGHAM—1 EDGELL RD (AT RTE 30); 781.209.2000; CHECK SCHEDULE ONLINE; FREE PARKING

MEDFIELD—10 N MEADOWS RD (AT MAIN ST); 508.242.9988; CHECK SCHEDULE ONLINE

NEWTON—109 OAK ST (AT CHESTNUT ST); 617.244.2988; CHECK SCHEDULE ONLINE; FREE PARKING

WALTHAM—3 CRESCENT ST (AT MOODY ST); 781.209.2000; CHECK SCHEDULE ONLINE

Habitat Education Center and Wildlife Sanctuary
Age range .... 2 yrs and up
WWW.MASSAUDUBON.ORG

BELMONT—10 JUNIPER RD (AT CONCORD AVE); 617.489.5050

Hudson Public Library ★★★★½
"...super fun and free... the 'lap time' is a librarian-led group for young children... the focus is on songs and games that can be played with your baby on your lap... a totally feel-good activity... we've made some good friends here, too..."

Customer service .... ❺ $ .... Prices
Age range .... 6 mths to 3 yrs

WWW.HUDSONPUBLICLIBRARY.COM

HUDSON—3 WASHINGTON ST /WOOD SQUARE AT THE ROTARY (AT FELTON ST); 978.568.9645; M-TH9-8:30, F 9-6, S 9-5

Isis Maternity ★★★★½

"...in addition to a great parenting center, they also offer lots of fun activities for new moms and dads... Kindermusik, baby yoga, play groups... as with everything else at Isis, everything is well organized and fun... a wonderful way to interact with my baby and make new friends... lots to do... a must-see for all new parents..."

Customer service.......................... ❸ $$$..Prices
WWW.ISISMATERNITY.COM
BROOKLINE —2 BROOKLINE PL (AT BROOKLINE AVE); 781.429.1500; M W-TH 9-9, T F-SA 9-5; GARAGE AT BROOKLINE PLACE

Jewish Community Center ★★★★☆

"...programs vary from facility to facility, but most JCCs have outstanding early childhood programs... everything from mom and me music classes to arts and crafts for older kids... a wonderful place to meet other parents and make new friends... class fees are cheaper (if not free) for members, but still quite a good deal for nonmembers... a superb resource for new families looking for fun..."

Customer service.......................... ❹ $$$..Prices
Age range................... 3 mths and up
WWW.JCCGB.ORG
BRIGHTON—50 SOUTHERLAND RD (AT BEACON ST); 617.278.1950; CALL FOR SCHEDULE
FRAMINGHAM—76 SALEM END RD (AT WINTER ST); 508.879.3300; CALL FOR SCHEDULE

Kids Place, The ★★★½☆

"...arts and crafts galore... they're great at helping everyone finish their projects to have something to take home... stuff your own animal, paint ceramics, get your hands dirty with plaster—so much fun... the staff knows how to get the creative juices flowing... be prepared for messy, stained clothes... super creative..."

Customer service.......................... ❹ $$$..Prices
Age range......................3 yrs and up
WWW.KIDSPLACEFORFUN.COM
NEWTON—188 NEEDHAM ST (AT CHRISTINA ST); 617.527.0500; M-SU 10-5:30; FREE PARKING

Marcie & Me ★★★★★

"...the activities are age-appropriate, and the opportunity to participate alongside my daughter is priceless... the first half of the hour is free play, followed by circle time... the atmosphere is so positive and nurturing... I have twins, so I really need to be impressed to pay double for a class—they are fantastic... a new 'playscape' every week... it helps get kids ready for preschool..."

Customer service.......................... ❺ $$$$......................................Prices
Age range................. 6 mths to 5 yrs
WWW.MARCIEANDME.COM
WELLESLEY—873 WORCESTER RD (AT RUSSELL RD); 781.235.6444; CHECK SCHEDULE ONLINE

Music Together ★★★★½

"...the best mom and baby classes out there... music, singing, dancing—even instruments for tots to play with... liberal make-up policy, great venues, take home books, CDs and tapes which are different each semester... it's a national franchise so instructors vary and have their own style... different age groups get mixed up which makes it a good learning experience for all involved... the highlight of

our week—grandma always comes along... be prepared to have your tot sing the songs at home, in the car—everywhere... "

Customer service .... ❹ $$$ .... Prices
Age range .... 2 mths to 5 yrs

WWW.MUSICTOGETHER.COM

ACTON—888.569.0712; CALL FOR SCHEDULE
AUBURNDALE—617.928.0190; CALL FOR SCHEDULE
BEDFORD—888.569.0712; CALL FOR SCHEDULE
BELMONT—617.254 9791; CALL FOR SCHEDULE
BROOKLINE—617.471.5779; CALL FOR SCHEDULE
CARLISLE—617.254 9791; CALL FOR SCHEDULE
CHESTNUT HILL—617.928.0190; CALL FOR SCHEDULE
CONCORD—888.569.0712; CALL FOR SCHEDULE
FRAMINGHAM—508.395.8751; CALL FOR SCHEDULE
MARLBOROUGH—508.395.8751; CALL FOR SCHEDULE
NATICK—508.655.8842; CALL FOR SCHEDULE
NEWTON—617.928.0190; CALL FOR SCHEDULE
SUDBURY—978.897.0874; CALL FOR SCHEDULE
WALTHAM—617.928.0190; CALL FOR SCHEDULE
WATERTOWN—617.928.0190; CALL FOR SCHEDULE
WAYLAND—978.440.8588; CALL FOR SCHEDULE
WELLESLEY—617.823.1450; CALL FOR SCHEDULE
WESTBOROUGH—978.568 9004; CALL FOR SCHEDULE
WESTFORD—978.761.5143; CALL FOR SCHEDULE
WESTON—978.440.8588; CALL FOR SCHEDULE

My Gym Children's Fitness Center ★★★★★

"*...a wonderful gym environment for babies with parents and older tots on their own... classes range from tiny tots to school-age children and the staff is great about making it fun for all ages... equipment and facilities are really neat—ropes, pulleys, swings, you name it... the kind of place your kids hate to leave... the staff's enthusiasm is contagious... great for memorable birthday parties... although it's a franchise, each gym seems to have its own individual feeling... awesome for meeting playmates and other parents...* "

Customer service .... ❹ $$$ .... Prices
Age range .... 3 mths to 9 yrs

WWW.MY-GYM.COM

FRAMINGHAM—855 WORCESTER RD (AT AUBURN ST); 508.370.9496; CHECK SCHEDULE ONLINE

NEWTON—188 NEEDHAM ST (AT INDUSTRIAL PL); 617.243.9496; CHECK SCHEDULE ONLINE

One Stop Fun Inc ★★★★☆

"*...a large activity center for kids—gymnastics, outdoor pool with slides, ball pits... a great indoor playground... if you want your kids to nap, let them run around here for a bit... there often are lots of other parties going on at the same time... they're pros at throwing a fun party for kids... the best part is the huge climbing and crawling structure...* "

Customer service .... ❸ $$$ .... Prices
Age range .... 18 mths and up

WWW.ONESTOPFUN.COM

WESTFORD—49 POWERS ROAD (OFF LITTLETON RD); 978.692.9907; CALL FOR SCHEDULE

Planet Gymnastics ★★★★½

"...a fun environment, totally designed for tots and kids... things to jump on, crawl through, hide in—it never gets boring... my son loves the huge foam pit... padded obstacle course and lots to climb on and hang from... my son has been taking lessons here for a couple of years and also had a birthday party here, which everyone loved... even the waiting area is decked out with stuff to do to keep little minds busy..."

Customer service..........................❹ $$$$......................................Prices
Age range.................12 mths to 6 yrs
WWW.PLANET-GYMNASTICS.COM

ACTON—10 GRANITE RD (AT QUARRY RD); 978.263.1900; SEE WEBSITE FOR SCHEDULES; FREE PARKING

NATICK—5 CHRYSLER RD (AT SPEEN ST); 508.647.1777; APPT ONLY

Puppet Showplace Theatre ★★★★☆

"...what a fun outing—it's a rare treat for my kids to see a professional puppet show... shows are geared toward very young kids as well as older ones... great puppets... a very memorable excursion—my daughter has been talking about the puppets for days now... fantastic staff—they take the time to explain things to the little ones..."

Customer service..........................❹ $$$..Prices
Age range.................. 3 yrs to 10 yrs
WWW.PUPPETSHOWPLACE.ORG

BROOKLINE—32 STATION ST (AT ROCKWOOD ST); 617.731.6400; SEPT-MAY W-TH 10:30, SA-SU 1-3, JUNE-AUG W-TH 10:30-1; STREET PARKING

Tumble Kids USA ★★★★☆

"...offers very active gymnastic classes for all ages... open gym a few times a week where tots can run, roll, tumble wherever they want... awesome inflatable and bouncy equipment for young tots... a bit serious for some 3-year-olds... class activities and intensity varies depending on the instructor... $10 per child for open gym (in addition to your class tuition)..."

Customer service..........................❸ $$$$......................................Prices
Age range.................15 mths to 6 yrs
WWW.TUMBLEKIDSUSA.COM

WATERTOWN—201 ARLINGTON ST (AT GROVE ST); 617.926.2640; CHECK SCHEDULE ONLINE

Warmlines Parent Resources ★★★★½

"...a nonprofit organization that provides a variety of resources to new parents including a music class for tots... the music program is outstanding—all of the children are interested and engaged throughout the class... six-week new mom and baby group... they offer wonderful community services for parents to meet one another, locate resources and learn more about parenting..."

Customer service..........................❹ $$...Prices
Age range................... 6 mths and up
WWW.WARMLINES.ORG

NEWTON—225 NEVADA ST (AT LINWOOD AVE); 617.244.6843; CHECK SCHEDULE ONLINE

Watertown Family Network ★★★★★

"...this is a free drop-in play space for Watertown residents, but nonresidents can join for only $15 per year... a great deal considering the vast array of offerings—new-mom support groups, music classes, mom and baby exercise, workshops on various parenting issues, etc... a

great resource for finding and engaging in numerous child-focused activities... **"**

Customer service .... ❺ $ .... Prices
Age range .... birth and up
WWW.WATERTOWN.K12.MA.US
WATERTOWN—460 MAIN ST (AT PRESCOTT ST); 617.926.1661

YMCA ★★★★☆

"...*most of the Ys in the area have classes and activities for kids... swimming, gym classes, dance—even play groups for the really little ones.... some facilities are nicer than others, but in general their programs are worth checking out... prices are more than reasonable for what is offered... the best bang for your buck... they have it all—great programs that meet the needs of a diverse range of families... check out their camps during the summer and school breaks....* **"**

Customer service .... ❹ $$ .... Prices
Age range .... 3 mths and up
WWW.YMCABOSTON.ORG

BRIGHTON—615 WASHINGTON ST (AT BRECK AVE); 617.782.3535; CALL FOR SCHEDULE

FRAMINGHAM—280 OLD CONNECTICUT PATH (AT HARDY ST); 508.879.4420; CALL FOR SCHEDULE; FREE PARKING

WALTHAM—725 LEXINGTON ST (AT COLLEGE FARM RD); 781.894.5295; CALL FOR SCHEDULE

NEWTON—276 CHURCH ST (AT RICHARDSON ST); 617.244.6050; CALL FOR SCHEDULE

Southern Suburbs

★★★★★
"lila picks"

- ★ Children's Museum
- ★ Family Music Makers
- ★ Gymboree Play & Music
- ★ Marcie & Me

Arnold's Gymnastics Academy ★★★★★

"...great tumbling and gymnastics classes for all ages... not too structured for the little ones, which definitely makes it more fun for them... the staff was engaged and friendly... call early, their classes fill up very quickly..."

Customer service.......................... ❺ $$$....................................... Prices
Age range.................. 6 mths and up
WWW.ARNOLDSGYMNASTICS.COM
MANSFIELD—249 OAKLAND ST (AT FRANCIS AVE); 508.339.6843; APPT ONLY; FREE PARKING

Barnes & Noble ★★★★☆

"...wonderful weekly story times for all ages and frequent author visits for older kids... lovely selection of books and the story times are fun and very well done... they have evening story times—we put our kids in their pjs and come here as a treat before bedtime... they read a story, and then usually have a little craft or coloring project related to the story... times vary by location so give them a call..."

Customer service.......................... ❹ $$.. Prices
Age range................. 6 mths to 5 yrs
WWW.BARNESANDNOBLE.COM
BRAINTREE—150 GRANITE ST (AT BRAINTREE HILL PARK); 781.380.3655; CALL FOR SCHEDULE
HINGHAM—96 DERBY ST (AT HINGHAM PLZ); 781.749.3319; CALL FOR SCHEDULE
WALPOLE—90 PROVIDENCE HWY (AT CONEY ST); 508.668.1303; CALL FOR SCHEDULE

Blue Hills Trailside Museum ★★★★☆

"...an inexpensive family outing with a great opportunity for up-close wildlife experiences... friendly staff that offers 'guess the animal' sessions every couple of hours... my daughter loved the birds being walked around by the guides throughout the museum... try Houghton's Pond nearby for pond swimming and a cute little playground..."

Customer service.......................... ❺ $ .... Prices
WWW.MASSAUDUBON.ORG

MILTON—1904 CANTON AVE (AT HEMENWAY DR); 617.333.0690; W-SU 10-5; FREE PARKING

Borders Books ★★★★☆

"...very popular weekly storytime held in most branches (check the web site for locations and times)... call before you go since they are very popular and get extremely crowded... kids love the unique blend of songs, stories, and dancing... Mr. Hatbox's appearances are a delight to everyone... large children's section is well categorized and well priced... they make it fun for young tots to browse through the board book section by hanging toys around the shelves... the low-key cafe is a great place to have coffee with your baby and leaf through some magazines..."

Customer service .... ❹ $$ .... Prices
Age range .... 6 mths to 6 yrs
WWW.BORDERSSTORES.COM

BRAINTREE—255 GROSSMAN DR (AT UNION ST); 781.356.5111; CALL FOR SCHEDULE

HANOVER—1316 WASHINGTON ST (AT MILL ST IN HANOVER MALL); 781.826.8526; CALL FOR SCHEDULE

KINGSTON—101 INDEPENDENCE MALL WY (IN INDEPENDENCE MALL); 781.582.8100; CALL FOR SCHEDULE

NORTH ATTLEBORO—1212 SOUTH WASHINGTON ST (AT ALLEN AVE); 508.699.7766; CALL FOR SCHEDULE

Boston Nature Center and Wildlife Sanctuary

Age range .... 2 yrs and up
WWW.MASSAUDUBON.ORG
MATTAPAN—500 WALK HILL ST (AT HARVARD ST); 617.983.8500

Build-A-Bear Workshop ★★★★☆

"...design and make your own bear—it's a dream come true... the most cherished toy my daughter owns... they even come with birth certificates... the staff is fun and knows how to play along with the kids' excitement... the basic stuffed animal is only about $15, but the extras add up quickly... great for field trips, birthdays and special occasions... how darling—my nephew is 8 years old now, and still sleeps with his favorite bear..."

Customer service .... ❹ $$$ .... Prices
Age range .... 3 yrs and up
WWW.BUILDABEAR.COM

BRAINTREE—250 GRANITE ST (AT SOUTH SHORE PLAZA); 781.356.8400; M-SA 10-10, SU 11-7; FREE PARKING

KINGSTON—101 INDEPENDENCE MALL WAY (AT INDEPENDENCE MALL); 877.560.2327; CHECK SCHEDULE ONLINE; PARKING LOT AT MALL

NORTH ATTLEBORO—999 S WASHINGTON ST (AT EMERALD SQUARE); 508.643.3443; M-SA 10-9:30, SU 11-6

Children's Museum ★★★★★

"...old-fashioned, hands-on fun... a nice little museum with lots for preschoolers and toddlers to do... the first floor has an open layout so your kids can move from exhibit to exhibit without disappearing... the second floor consists of individual rooms... fun workshops... the interactive golf ball maze is a crowd favorite... $6 for adults; free for children under 1 ..."

Customer service .... ❹ $$ .... Prices
Age range .... 3 mths to 5 yrs
WWW.CHILDRENSMUSEUMINEASTON.ORG

www.lilaguide.com

NORTH EASTON—9 SULLIVAN AVE (AT MAIN ST); 508.230.3789; T-SA 10-5, SU 12-5; FREE PARKING

Chuck E Cheese's ★★★☆☆

"...lots of games, rides, playrooms and very greasy food... the kids can play and eat and parents can unwind a little... a good rainy day activity... the kids love the food, but it's a bit greasy for adults... always crowded and crazy—but that's half the fun... can you ever go wrong with pizza, games and singing?.. although they do have a salad bar for adults, remember, you're not going for the food—you're going because your kids will love it... just about the easiest birthday party around—just pay money and show up...**"**

Customer service.......................... ❸ $$.. Prices
Age range................12 mths to 7 yrs
WWW.CHUCKECHEESE.COM

ATTLEBORO—287 WASHINGTON ST SOUTH (AT SOUTH ATTLEBORO SQ); 508.399.8445; SU-TH 9-10, F-SA 9-11

Clayroom ★★★☆☆

"...arts and crafts that go beyond just glue and paper... not specifically geared towards kids, but the staff is great and will help make it fun... better for older kids who have better coordination and can be independent... you can make things from scratch, or simply paint what they have in stock... a fun birthday party outing...**"**

Customer service.......................... ❸ $$$.. Prices
Age range......................3 yrs and up
WWW.CLAYROOM.COM

EASTON—20 ROCHE BROS WAY—RT 138 (UNION ST); 508.238.3666; M-W 10-6, TH 10-9, F 10-6, SA 11-6, SU 12-4

NEEDHAM—330 CHESTNUT ST (AT MARSH RD); 781.449.6677; SU-TH 12-7, F-SA 12-9; FREE PARKING

WALPOLE—930 MAIN STREET (AT EAST ST); 508.660.1110; TH-TU 10-6, W 10-10

Creative Movement Arts Center ★★★★☆

"...this center offers music, art, exercise and dance classes for babies and young children... the staff is friendly and open to suggestions... low staff turnover, so kids become comfortable with the teachers from one session to the next... lots of classes to choose from... fun for birthday parties...**"**

Customer service.......................... ❹ $$$.. Prices
Age range................3 mths to 10 yrs

NEEDHAM—145 ROSEMARY ST (AT HILLSDALE AVE); 781.449.2707; CHECK SCHEDULE ONLINE; FREE PARKING

Family Music Makers ★★★★★

"...fun classes with lots of music, clapping and singing... many locations... variety of instruments and activities... parents have to be willing to sing and dance, too... the class price includes a free music book and CD for the session... we've been going since my son was 3 months old, and it has been terrific fun...**"**

Customer service.......................... ❺ $$$.. Prices
Age range................. 3 mths to 3 yrs
WWW.FAMILYMUSICMAKERS.COM

NEEDHAM—1154 GREAT PLAIN AVE (AT LINDEN STREET); 617.783.9818; CALL FOR SCHEDULE

NORWOOD—71 BOND STREET (WALPOLE STREET/); 617.783.9818; CALL FOR SCHEDULE

Gymboree Play & Music ★★★★★

"...we've done several rounds of classes with our kids and they absolutely love it... colorful, padded environment with tons of things to climb and play on... a good indoor place to meet other families and for kids to learn how to play with each other... the equipment and play areas are generally neat and clean... an easy birthday party spot... a guaranteed nap after class... costs vary, so call before showing up..."

Customer service ❹ $$$ .... Prices
Age range .... 3 mths to 5 yrs
WWW.GYMBOREE.COM

CANTON—95 WASHINGTON ST (AT THOMAS FLATLEY VILLAGE MALL); 781.828.6620; CHECK SCHEDULE ONLINE; PARKING LOT AT MALL

NORWELL—293 WASHINGTON ST (AT HALL DR); 781.659.2208; CHECK SCHEDULE ONLINE

QUINCY—101 FALLS BLVD (AT QUINCY AVE); 617.479.5444; CHECK SCHEDULE ONLINE; FREE PARKING

Isis Maternity ★★★★½

"...in addition to a great parenting center, they also offer lots of fun activities for new moms and dads... Kindermusik, baby yoga, play groups... as with everything else at Isis, everything is well organized and fun... a wonderful way to interact with my baby and make new friends... lots to do... a must-see for all new parents..."

Customer service ❸ $$$ .... Prices
WWW.ISISMATERNITY.COM

NEEDHAM —110 2ND AVE (AT HIGHLAND AVE); 781.429.1500; M-TU 9-9, W 9-5, TH 9-9, F-SU 9-5; 2 LOTS ON EITHER SIDE OF BUILDING

Jewish Community Center ★★★★☆

"...programs vary from facility to facility, but most JCCs have outstanding early childhood programs... everything from mom and me music classes to arts and crafts for older kids... a wonderful place to meet other parents and make new friends... class fees are cheaper (if not free) for members, but still quite a good deal for nonmembers... a superb resource for new families looking for fun..."

Customer service ❹ $$$ .... Prices
Age range .... 3 mths and up
WWW.STRIARJCC.ORG

STOUGHTON—445 CENTRAL ST (AT TURNPIKE ST); 781.341.2016; CALL FOR SCHEDULE

Kids Club Fun Land ★★★☆☆

"...a loud and colorful kid's 'fun land'... a maze, slides, tubes to crawl through and pits with thousands of colored balls... super easy to throw a party here—they pretty much organize it all... ever wonder how they clean all those balls?.. pinball machines and video games, too... they charge $8 for admission plus tokens..."

Customer service ❸ $$$ .... Prices
Age range .... 12 mths to 12 yrs
WWW.KIDSCLUBFUNLAND.COM

NORWOOD—500 PROVIDENCE TURNPIKE (AT NEPONSET ST); 781.762.7007; M-TH 11-7, F-SA 10-8, SU 12-8; FREE PARKING

Kidz Planet Gymnastics

SOUTH EASTON—15 PLYMOUTH DR (AT EASTON INDUSTRIAL COMPLEX); 508.238.0439; CALL FOR SCHEDULE; FREE PARKING

Little Gym, The ★★★★☆

"...a well thought-out program of gym and tumbling geared towards different age groups... a clean facility, excellent and knowledgeable staff... we love the small-sized gym equipment and their willingness to work with kids with special needs... activities are fun and personalized to match the kid's' age... great place for birthday parties with a nice party room—they'll organize and do everything for you..."

Customer service.......................... ❹ $$$...................................... Prices
Age range................4 mths to 12 yrs
WWW.THELITTLEGYM.COM

RAYNHAM—1510 NEW STATE HWY (AT CHURCH ST); 508.880.5408; CALL FOR SCHEDULE; FREE PARKING

Marcie & Me ★★★★★

"...the activities are age-appropriate, and the opportunity to participate alongside my daughter is priceless... the first half of the hour is free play, followed by circle time... the atmosphere is so positive and nurturing... I have twins, so I really need to be impressed to pay double for a class—they are fantastic... a new 'playscape' every week... it helps get kids ready for preschool..."

Customer service.......................... ❺ $$$$...................................... Prices
Age range................. 6 mths to 5 yrs
WWW.MARCIEANDME.COM

WESTWOOD—615 HIGH ST (AT GAY ST); 781.329.0778; CHECK SCHEDULE ONLINE; STREET PARKING

Music Together ★★★★½

"...the best mom and baby classes out there... music, singing, dancing—even instruments for tots to play with... liberal make-up policy, great venues, take home books, CDs and tapes which are different each semester... it's a national franchise so instructors vary and have their own style... different age groups get mixed up which makes it a good learning experience for all involved... the highlight of our week—grandma always comes along... be prepared to have your tot sing the songs at home, in the car—everywhere..."

Customer service.......................... ❹ $$$...................................... Prices
Age range................. 2 mths to 5 yrs
WWW.MUSICTOGETHER.COM

ATTLEBORO—508.222.3321; CALL FOR SCHEDULE
BRAINTREE—781.961 3460; CALL FOR SCHEDULE
BRIDGEWATER—508.222.3321; CALL FOR SCHEDULE
CANTON—781.769 9827; CALL FOR SCHEDULE
DEDHAM—617.469.0669; CALL FOR SCHEDULE
EAST BRIDGEWATER—508.222.3321; CALL FOR SCHEDULE
HINGHAM—617.696.5200; CALL FOR SCHEDULE
MILTON—617.770.3347; CALL FOR SCHEDULE
NEEDHAM—781.769 9827; CALL FOR SCHEDULE
NORWOOD—CALL FOR SCHEDULE
WESTPORT—508.493.0355; CALL FOR SCHEDULE

My Gym Children's Fitness Center ★★★★☆

"...a wonderful gym environment for babies with parents and older tots on their own... classes range from tiny tots to school-age children and the staff is great about making it fun for all ages... equipment and facilities are really neat—ropes, pulleys, swings, you name it... the kind of place your kids hate to leave... the staff's enthusiasm is contagious...

great for memorable birthday parties... although it's a franchise, each gym seems to have its own individual feeling... awesome for meeting playmates and other parents... "

Customer service .... ❹ $$$ .... Prices
Age range .... 3 mths to 9 yrs
WWW.MY-GYM.COM

DEDHAM—622 WASHINGTON ST (AT DEDHAM PLAZA); 781.320.9496; CHECK SCHEDULE ONLINE; FREE PARKING

KINGSTON—182 SUMMER ST (AT TREMONT ST); 781.582.2255; CHECK SCHEDULE ONLINE; FREE PARKING

Sheep Pasture ★★★★☆

"...if you like sheep, then you've come to the right place... lots of free fun—only bring quarters if you want to feed the animals... walk the trails, sit by the frog pond and just spend time outdoors... bring wipes, because the hand sanitizers are sometimes empty... wear boots or bring a change of shoes and socks... lots of guided and educational programs for older kids..."

Customer service .... ❹ $$ .... Prices
Age range .... 3 yrs and up
WWW.NRTOFEASTON.ORG

NORTH EASTON—307 MAIN ST (AT STONEHILL COLLEGE); 508.238.6049; DAWN TO DUSK

Showcase Cinema—Baby Pictures ★★★★☆

"...the whole time I was on maternity leave, I looked forward to Tuesdays when the Baby Pictures are on... not only do you get to interact with other moms and babies, but you also get to enjoy a movie... when your baby cries, no one tells you to shush... dim—not dark—lighting for the babies, sound is low and there is a play area for the little ones... bagel and coffee cart for adults... diaper changing station... babies get in free... adults pay $5.50..."

Customer service .... ❹ $$ .... Prices
WWW.SHOWCASECINEMAS.COM

RANDOLPH—73 MAZZEO DR; 781.963.0769; CHECK SCHEDULE ONLINE; FREE PARKING

Smith Farm ★★★★☆

"...a working family farm with an outdoor zoo of farm animals for the kids to feed (bring quarters)... lots of greenhouses to walk through and check out... friendly dogs roam throughout the farm and like to be petted... pick your own strawberries, blueberries, apples and, of course, pumpkins... I like seeing my toddlers discover where fruits and vegetables come from..."

Customer service .... ❸ $ .... Prices
Age range .... 2 yrs and up
WWW.CNSMITHFARMINC.COM

EAST BRIDGEWATER—325 SOUTH ST (AT BRIDGE ST); 508.378.2270; M-SA 9-6, SU 9-5

Wards Berry Farm ★★★★★

"...a fantastic summer outing for kids... a family-run operation with farm animals, hay rides, strawberry picking, sand box, hay piles and more... they also have a farm store with great produce, smoothies, sandwiches and tasty baked goods... we attended a birthday party here and had a blast... great staff—lots of fun..."

Customer service .... ❺ $$ .... Prices
Age range .... 6 mths and up

www.lilaguide.com

SHARON—614 S MAIN ST (AT WALPOLE ST); 781.784.6939; DAILY 8:30-6:30

YMCA ★★★★☆

"...most of the Ys in the area have classes and activities for kids... swimming, gym classes, dance—even play groups for the really little ones.... some facilities are nicer than others, but in general their programs are worth checking out... prices are more than reasonable for what is offered... the best bang for your buck... they have it all—great programs that meet the needs of a diverse range of families... check out their camps during the summer and school breaks..."

Customer service.......................... ❹ $$..Prices
Age range.................. 3 mths and up
WWW.YMCABOSTON.ORG

NEEDHAM—863 GREAT PLAIN AVE (AT WARREN ST); 781.444.6400; CALL FOR SCHEDULE

parks & playgrounds

City of Boston

★★★★★
"lila picks"

- ★ Arnold Arboretum
- ★ Castle Island & Fort Independence
- ★ Myrtle Street Playground
- ★ Pope John Paul II Park
- ★ Ringgold Park

Arnold Arboretum ★★★★★
"...a gorgeous natural park maintained with utmost care... open space for the kids to run and play... an excellent choice for an after-dinner family walk... great for nature hunts, riding bikes and playing frisbee... don't miss the lilacs at the Arboretum... the roads are paved and plowed in the winter... see the Boston skyline at the end of one path..."
Equipment/play structures............❹ ❺.............................Maintenance
WWW.ARBORETUM.HARVARD.EDU
JAMAICA PLAIN—125 ARBORWAY (AT CENTRE ST); 617.524.1717

Boston Common ★★★★☆
"...lots of grassy areas good for picnics and walks... nothing beats the spring flowers and swan boat rides... lots of people watching, playgrounds, swan boats and the Frog Pond, for wading on hot summer days!... nice and quiet right in the middle of the city... one of the most beautiful parks in the world... no restrooms available..."
Equipment/play structures............❹ ❹.............................Maintenance
WWW.CITYOFBOSTON.GOV
DOWNTOWN—147 TREMONT ST (AT WEST ST); 617.635.7383

Brewer/Burroughs Tot Lot ★★★★☆
"...great playground for children... it is nicely maintained, and parents frequently donate toys to the playground..."
Equipment/play structures............❹ ❹.............................Maintenance
WWW.CI.BOSTON.MA.US
JAMAICA PLAIN—BURROUGHS ST (AT BREWER ST)

Castle Island & Fort Independence ★★★★★
"...nothing better on a hot summer day... there is a beach, a playground and plenty of room for biking and skating... my son loved watching all the airplanes from the nearby airport zoom by... there's a picnic area and food stands... can get crowded in the evenings..."
Equipment/play structures............❹ ❹.............................Maintenance

participate in our survey at

DORCHESTER—WILLIAM J DAY BLVD (AT E END OF WJD BLVD); 617.973.8800

Christopher Columbus Waterfront Park ★★★½☆

"...wonderful location—right on Boston Harbor and a short walk to the North End for the best food in town... the playground has tons to climb on and around (no swings though)... my kids hardly notice the waterfront, but my husband and I love going there... the only downside is that it can get really crowded with tourists..."

Equipment/play structures .... ❹   ❹ .... Maintenance
WWW.CITYOFBOSTON.GOV
NORTH END—ATLANTIC AVE (AT NORTH ST)

Georges Island ★★★★☆

"...a day adventure my two-year-old loves... the ferry ride alone is worth it... you end up at a great spot to spend the day and have a picnic... the gravel beach is good for digging and building things... dress in layers and warm clothes—it gets quite windy at times and you'll want to be sure your tots are warm..."

Equipment/play structures .... ❹   ❹ .... Maintenance
WWW.BOSTONISLANDS.ORG/ISLE_GEORGES.HTML
BOSTON—7 MI FROM DOWNTOWN BOSTON; 617.223.8666; 9-SUNSET

Jamaica Pond ★★★★½

"...the jewel of the Emerald Necklace!... we love the Jamaica Pond... a lovely place to walk, stroll around, bring a jogger... plenty of ducks and other assorted birds for the kids to feed, bring bread/food... there are also places to sit, boats to ride in... once around the park is about 1 1/2 miles—perfect outdoor place to get in shape..."

Equipment/play structures .... ❸   ❹ .... Maintenance
WWW.CITYOFBOSTON.GOV/PARKS
JAMAICA PLAIN—507 JAMAICA WY (AT POND ST); 617.522.6258

Joe Moakley Park ★★★★☆

"...a couple of playgrounds and basketball courts filled with kids of all ages... the playgrounds are fenced in... one of the basketball courts is generally crowded with teens, while the other one is used by tots on their tricycles... easy to meet other families with toddlers..."

Equipment/play structures .... ❺   ❺ .... Maintenance
WWW.CITYOFBOSTON.GOV/PARKS/OPENSPACES/MAIN.ASP?ID=483
SOUTH BOSTON—COLUMBUS RD

Millennium Park ★★★★½

"...incredible!... two great play spaces... beautiful fields... paved areas for walking or trikes... beautiful spot to fly a kite, a bit lonely at the children's park at the top when no one else is there... unbelievable sunsets, a great family park... recommend going with someone, it's got a secluded feel..."

Equipment/play structures .... ❹   ❹ .... Maintenance
WWW.CITYOFBOSTON.GOV/MAINSTREETS/WESTROXBURY.ASP
WEST ROXBURY—180 CHARLES PARK RD (AT RIVERMONT ST); 617.325.6400

Myrtle Street Playground ★★★★★

"...this city-owned playground is meticulously maintained by a private neighborhood group... the play equipment is in great shape and locals are constantly donating new toys and playthings for the kids... very convenient for downtown families..."

Equipment/play structures .... ❺   ❹ .... Maintenance

WWW.GOCITYKIDS.COM/BROWSE/ATTRACTION.JSP?ID=2156
BEACON HILL/WEST END—MYRTLE ST (AT IRVING ST)

Pope John Paul II Park ★★★★★

"...located next to the freeway, but don't really notice it at all—it's surprisingly quiet... pathways are smooth and well taken care of—perfect for strolls with the pram... nice play area, but the best part is bird watching right next to the water ..."

Equipment/play structures............❹ ❺...............................Maintenance

WWW.STATE.MA.US/MDC/PJP.HTM
DORCHESTER—GALLIVAN BLVD (AT NEPONSET CIR); 617.727.6034

Ringgold Park (Hanson Street Play Area) ★★★★★

"...a great, out of the way park, newly renovated, beautiful setting in secure, dog-free enclosed area... nice mommies and kids at this little neighborhood park... mostly used by toddlers and infants... it gets crowded with daycare groups in the late morning—that means lots of playmates for my 2-year-old... mostly used by toddlers, not much for 5+ kids..."

Equipment/play structures............❺ ❹...............................Maintenance

WWW.CITYOFBOSTON.GOV/PARKS
BOSTON—WALTHAM ST & HANSON ST (AT BRADFORD ST)

Titus Sparrow Park ★★★★☆

"...great playground for little ones, with a large sandbox, swings, climbing equipment... also a nice grassy area for picnics and playing... live music concerts for kids every Wednesday morning—very entertaining and fun... bring the sunscreen—there's very little shade..."

Equipment/play structures............❺ ❺...............................Maintenance

WWW.TITUSSPARROWPARK.ORG
BACK BAY—W NEWTON ST (BTWN COLUMBUS & HUNTINGTON AVES)

participate in our survey at

Northern Suburbs

★★★★★

"lila picks"

★ Lake Quannapowitt
★ Raymond Park
★ Robbins Farm/Skyline Park

parks & playgrounds

Ames Playground ★★★★☆
"...*equipment for ages up to 12, including climbing structure, swings and sandbox... on-street parking available... baseball field and basketball nets...* **"**
Equipment/play structures .... ❸   ❸ .... Maintenance
WWW.CI.LYNN.MA.US
LYNN—BOSTON ST (BTWN CONGRESS AND FRANKLIN STS)

Boy Scout Park ★★★★☆
"...*this park was created with a castle in the middle... lots of tunnels, secret passages... ways to explore... very safe, clean and entertaining for kids of all ages...* **"**
Equipment/play structures .... ❺   ❺ .... Maintenance
BOXFORD—CAHOUN ST

Brackett School Playground ★★★★★
"...*this is a fantastic park for children of all ages... there's a large field with a great view of Boston... a slide built into the ground takes you to the lower playground... there are swings and activities for all ages... lots of street parking ...* **"**
Equipment/play structures .... ❺   ❺ .... Maintenance
WWW.ARLINGTON.K12.MA.US/BRACKETT/
ARLINGTON—66 EASTERN AVE (AT FAYETTE ST); 781.316.3702

Callery Park ★★☆☆☆
"...*play area adjacent to the Little League ball fields... merry-go-round structure, swings... slide is a fairly high, old-fashioned metal one, it can get pretty hot... the area seems clean, and the mulch surface is new... keep a close eye on children, as the play area is not fenced off from the road...* **"**
Equipment/play structures .... ❷   ❷ .... Maintenance
WWW.LOWELLMA.GOV
LOWELL—200 B ST (AT STEVENS ST)

Cambridge Common ★★★★☆
"...*plenty of play structures for children of all ages... located right in Harvard Square... the wooden play structures could use a face lift... bridges, slides and even a big model car with a steering wheel... the whole playground is fenced in, so parents can relax a little...* **"**

www.lilaguide.com

Equipment/play structures............ **4**   **4** ....Maintenance
WWW.CAMBRIDGEMA.GOV

CAMBRIDGE—GARDEN ST (AT WATERHOUSE ST)

Dana Park ★★★★★

"...a newly renovated public park with a big grassy lawn, play equipment for kids of all ages, a basketball court, a sand play area and water spray area..."
Equipment/play structures............ **5**   **4** ....Maintenance
WWW.CAMBRIDGEMA.GOV

CAMBRIDGE—MAGAZINE ST (AT LAWRENCE ST); 617.349.4603

Danehy Park ★★★★☆

"...wonderful, child-friendly park... great place for strollers and there are a bunch of age-appropriate playgrounds... usually the first to turn their sprinklers on in the summer... plenty of green space for running and playing catch... my only caveat would be its a bit bare and unwelcoming aesthetically..."
Equipment/play structures............ **5**   **4** ....Maintenance
WWW.CAMBRIDGEMA.GOV

CAMBRIDGE—99 SHERMAN ST (AT CADBURY RD); 617.349.4895

Friendship Park Playground ★★★★☆

"...limited sun in the mornings, but very shaded in the afternoon... a porta-potty is located at the firehouse across the field... wonderful for all ages..."
Equipment/play structures............ **4**   **4** ....Maintenance
WWW.TOWNOFCHELMSFORD.US

CHELMSFORD—OLD WESTFORD RD; 978.250.5262

Ginn Field ★★★★☆

"...small but very friendly playground and great place to meet new moms... midday shade is nonexistent, but afternoons and mornings are much more comfortable on a hot summer day... ice cream trucks arrive at regular intervals to cool the kiddies off... very cute playground..."
Equipment/play structures............ **4**   **3** ....Maintenance
WWW.WINCHESTER.US/PROJECTS.ASP

WINCHESTER—BACON ST (OFF MYSTIC VALLEY PKWY); 781.721.7126

Hancock Park ★★★★☆

"...a hidden gem for families in the middle of Cambridge... a truly international playground, where we've made lots of foreign friends... big enough so it doesn't get overly crowded... sprinklers spray in the warmer months... a canopied sandbox... nice variety of play equipment so kids of all ages are happy..."
Equipment/play structures............ **5**   **4** ....Maintenance
WWW.CAMBRIDGEMA.GOV

CAMBRIDGE—HANCOCK (BTWN MASSACHUSETTS AVE AND HARVARD ST)

Kingsley Park ★★★★☆

"...a great park for walkers and parents who want to get some exercise... a paved trail runs around the reservoir, which is completely fenced in... a beautiful setting... lots of off-leash dogs, which is good or bad, depending on the age of your tot... the play area has some swings and a seesaw..."
Equipment/play structures............ **4**   **5** ....Maintenance
WWW.CAMBRIDGEMA.GOV

CAMBRIDGE—FRESH POND PKWY (AT CONCORD AVE)

Lake Quannapowitt ★★★★★

"...my daughter loves walking around this lake ... great 3-1/2 mile walk, with a great playground... plenty of parking in a public lot, and a lot of good donut stores for a nosh on the way... the lake is the perfect place to walk... park and greens are always active..."

Equipment/play structures .... ❹   ❹ .... Maintenance
WWW.WAKEFIELDMA.ORG/WAKEFIELD_HISTORY.HTML
WAKEFIELD—RT 128 (AT RT 129); 781.246.6389

Lynch Park ★★★★☆

"...two beaches, picnic tables, playground structure, grassy fields, snack bar, public bathrooms... this is a wonderful place to spend a summer day... watch the kayaks and sailboats go by while your children build sand castles, hunt for crabs and wade in the ocean...."

Equipment/play structures .... ❹   ❺ .... Maintenance
WWW.BEVREC.COM
BEVERLY—55 OBER ST (AT OCEANSIDE DR); 978.921.6067

Melrose Common ★★★★☆

"...super kid-friendly park with something for everyone... baseball fields and basketball courts for the bigger kids and a large fenced-in play area for the smaller kids... sandbox, complete with trucks, pails, shovels and rakes is a huge hit... a very nice park..."

Equipment/play structures .... ❹   ❹ .... Maintenance
WWW.CITYOFMELROSE.ORG/DEPARTMENTS/PARKS.HTM
MELROSE—LAUREL ST (AT FOSTER ST); 781.662.9511

Minute Man Trail ★★★★☆

"...visitors walk and rest along the 5 1/2-mile Minute Man trail... trail is part of the Minute Man National Historical Park, which marks Revolutionary War sites throughout Lexington and Concord... nice paved trail, great for strollers. ..."

Equipment/play structures .... ❹   ❹ .... Maintenance
WWW.NPS.GOV
ARLINGTON—EXIT 30B OFF RT 128/I-95 (AT LIBERTY ST)

Penguin Park ★★★★☆

"...want to see penguins play? take the kids to Penguin Park, one of the city's perpetually popular family attractions... great for toddlers and new walkers..."

Equipment/play structures .... ❸   ❸ .... Maintenance
WWW.ANDOVERMA.GOV
ANDOVER—BURNHAM RD (OFF HAVERHILL ST); 978.623.8276

Raymond Park ★★★★★

"...small neighborhood park with play structures for different age groups... quiet, easy to get to... nice open space... aside from being a great place to play during the day, they also have great activities such as movie night in the summer and tree lighting at Christmas..."

Equipment/play structures .... ❹   ❹ .... Maintenance
WWW.CAMBRIDGEMA.GOV
CAMBRIDGE—WALDEN ST (AT UPTON ST)

Robbins Farm/Skyline Park ★★★★★

"...wow, what a park and what a view!.. absolutely fantastic—there are two very long slides built right into the hill... lots of climbing structures, a sandbox and plenty of swings for toddlers and infants... an amazing view of the Boston skyline to boot... there's a school park *across the street with a basketball court (great for tricycles) and other climbing structures...* "

Equipment/play structures............**4**   **4** ....Maintenance
WWW.ARLINGTONFAMILYCONNECTION.ORG/RESOURCES/PARKS.HTML
ARLINGTON—EASTERN AVE (AT FAYETTE ST); 781.316.3880

Shedd Park ★★★☆☆

"...this park isn't astounding except in winter, when it is the best sledding hill in the area... you'll want to supervise your kids closely, as there is a lot of ground to cover, but this is a well-loved winter spot... "

Equipment/play structures............**3**   **3** ....Maintenance
LOWELL—RT 38 (AT BOYLSTON ST)

Simonds Park ★★★★☆

"...a nice, fenced-in playground with a wading pool in the summer... it's been here forever—I played here as a kid and I love seeing my son having fun here too... newly renovated equipment... the little- and big-kid areas are close to each other, so I can come here with both of my children... my son loves watching all the action in the skate park nearby... "

Equipment/play structures............**5**   **5** ....Maintenance
WWW.BURLINGTON.ORG
BURLINGTON—BEDFORD ST (AT RT 62); 781.270.1695

Spy Pond Playground ★★★★☆

"...a good fenced-in playground, which makes it perfect for toddlers and preschoolers... kids can watch the ducks, geese and swans in the pond... parking can be a hassle, especially during the busy times at the Boys and Girls Club... "

Equipment/play structures............**3**   **4** ....Maintenance
WWW.ARLINGTONFAMILYCONNECTION.ORG/RESOURCES/PARKS.HTML
ARLINGTON—POND LN (AT MASSACHUSETTS AVE); 781.316.3880

Stoughton St Park ★★★★☆

"...this little park is great—it's at the end of a dead-end street and rarely crowded... mostly frequented by neighborhood families... all the standard facilities, plus a bubble day and sprinklers in the summer... "

Equipment/play structures............**4**   **4** ....Maintenance
SOMERVILLE—UNION SQ (AT WARREN AVE)

Sullivan Park ★★★★★

"...this is the perfect park for toddlers... fenced-in with toddler swings and climbing structures... it's very popular—the kids love it... there are a few benches around... ground cover consists of wood chips... "

Equipment/play structures............**5**   **5** ....Maintenance
WAKEFIELD—SILVER LAKE RD

Warren-Manning State Forest ★★★★☆

"...a woodsy state park which boasts a small, but fun sprinkler park... the water turns on at 10am, press the top of the hydrant to get it started and re-started if the timer runs out... the shaded park is nice, but don't forget the bug spray... they're not always good about opening the bathrooms... sometimes they charge $3 per vehicle for parking... "

Equipment/play structures............**3**   **2** ....Maintenance
BILLERICA—129 CHELMSFORD RD (AT BRICK KILN RD); 508.369.6312

Western Suburbs

"lila picks"
★★★★★

- ★ Auburndale Playground (The Cove)
- ★ Casey Park
- ★ Haskell Tot Lot Playground
- ★ Larz Anderson Park

Auburndale Playground (The Cove)
★★★★★

"...a beautiful playground with a special setting, next to the Charles, with picnic tables, swings and lots of ducks to feed... nature walks... varied age-appropriate playground equipment... there are restrooms by the softball diamond... the playground is nicely set away from the street and there is plenty of shade for those sunny afternoons... I worry that my 18-month-old is going to fall into the river... also, watch out for aggressive geese!..."

Equipment/play structures .... ❹   ❹ .... Maintenance
WWW.CI.NEWTON.MA.US
AUBURNDALE—W PINE ST (AT EDGEWATER PARK); 617.796.1500

Baker School Playground
★★★★☆

"...two separate playgrounds, one for younger kids... gives good options depending on time of day (school recess) and sun location (not a lot of shade)... ball field attached to older-kids playground... great for kids of all ages..."

Equipment/play structures .... ❹   ❹ .... Maintenance
WWW.TOWN.BROOKLINE.MA.US
BROOKLINE—BEVERLY RD (OFF NEWTON ST); 617.730.2069

Callahan State Park
★★★★☆

"...fantastic outdoor hiking area... no playground equipment, but lots of trails, streams and rocks to climb... the pond has lots of birds to feed and watch... lots of dogs here, so prepare your kids... dog poop is pretty much the only thing you need to watch out for..."

Equipment/play structures .... ❸   ❸ .... Maintenance
WWW.STATE.MA.US/DEM/PARKS/CALL.HTM
FRAMINGHAM—MILLWOOD ST (AT WINCH ST); 508.653.9641

Casey Park
★★★★★

"...excellent playground for all ages... great for picnic lunches... great parking... the jungle gym is well maintained and there is a basketball court and field to play in... the park is enclosed by a gate, so the kids can play without your being afraid of their darting into traffic... instead

of grass, the playground is on a rubbery, springy, soft mat—no skinned knees or grass stains... "

Equipment/play structures............ ❺ ❺ ....Maintenance

WWW.CI.WATERTOWN.MA.US

WATERTOWN—WATERTOWN ST (AT WATERTOWN SQ); 617.972.6494

Cochituate State Park ★★★☆☆

"*...main attraction is the lake in the park... boat rental is always fun... great beach area with lots of shade for little ones... beach and bathrooms are clean... no membership required... parking is a little ways away from the beach—the walk isn't too far, but it can be tough with kids and stuff in tow...* "

Equipment/play structures............ ❸ ❸ ....Maintenance

WWW.STATE.MA.US/DEM/PARKS/COCH.HTM

NATICK—RTE 30 (AT SPLEEN ST); 508.653.9641

Cold Spring Park ★★★★☆

"*...lovely for a little stroll... the playing fields of Cold Springs Park are the place in Newton to come for kids and family team sports... there is also a wooded area with paths... great location; beautiful grounds... during the summer, the park has wonderful farmer's market on Tuesdays...* "

Equipment/play structures............ ❸ ❸ ....Maintenance

WWW.CI.NEWTON.MA.US

NEWTON—BEACON ST (OFF RT 90)

Fairbanks Community Center Playground ★★★★⯪

"*...great playground for toddlers equipped with lots of trucks, pails and shovels in a huge sandbox... the fields allow children to run around before heading into the playground... love that it is fenced in... sunscreen and a hat are a must... there is a gazebo for shade...* "

Equipment/play structures............ ❹ ❹ ....Maintenance

WWW.BOSTONCENTRAL.COM

SUDBURY—40 FAIRBANK RD (AT BUTLER RD)

Fillipello Park ★★★★☆

"*...squishy flooring under the swing and play sets... age-appropriate play sets and a great sprinkler in the summer... it can get quite crowded, but that never seems to detract from the fun... facilities include parking, picnic tables, lots of green grass and a great water park in the summer... great place to bring the kids...* "

Equipment/play structures............ ❺ ❺ ....Maintenance

WWW.CI.WATERTOWN.MA.US/INDEX.ASP

WATERTOWN—ARLINGTON ST (AT ELM ST); 617.972.6494

Great Brook Farm State Park ★★★★⯪

"*...lots of great hiking trails, but the biggest hit with the kids is the ice cream stand and the animal farm... two big thumbs up for a very pleasant and exciting family outing... my kids love the horses and we always have a picnic... fun all year round... good for easy hikes with the little ones—an all-terrain jogger or carrier is needed...* "

Equipment/play structures............ ❸ ❹ ....Maintenance

WWW.STATE.MA.US/DEM/PARKS/GBFM.HTM

CARLISLE—984 LOWELL RD (AT CURVE ST); 978.369.6312

Haskell Tot Lot Playground ★★★★★

"*...nice outdoor playground next to the Sudbury Shaws and CVS stores, so there is ample parking... open seasonally... great jungle gym*

(better for older kids), rocking animals for preschoolers and swings for both infants and young children... this is a nice quiet playground that doesn't get a ton of traffic. ..."
Equipment/play structures .... ❺   ❹ .... Maintenance
SUDBURY—RTE 20 (AT SUDBURY SHAWS)

Larz Anderson Park ★★★★★
"...an absolutely beautiful park with walking paths and a playground... be sure to bring your sled for some wintertime fun... plenty of green grass to run or fly a kite, a pond to feed the ducks... a lovely pond, a covered picnic area and an automobile museum... dogs are welcome and numerous..."
Equipment/play structures .... ❹   ❹ .... Maintenance
WWW.TOWNOFBROOKLINEMASS.COM
BROOKLINE—140 GODDARD AVE (AT ROCKWOOD ST)

Memorial-Spaulding Elementary School Playground ★★★★☆
"...playground caters to all ages in separate sections... on one side of the park, there are toddler swings that are really low to the ground, a nice sandpit with scoop digger, a little climbing structure for little toddlers and several spring riders... fairly new playground... good for all ages..."
Equipment/play structures .... ❹   ❺ .... Maintenance
WWW.CI.NEWTON.MA.US
NEWTON—250 BROOKLINE ST (AT WALNUT ST); 617.559.9600

Nara Park & Swim Area ★★★★☆
"...a nice little, man-made beach... they have paddle boats, playgrounds and a beach... always clean and fun... the only drawback is that there's no shade... a great place to spend the day... relatively new, well maintained playground equipment... a nice spot for a day trip and picnic..."
Equipment/play structures .... ❹   ❺ .... Maintenance
ACTON—LEDGE ROCK RD (OFF MAIN ST); 978.264.9608

Percy Rideout Playground ★★★★★
"...an enormous playground structure... the structure is wooden so be prepared for the occasional splinter... they don't make playground structures like this anymore—it's got so much character and the kids have a blast... a good amount of shade is provided by the tall trees nearby..."
Equipment/play structures .... ❺   ❺ .... Maintenance
CONCORD—CONANT RD (AT LAWSBROOK RD)

Perrin Park ★★★★☆
"...great for toddlers... this is a wonderful park for infants through pre-school... equipment is all smaller in scale... there is a sandbox... much of the equipment is shaded by trees which is nice in the heat of the summer... park is located at the end of a dead-end street, so there is not a lot of traffic nearby and plenty of parking..."
Equipment/play structures .... ❹   ❹ .... Maintenance
HTTP://REASITE.COM/PORTFOLIO/PROJECTS/PERRIN.HTM
WELLESLEY—THOMAS RD (OFF RT 9)

Walden Pond ★★★★☆
"...a terrific place to take the kids... calm beach setting for young kids to play in... parking can sometimes be challenging in the peak

summertime hours... easy parking, clean water, plenty of sand... always a fun trip, and the price is right... **"**

Equipment/play structures............**❹**   **❹**...............................Maintenance

WWW.MASSPARKS.ORG

CONCORD—915 WALDEN ST (RTE126, NEAR RTE 2); 978.369.3254; DAILY 8-SUNSET

Winthrop Square Park ★★★★☆

"...*lovely settings... great playground with equipment for all ages... there's also a wading pool for the warmer months... unused portion of pavement at the tip of Winthrop Square park is pedestrianized, allowing better access to and from the high-volume Winthrop Lane walkway...* **"**

Equipment/play structures............**❹**   **❹**...............................Maintenance

WWW.TOWNOFBROOKLINEMASS.COM

BROOKLINE—ST PAUL ST (OFF BEACON ST)

Southern Suburbs

Caryl Park ★★★★★
"...Caryl Park is the best in the area... it's right alongside the woods, so it's always cool and shaded... the equipment is fabulous because it's well-maintained and fairly new... even has a porta-potty... nearby wooded area makes this park great for picnics..."
Equipment/play structures .... ❺ ❺ .... Maintenance
WWW.DOVERREC.COM
DOVER—DEDHAM ST (AT WILLOW ST)

Defazio Tot Lot ★★★★☆
"...this is a great playground for little ones... it's rather large—so big that if you are going with more than one child, you may be struggling to keep up with them... clean, friendly and a wide variety of play equipment... perfect for younger tots as well as older ones..."
Equipment/play structures .... ❹ ❹ .... Maintenance
WWW.TOWN.NEEDHAM.MA.US
NEEDHAM—DEDHAM AVE (AT SOUTH ST); 781.455.7521; DAYLIGHT HOURS; PARKING AT PARK

DW Field Park
WWW.BROCKTON.NET
BROCKTON—DW FIELD PKWY W

Francis William Bird Park ★★★★☆
"...beautiful and fun... plenty of space for walking and riding tricycles and a great playground for ages 2 through 5... miles and miles of trails for easy walks with or without a stroller... a couple of ponds feature plenty of birds to watch and feed... bird park is awesome..."
Equipment/play structures .... ❹ ❹ .... Maintenance
WWW.WALPOLE.MA.US/EFRANCISWILLIAM.HTM
EAST WALPOLE—WASHINGTON ST (AT JUNE ST); 508.668.6136

Friendship Park ★★★★☆
"...a nice fenced-in park with many different play structures... good for different age groups... something for all kids... clean and well-kept... ample parking makes this a no-brainer to drive to..."
Equipment/play structures .... ❸ ❹ .... Maintenance
WWW.TOWN.WEST-BRIDGEWATER.MA.US/
WEST BRIDGEWATER—97 W CENTER ST (AT HOWARD ST); 508.894.1217

Perry Park ★★★★☆
"...relatively new equipment makes this a wonderful spot for tots of all ages... small enough so you can keep an eye on multiple kids... very little shade so it's not ideal on really hot days... plenty to keep my 2- and 4- year olds busy for several hours..."
Equipment/play structures .... ❹ ❹ .... Maintenance
WWW.TOWN.NEEDHAM.MA.US/PARKREC/INDEX.HTM
NEEDHAM—BEAUFORT AVE (AT GREAT PLAIN AVE); 781.455.7500

Tufts Library Park ★★★★☆
"...I've taken my twins here a few times and they absolutely love it... there are a couple of issues with this park—it's not enclosed and it's always crowded... tons of children from all around—there's always someone for my kids to play with..."

www.lilaguide.com

Equipment/play structures............ ❹   ❸ ....Maintenance
WWW.OCLN.ORG
WEYMOUTH—46 BROAD ST (AT STETSON ST); 781.337.1402; M-TH 9-9, F-S 9-5

restaurants

City of Boston

★★★★★
"lila picks"

★ Jasper White's Summer Shack
★ Vinny T's Of Boston

Barking Crab ★★★½☆

"...New England crab bake that you can get to from land or sea... very casual... lots of noise and things for kids to look at... I have been going for years—prices are now outrageous since the Federal Courthouse opened next door... great seafood and access for stroller... bathroom is not the greatest... you must park your stroller outside in the summer..."

Children's menu	✓	$$$	Prices
Changing station	✗	❹	Customer service
Highchairs/boosters	✓	❹	Stroller access

WWW.BARKINGCRAB.COM

SOUTH BOSTON—88 SLEEPER ST (AT SEAPORT BLVD); 617.426.2722; SU-W 11:30-9, TH-SA 11:30-10

Bennigan's Grill & Tavern ★★★★☆

"...great kid-friendly atmosphere with an array of choices for your child... loud enough to relax and not worry about your child standing out with the crying... great service... plenty of room for strollers, and something for everyone on the menu..."

Children's menu	✓	$$$	Prices
Changing station	✓	❹	Customer service
Highchairs/boosters	✓	❸	Stroller access

WWW.BENNIGANS.COM

DOWNTOWN—191 STUART ST (AT CHARLES ST); 617.227.3754; SU-TH 11-12:30, F-SA 11-1:30AM

Bertucci's Brick Oven Pizzeria ★★★½☆

"...a laid-back Italian eatery with delicious Italian grub... pizza, pasta, something for everyone... get the olive oil for dipping, this makes waiting for the pizza a bearable experience with hungry tots... not an obviously kid-friendly restaurant, but they do a good job of accommodating parents with tots... great kids' menu... it can get busy, so go early... finding room for strollers can be challenging, but the staff is very accommodating..."

Children's menu	✓	$$	Prices
Changing station	✓	❹	Customer service
Highchairs/boosters	✓	❹	Stroller access

WWW.BERTUCCIS.COM

BACK BAY—39-45 STANHOPE ST (AT BERKELEY ST); 617.247.6161; M-TH 11-11, F-SA 11-12, SU 12-10

BACK BAY—533 COMMONWEALTH AVE (AT KENMORE ST); 617.236.1030; M-TH 11-11, F-SA 11-12, SU 12-10; FREE PARKING

DOWNTOWN—22 MERCHANTS ROW (AT STATE ST); 617.227.7889; M-TH 11-11, F-SA 11-12, SU 12-10

FENWAY/KENMORE—ONE BLACKFAN CIR (AT LONGWOOD AVE); 617.739.2492; M-TH 11-11, F-SA 11-12, SU 12-10

WEST ROXBURY—683 VFW PKWY (AT COREY ST); 617.327.0898; M-SA 11-10; FREE PARKING

Brigham's   ★★★½☆

"...eating at an ice cream parlor—what could be better?.. wide selection of decent food... try to avoid the main lunch hour, that's when they are at their busiest and the service is slowest... an inexpensive option that works great for moms and babies..."

Children's menu	✗	$$$	Prices
Changing station	✗	❹	Customer service
Highchairs/boosters	✗	❹	Stroller access

WWW.BRIGHAMS.COM

DOWNTOWN—109 HIGH ST (AT WATER ST); 617. 482.3524; M-F 6-5:30

Brown Sugar Cafe   ★★★★☆

"...delicious.... staff is very attentive... great food.... a few steps to get up with the stroller, but great, friendly staff and delicious food at great prices..."

Children's menu	✗	$$	Prices
Changing station	✗	❺	Customer service
Highchairs/boosters	✓	❹	Stroller access

WWW.BROWNSUGARCAFE.COM

BACK BAY—1033 COMMONWEALTH AVE (AT BRIGHTON AVE); 617.787.4242; M-TH 11-10, F 11-11, SA 12-11, SU 12-10

California Pizza Kitchen   ★★★★½

"...you can't go wrong with their fabulous pizza... always clean... the food's great, the kids drinks all come with a lid... the staff is super friendly to kids.... crayons and coloring books keep little minds busy... most locations have a place for strollers at the front... no funny looks or attitude when breastfeeding... open atmosphere with friendly service... tables are well spaced so you don't feel like your kid is annoying the diners nearby (it's usually full of kids anyway)..."

Children's menu	✓	$$	Prices
Changing station	✓	❹	Customer service
Highchairs/boosters	✓	❹	Stroller access

WWW.CPK.COM

BACK BAY—137 STUART ST (AT WARRENTON ST); 617.720.0999; M-TH 11:30-10, F-SA 11:30-11, SU 11:30-10

BACK BAY—800 BOYLSTON ST (AT PRUDENTIAL CTR); 617.247.0888; M-TH 11:30-10, F-SA 11:30-11, SU 11:30-10

Centre Street Cafe   ★★★★☆

"...the staff at Centre Street Cafe were very accommodating to our newborn... helped get us an accessible table... great food for hungry breastfeeding moms... they're always helpful and accommodating to us and other parents ... food is great with quick, pleasant service..."

Children's menu	✗	$$$	Prices
Changing station	✗	❹	Customer service
Highchairs/boosters	✗	❸	Stroller access

JAMAICA PLAIN—669 CENTRE ST (AT GREEN ST.); 617.524.9217; M-F 11:30-3 5-10, SA 9-3 5-10

Charley's ★★★★★

"...staff are extremely helpful, in providing hot water, high chairs... will also try and accommodate strollers next to the tables if need be... disabled access... go midweek for a late lunch and you really don't feel like you are encroaching on other eaters..."

Children's menu	✓	$$	Prices
Changing station	✗	❺	Customer service
Highchairs/boosters	✓	❸	Stroller access

WWW.BBRGINC.COM

BACK BAY—284 NEWBURY ST (AT GLOUCESTER ST); 617.266.3000; SU-TH 11:30-1, F 11:30-12, SA-SU 9-12

Charlie's Sandwich Shoppe ★★★★☆

"...fun and crowded... sometimes you have to share a table, which is nerve-racking if your toddler likes throwing food... it's a tight fit so strollers aren't easy... staff is very accommodating towards kids... delicious breakfast... they open early, but are closed on Sundays... good burgers and beers..."

Children's menu	✗	$$	Prices
Changing station	✗	❹	Customer service
Highchairs/boosters	✓	❷	Stroller access

SOUTH END/BAY VILLAGE—429 COLUMBUS AVE (AT DARTMOUTH ST); 617.536.7669

Doyles Cafe ★★★★☆

"...classic Irish pub scene, but very family-friendly... big, hearty meals without frills, children's menu, quick service... changing table in the bathroom... noise level is a dull roar, so baby can occasionally scream..."

Children's menu	✓	$$	Prices
Changing station	✓	❹	Customer service
Highchairs/boosters	✓	❸	Stroller access

WWW.DOYLESCAFE.COM

JAMAICA PLAIN—3484 WASHINGTON ST (AT WILIAMS ST); 617.524.2345; DAILY 9-2AM

Friendly's ★★★★☆

"...we love Friendly's because it's fast, fun and the food is pretty good... you may wait a bit for your service but given the promise of a sundae most kids will persevere... colorful menu and M&M pancakes... desert and a drink are included with some kids' meals... convenient if you have kids of varying ages—there's something good for everyone... burgers, sandwiches and more fries than you'll know what to do with..."

Children's menu	✓	$$	Prices
Changing station	✓	❸	Customer service
Highchairs/boosters	✓	❸	Stroller access

WWW.FRIENDLYS.COM

WEST ROXBURY—1985 CENTRE ST (AT BELLEVUE ST); 617.327.2469; DAILY 11-9; FREE PARKING

Garden Of Eden

Children's menu	✗	✓	Changing station
Highchairs/boosters	✓		

WWW.GOEBOSTON.COM

ROXBURY—571 TREMONT ST (AT UNION PARK ST); 617.247.8377; M-F 7-11, SA 7:30-11, SU 7:30-10; STREET PARKING

Hard Rock Cafe ★★★½☆

❝...fun and tasty if you can get in... the lines can be horrendous so be sure to check in with them first... a good spot if you have tots in tow— food tastes good and the staff is clearly used to messy eaters... hectic and loud... fun for adults as well as kids...❞

Children's menu	✓	$$$	Prices
Changing station	✓	❹	Customer service
Highchairs/boosters	✓	❸	Stroller access

WWW.HARDROCK.COM

BACK BAY—131 CLARENDON ST (AT STUART ST); 617.424.7625; SU-TH 11-11AM, F-SA 11-12AM

Jasper White's Summer Shack ★★★★★

❝...picnic tables are covered in brown paper and far enough apart that we didn't seem to annoy our neighbors...great seafood in a casual atmosphere... kids can see and sometimes touch the lobsters... there's lots for kids to look around at... on arrival, your child gets a balloon and crayons (so they can draw on the paper-covered tables)... no need to worry about the noise level... servers are very patient with kids... large portions will serve a big group or family...❞

Children's menu	✗	$$$$	Prices
Changing station	✗	❹	Customer service
Highchairs/boosters	✓	❹	Stroller access

WWW.SUMMERSHACKRESTAURANT.COM

BACK BAY—50 DALTON ST (AT BELVEDERE ST); 617.520.9500; M-TH 11:30-10, F 11:30-11, SA 12-11

Joe's American Bar & Grill ★★★★½☆

❝...great bar food and friendly atmosphere—avoid peak times as it gets very busy... they brought our food quickly and also helped us pack up quickly when the meltdown began... the waiter just smiled as our daughter tossed all of her food on the floor... no attitude, just helpful service... it's easy to find food here for the whole family...❞

Children's menu	✗	$$$	Prices
Changing station	✗	❹	Customer service
Highchairs/boosters	✓	❸	Stroller access

WWW.JOESAMERICAN.COM

BACK BAY—279 DARTMOUTH ST (AT NEWBURY ST); 617.536.4200; M-TH 10-11, F-SA 10-12, SU 10-10

NORTH END—100 ATLANTIC AVE (AT COMMERCIAL WATERFRONT); 617.367.8700; M-TH 10-11, F-SA 10-12, SU 10-10

Kaya Restaurant ★★★★½☆

❝...waiters were very friendly to my daughter, food is fresh and good .... great Korean food, open all kinds of hours... very family-friendly...❞

Children's menu	✗	$$$	Prices
Changing station	✗	❸	Customer service
Highchairs/boosters	✓	❺	Stroller access

WWW.KAYAUSA.COM

BACK BAY—581 BOYLSTON ST (AT DARTMOUTH ST); 617.236.5858; M-SU 11:30-1

King & I ★★★★☆

❝...superb Thai food... staff is willing to accommodate babies and toddlers... the decor makes you feel like you are dining in Thailand... we have been going there for 14 years and have never had a bad dinner...❞

Children's menu	✗	$	Prices
Changing station	✗	❹	Customer service

Highchairs/boosters .... ✓   ❹ .... Stroller access
WWW.KINGANDI-BOSTON.COM

BEACON HILL/WEST END—145 CHARLES ST (AT CAMBRIDGE ST);
617.227.3320; M-TH 11:30-9:30, F 11:30-10:30, SA 12-10:30, SU 5-9:30

Longhorn Steakhouse ★★★★☆

"...for meat and seafood lovers... the staff totally gets 'the kid thing' here... they bring out snacks, get the orders going quickly, and frequently check back for things like new spoons and napkins... lots of things for baby to look at... get there early or call ahead to avoid the wait..."

Children's menu .... ✓ $$$ .... Prices
Changing station .... ✓   ❹ .... Customer service
Highchairs/boosters .... ✓   ❸ .... Stroller access
WWW.LONGHORNSTEAKHOUSE.COM

BACK BAY—401 PARK DR (AT BROOKLINE AVE); 617.247.9199; SU-TH 11-10, F-SA 11-11

McCormick & Schmicks ★★★★☆

"...steak and seafood are the mainstay but the menu is broad... terrific happy hour menu... a little more formal than your regular 'tot-friendly' restaurant, but the staff is great and goes out of their way to make sure you're comfortable... try to get one of the banquet rooms—it makes breastfeeding much easier... good food for adults and more than enough for the little ones too..."

Children's menu .... ✓ $$$ .... Prices
Changing station .... ✓   ❹ .... Customer service
Highchairs/boosters .... ✓   ❹ .... Stroller access
WWW.MCCORMICKANDSCHMICKS.COM

DOWNTOWN—34 COLUMBUS AVE (OFF STUART ST); 617.482.3999; DAILY 11:30-11

DOWNTOWN—FANEUIL HALL MARKETPLACE (OFF RT 3); 617.720.5522; DAILY 11:30-11

No Name Restaurant ★★★★☆

"...famous restaurant, but not for its decor... location is nice, but people really go for the food... hard to get up the narrow stairwell to the dining room with a stroller..."

Children's menu .... ✓ $$ .... Prices
Changing station .... ✗   ❹ .... Customer service
Highchairs/boosters .... ✓   ❸ .... Stroller access

SOUTH BOSTON—15 FISH PIER ST W (AT NORTHERN AVE.); 617.423.2705; M-SA 11-10, SU 11-9

Parish Cafe ★★★★★

"...this place takes sandwiches seriously... the super staff helped us find a good spot and made us feel welcome... especially nice to sit on the patio, have some lunch and chat with friends..."

Children's menu .... ✗ $$$ .... Prices
Changing station .... ✗   ❹ .... Customer service
Highchairs/boosters .... ✓   ❸ .... Stroller access
WWW.PARISHCAFE.COM

BACK BAY—361 BOYLSTON ST (AT ARLINGTON ST); 617.247.4777; DAILY 10-1AM

Picco Pizza & Ice Cream Co ★★★★☆

"...fantastic pizza and ice cream—kid-friendly staff and food... tables are a bit tight but they make it work... one of the South End's best restaurants for families... it's next door to a theater, so watch out for the pre-performance rush..."

Children's menu	✗	$$	Prices
Changing station	✗	❺	Customer service
Highchairs/boosters	✓	❸	Stroller access

WWW.PICCOBOSTON.COM

BACK BAY—513 TREMONT ST (AT DWIGHT ST); 617.927.0066; DAILY 11-11

Sonsie Restaurant ★★★★☆

"...good pizza and nice outside seating... friendly staff that is happy to accommodate baby strollers... lunch is better than brunch...**"**

Children's menu	✗	$$$	Prices
Changing station	✗	❹	Customer service
Highchairs/boosters	✓	❹	Stroller access

HTTP://SONSIEBOSTON.COM

BACK BAY—327 NEWBURY ST (AT HEREFORD ST); 617.351.2500; DAILY 11:30-12:30

TGI Friday's ★★★★☆

"...good old American bar food with a reasonable selection for the healthier set as well... I love that the kids meal includes salad... my daughter requests the potato skins on a regular basis (which is good because they are also my favorite)... moderately priced... cheerful servers are used to the mess my kids leave behind... relaxed scene... I'd steer clear on a Friday night unless you don't mind waiting and watching the singles scene...**"**

Children's menu	✓	$$	Prices
Changing station	✓	❹	Customer service
Highchairs/boosters	✓	❸	Stroller access

WWW.TGIFRIDAYS.COM

BACK BAY—26 EXETER ST (AT PUBLIC ALLEY 434); 617.266.9040; SU-W 11:30-12, TH-SA 11:30-1

Thorton's Restaurant ★★★★☆

"...great diner in downtown area, where you won't see many babies but you'll find that they are welcoming to yours... high chairs are a bit rickety, but get the job done... friendly staff makes you feel comfortable, despite the mess you leave behind... window seats provide baby with plenty of distraction...**"**

Children's menu	✗	$$	Prices
Changing station	✗	❹	Customer service
Highchairs/boosters	✓	❹	Stroller access

BACK BAY—150 HUNTINGTON AVE (AT BELVEDERE ST); 617.267.6336

Tia's On The Waterfront ★★★☆☆

"...wonderful to go for lunch on sunny day... nice outdoor seating area... lobster special is great... do not recommend Tia's for families with young children... they close down for the winter season so call first to make sure they're open...**"**

Children's menu	✗	$$$	Prices
Changing station	✗	❹	Customer service
Highchairs/boosters	✓	❷	Stroller access

WWW.TIASWATERFRONT.COM

NORTH END—200 ATLANTIC AVE (AT STATE ST); 617.227.0828; M-SA 11:30-CLOSE, SU 11-CLOSE

Tremont 647 ★★★☆☆

"...not very stroller-friendly but the staff is very accommodating and efficient... we felt comfortable even when the baby had a meltdown... no changing station though...this is a date-night restaurant... if your kids are extremely well-behaved and you're thick-skinned, you might *survive a quick appetizer course... I love to eat here, but I get a babysitter first...* **"**

Children's menu........................... ✗ $$$...Prices
Changing station .... ✗ ❸ ....Customer service
Highchairs/boosters .... ✓ ❸ .... Stroller access

WWW.TREMONT647.COM

ROXBURY—647 TREMONT ST (AT W BROOKLINE ST); 617.266.4600; M-TH 5:30-10, F 5:30-10:30, SA 10:30-10:30, SU 10:30-10; VALET

Vinny T's Of Boston ★★★★★

"*...delicious, family style Italian... inexpensive, good food... excellent place for a celebration-type meal... very large serving sizes... no kids' menu but there are many things that they can eat off of their parents' plates... brought my two girls (both under 2 and a half) in for lunch - the staff was great, very kid-friendly...they usually give you lots of extra spaghetti so you don't even have to order a kids meal...* **"**

Children's menu........................... ✓ $$$...Prices
Changing station .... ✓ ❹ ....Customer service
Highchairs/boosters .... ✓ ❹ .... Stroller access

WWW.VINNYTSOFBOSTON.COM

BACK BAY—867 BOYLSTON ST (AT GLOUCESTER ST); 617.262.6699; M-W 11:30-11, TH-SA 11:30-12, SU 12-10; STREET/METERED

Northern Suburbs

★★★★★ "lila picks"

- ★ Full Moon
- ★ Jasper White's Summer Shack
- ★ Johnny Rockets
- ★ Not Your Average Joe's
- ★ Vinny T's Of Boston

Amelia's Kitchen ★★★★★
"...not a place you would expect to be kid-friendly—small, quiet, personal restaurant with good, home-cooked Italian gourmet food... the owners seem to love kids... one of the few restaurants we really loved before our first child and that we can still attend with tots in tow..."

Children's menu	✗	$$	Prices
Changing station	✗	❺	Customer service
Highchairs/boosters	✓	❺	Stroller access

WWW.AMELIASKITCHEN.COM

SOMERVILLE—1137 BROADWAY (AT HOLLAND ST); 617.776.2800; M-SA 11-11, SU 5-10

Applebee's Neighborhood Grill ★★★★☆
"...geared to family dining—they expect you to be loud and leave a mess... macaroni & cheese, hot dogs, and tasty grilled cheese... activity book and special kids cup are a bonus... service can be slow, but they will cover you with things to snack on... stay clear on Friday and Saturday nights... comfort food in a casual atmosphere... even though it's part of a very large chain you get the feeling it's a neighborhood-type place..."

Children's menu	✓	$$	Prices
Changing station	✓	❹	Customer service
Highchairs/boosters	✓	❸	Stroller access

WWW.APPLEBEES.COM

DANVERS—50 INDEPENDENCE WY (AT LIBERTY TREE MALL); 978.777.5447; SU-TH 11-11, F-SA 11-12:30; MALL PARKING

MALDEN—95 MIDDLESEX ST (AT HIGHWAY 60); 781.322.8521; SU-TH 11-11:30, F-SA 11-12

SAUGUS—214 BROADWAY (AT WALNUT ST); 781.231.0137; SU-TH 11-11:30, F-SA 11-12

Arlington Restaurant & Diner ★★★★☆
"...wouldn't go during busy times as the service is too slow for toddlers... this is a great diner for families with kids... they've got all the basics for breakfast and lunch... strollers are usually parked outside,

and you're free to use one of their high chairs or bring your own... we've got a 12-month-old, and go there at least once a month... **"**

Children's menu	✓	$$	Prices
Changing station	✗	❹	Customer service
Highchairs/boosters	✓	❸	Stroller access

ARLINGTON—134 MASSACHUSETTS AVE (AT MILTON ST); 781.646.9266; M-F 6:30-9, SA 6-9, SU 6-1; STREET PARKING

Bertucci's Brick Oven Pizzeria ★★★½☆

"...*a laid-back Italian eatery with delicious Italian grub... pizza, pasta, something for everyone... get the olive oil for dipping, this makes waiting for the pizza a bearable experience with hungry tots... not an obviously kid-friendly restaurant, but they do a good job of accommodating parents with tots... great kids menu... it can get busy, so go early... finding room for strollers can be challenging, but the staff is very accommodating...* **"**

Children's menu	✓	$$	Prices
Changing station	✓	❹	Customer service
Highchairs/boosters	✓	❹	Stroller access

WWW.BERTUCCIS.COM

ANDOVER—90 MAIN ST (OFF CHESTNUT ST); 978.470.3939; M-TH 11-10, F-SA 11-11, SU 12-10

BEVERLY—27 ENON ST (OFF DODGE ST); 978.927.6866; M-TH 11-10, F-SA 11-11, SU 12-10; FREE PARKING

CAMBRIDGE—21 BRATTLE ST (AT CHURCH ST); 617.864.4748; M-TH 11-10, F-SA 11-11, SU 12-10

CAMBRIDGE—5 CAMBRIDGE PARK DR (AT RINGE AVE); 617.876.2200; M-TH 11-10, F-SA 11-11, SU 12-10

CAMBRIDGE—799 MAIN ST (AT CHERRY ST); 617.497.5393; M-TH 11-10, F-SA 11-11, SU 12-10; FREE PARKING

CHELMSFORD—14 LITTLETON RD (AT CHELMSFORD ST); 978.250.8800; M-TH 11-10, F-SA 11-11, SU 12-10

MEDFORD—4054 MYSTIC VALLEY PKWY (AT COMMERCIAL ST); 781.396.9933; M-TH 11-10, F-SA 11-11, SU 12-10

NORTH ANDOVER—435 ANDOVER ST (AT HIGHLAND TER); 978.685.4498; M-TH 11-10, F-SA 11-11, SU 12-10; FREE PARKING

PEABODY—15 NEWBURY ST (NEAR LAKE ST); 978.535.0969; M-TH 11-10, F-SA 11-11, SU 12-10

SWAMPSCOTT—450 PARADISE RD (AT SWAMPSCOTT MALL); 781.581.6588; M-TH 11-10, F-SA 11-11, SU 12-10; FREE PARKING

WOBURN—17 COMMERCE WAY (AT ACROOS FROM WOBURN MALL); 781.933.1440; M-TH 11-10, F-SA 11-11, SU 12-10; FREE PARKING

Blue Ribbon Bar-B-Q ★★★★☆

"...*excellent barbecue for mom and dad... if your little one likes macaroni and cheese, they have some of the best around... laid-back take-out atmosphere and outdoor seating make it perfect for restless toddlers... generous portions...* **"**

Children's menu	✗	$$	Prices
Changing station	✗	❹	Customer service
Highchairs/boosters	✓	❸	Stroller access

WWW.BLUERIBBONBBQ.COM

ARLINGTON—908 MASSACHUSETTS AVE (AT HIGHLANDS AVE); 781.648.7427; M-SA 11:30-9, SU 12-8

Border Cafe ★★★★☆

"...*a good spot for kids of all ages... Mexican cuisine... fabulous food, and there is enough noise that crying babies aren't too big of a deal...*

special holders for car seats... my kids love the plain cheese quesadillas... fast service... balloons and toys for the kids... "

Children's menu	✗	$$	Prices
Changing station	✗	❹	Customer service
Highchairs/boosters	✓		Stroller access

CAMBRIDGE—32 CHURCH ST (AT JF KENNEDY ST); 617.864.6100; M-TH 11-1, F-SA 11-2, SU 12-1; LOT, STREET

SAUGUS—817 BROADWAY (AT THOMAS ST); 781.233.5308; SU-TH 11:30-11, F-SA 11:30-12AM

Brigham's Inc ★★★⯨☆

"*...eating at an ice cream parlor—what could be better?.. wide selection of decent food... try to avoid the main lunch hour, that's when they are at their busiest and the service is slowest... an inexpensive option that works great for moms and babies... service tends to be inconsistent...* "

Children's menu	✓	$$	Prices
Changing station	✗	❸	Customer service
Highchairs/boosters	✓	❸	Stroller access

WWW.BRIGHAMS.COM

ARLINGTON—1328 MASSACHUSETTS AVE (AT PARK AVE); 781.648.9892; DAILY 10-10

ARLINGTON—46 MILL ST (AT MILBROOK DR); 781.648.9000; M-SA 7:30-10, SA 8-10

BURLINGTON—75 MIDDLESEX TPKE (AT WOODS CORNER); 781.272.7870; M-SA 9-10. SU 11-7

Bugaboo Creek Steak House ★★★★☆

"*...a definite must-go place for families with children... delicious food for grown-ups and a nice selection of food on the kids' menu... all kids' meals come with ice cream... all the hustle and bustle around us kept my son entertained while we waited for our meal... the singing tree (and moose) will either delight your child or scare the bejesus out of him... terrific service—the staff goes out of their way to cater to families... fun for birthdays—staff sings and brings out the birthday moose, which the honored one is supposed to kiss...* "

Children's menu	✓	$$$	Prices
Changing station	✓	❹	Customer service
Highchairs/boosters	✓	❹	Stroller access

WWW.BUGABOOCREEKSTEAKHOUSE.COM

METHUEN—90 PLEASANT VALLEY ST (AT THE LOOP); 978.794.9713; M-TH 11:30-10, F-SA 11:30-10:30, SU 12-9

PEABODY—210 ANDOVER ST (AT PROSPECT ST); 978.538.0100; M-TH 11:30-10, F-SA 11:30-10:30, SU 12-9

Burlington Mall ★★★⯨☆

"*...very clean, bright, and spacious... noisy, fun, fascinating atmosphere—food is great... noise and a flashing lights may frighten the very little set...* "

Children's menu	✗	$$	Prices
Changing station	✗	❸	Customer service
Highchairs/boosters	✗	❹	Stroller access

WWW.SIMON.COM/MALL/MALL_INFO.ASPX?ID=146

BURLINGTON—75 MIDDLESEX ST (AT BURLINGTON MALL RD); 781.272.8667; M-SA 10-10, SU 11-7

Cafe Barada ☆☆☆☆☆

"*...good food... small place... great for take out...* "

Children's menu	✗	$$	Prices

| Changing station | ✗ | ❺ | Customer service |
| Highchairs/boosters | ✓ | ❸ | Stroller access |

CAMBRIDGE—2269 MASSACHUSETTS AVE (AT DOVER ST.); 617.354.2112; M-SA 11-9

California Pizza Kitchen ★★★★☆

"...you can't go wrong with their fabulous pizza... always clean... the food's great, the kids' drinks all come with a lid... the staff is super friendly to kids.... crayons and coloring books keep little minds busy... most locations have a place for strollers at the front... no funny looks or attitude when breastfeeding... open atmosphere with friendly service... tables are well spaced so you don't feel like your kid is annoying the diners nearby (it's usually full of kids anyway)..."

Children's menu	✓	$$	Prices
Changing station	✓	❹	Customer service
Highchairs/boosters	✓	❹	Stroller access

WWW.CPK.COM

CAMBRIDGE—100 CAMBRIDGESIDE PL (AT CAMBRIDGESIDE GALLERIA); 617.225.2772; M-TH 11:30-10, F-SA 11:30-11, SU 11:30-10

Cheddars Pizzeria ★★★★★

"...best sub shop ever .... salads made with fresh ingredients and mesclun greens ..."

Children's menu	✗	$$$	Prices
Changing station	✗	❹	Customer service
Highchairs/boosters	✓	❸	Stroller access

CAMBRIDGE—201 ALEWIFE BROOK PKY (AT FRESH POND SHOPPING CTR); 617.661.3366; M-F 10-8, SA 10-4

Cheesecake Factory, The ★★★★☆

"...although their cheesecake is good, we come here for the kid-friendly atmosphere and selection of good food... eclectic menu has something for everyone... they will bring your tot a plate of yogurt, cheese, bananas and bread free of charge... we love how flexible they are—they'll make whatever my kids want... lots of mommies here... always fun and always crazy... no real kids menu, but the pizza is great to share... waits can be really long..."

Children's menu	✗	$$$	Prices
Changing station	✓	❹	Customer service
Highchairs/boosters	✓	❸	Stroller access

WWW.THECHEESECAKEFACTORY.COM

CAMBRIDGE—100 CAMBRIDGESIDE PL (AT CAMBRIDGESIDE GALLERIA); 617.252.3810; M-TH 11:30-11:30, F-SA 11:30-12:30, SU 10-11

Friendly's ★★★★☆

"...we love Friendly's because it's fast, fun and the food is pretty good... you may wait a bit for your service but given the promise of a sundae most kids will persevere... colorful menu and M&M pancakes... desert and a drink are included with some kids' meals... convenient if you have kids of varying ages—there's something good for everyone... burgers, sandwiches and more fries than you'll know what to do with..."

Children's menu	✓	$$	Prices
Changing station	✓	❸	Customer service
Highchairs/boosters	✓	❸	Stroller access

WWW.FRIENDLYS.COM

AMESBURY—111 MACY ST RTE 110 (AT ELM ST); 978.388.0378; DAILY 11-9; FREE PARKING

ANDOVER—32 N MAIN ST (AT PEARSON ST); 978.475.4505; DAILY 11-9

ARLINGTON—105-109 BROADWAY (AT OXFORD ST); 781.648.1480; DAILY 11-9

BILLERICA—510 BOSTON RD (AT INNIS DR); 978.667.5837; DAILY 11-9; FREE PARKING

CHELMSFORD—20 BOSTON RD (AT SUMMER ST); 508.256.5351; DAILY 11-9; FREE PARKING

GLOUCESTER—226 WASHINGTON ST (AT GLOUCESTER AVE); 978.281.1323; DAILY 11-9

HAVERHILL—1160 MAIN ST (AT ROSEDALE AVE); 978.373.6120; DAILY 11-9; FREE PARKING

LAWRENCE—222 WINTHROP AVE (AT HWY 495); 978.689.8565; DAILY 11-9; FREE PARKING

MEDFORD—385 MYSTIC VALLEY PKWY (AT MEADOW GLEN MALL); 781.396.9534; DAILY 11-9; FREE PARKING

METHUEN—255 BROADWAY, RT 28 (AT GLEASON ST); 978.686.0811; DAILY 11-9; FREE PARKING

PEABODY—250 ANDOVER ST (AT WALTER RD); 978.532.1445; DAILY 11-9; FREE PARKING

REVERE—128 SQUIRE (AT N GATE SHOPPING CTR); 781.289.4228; DAILY 11-9; FREE PARKING

SAUGUS—777 BROADWAY (AT THOMAS ST); 781.231.2738; DAILY 11-9; FREE PARKING

STONEHAM—611 MAIN ST (AT N BORDER RD); 781.438.5444; DAILY 11-9

SWAMPSCOTT—VINNIN SQ PLAZA PARADISE RD (AT VINNIN SQ); 781.599.2389; DAILY 11-9; FREE PARKING

WOBURN—303 MONTVALE AVE (AT WASHINGTON ST); 781.935.0576; DAILY 11-9; FREE PARKING

Fuddruckers ★★★★☆

"...a super burger chain with fresh and tasty food... colorful and noisy with lots of distraction until the food arrives... loads of fresh toppings so that you can make your perfectly cooked burger even better... great kids' deals that come with a free treat... noise not a problem in this super casual atmosphere... some locations have video games in the back which will buy you an extra half hour if you need it... low-key and very family-friendly..."

Children's menu	✓	$$	Prices
Changing station	✓	❹	Customer service
Highchairs/boosters	✓	❹	Stroller access

WWW.FUDDRUCKERS.COM

NORTH ANDOVER—550 TURNPIKE ST (AT ANDOVER BYP); 978.557.1100; SU-TH 11-9, F-SA 11-10

SAUGUS—900 BROADWAY (AT THOMAS ST); 781.233.6399; SU-TH 11-9, F-SA 11-10

Full Moon ★★★★★

"...caters to kids with great food for everyone... a play area, toys, crayons on the tables and a kids' menu... the menu for adults is sophisticated and healthy... snazzy nonalcoholic beverages are perfect for pregnant and nursing moms... upscale and a bit pricey but a fun outing... so fabulous to be able to eat while your kids play..."

Children's menu	✓	$$$	Prices
Changing station	✓	❹	Customer service
Highchairs/boosters	✓	❹	Stroller access

WWW.FULLMOONRESTAURANT.COM

CAMBRIDGE—344 HURON AVE (AT FAYERWEATHER ST); 617.354.6699; M-F 11-3 5-9, SA-SU 9-2:30 5-9; STREET PARKING

It Rains Fishes ★★★★☆
"...Thai restaurant with an American menu for kids... very accommodating; for instance, they'll seat the kids near the waterfall...**"**

Children's menu...................... ✓	$$$..Prices
Changing station .... ✗	❹...................Customer service
Highchairs/boosters .... ✓	❹............................ Stroller access

WWW.ITRAINSFISHES.COM

WINCHESTER—14 THOMPSON ST (AT MAIN ST); 781.721.2535; SU-TH 11:30-9:30, F-SA 11:30-10

Jasper White's Summer Shack ★★★★★
"...picnic tables are covered in brown paper and far enough apart that we didn't seem to annoy our neighbors...great seafood in a casual atmosphere... kids can see and sometimes touch the lobsters... there's lots for kids to look around at... on arrival, your child gets a balloon and crayons (so they can draw on the paper-covered tables)... no need to worry about the noise level... servers are very patient with kids... large portions will serve a big group or family...**"**

Children's menu...................... ✗	$$$$......................................Prices
Changing station .... ✗	❹...................Customer service
Highchairs/boosters .... ✓	❹............................ Stroller access

WWW.SUMMERSHACKRESTAURANT.COM

CAMBRIDGE—149 ALEWIFE BROOK PKWY (AT RINDGE AVE); 617.520.9500; M-TH 11:30-10, F 11:30-11, SA 12-11

Joe Fish Seafood Restaurant ★★★★☆
"...great food, great service, great prices.......**"**

Children's menu...................... ✗	$$..Prices
Changing station .... ✗	❺...................Customer service
Highchairs/boosters .... ✓	❹............................ Stroller access

WWW.JOEFISH.NET

NORTH ANDOVER—1120 OSGOOD ST (AT CLARK ST); 978.685.3663; M-TH 11:30-9:30, F-SA 11:30-10, SU 12-9

Joe's American Bar & Grill ★★★★⯪☆
"...great bar food and a friendly atmosphere—avoid peak times, as it gets very busy... they brought our food quickly and also helped us pack up quickly when the meltdown began... the waiter just smiled as our daughter tossed all of her food on the floor... no attitude, just helpful service... easy to find food here for the whole family...**"**

Children's menu...................... ✗	$$$..Prices
Changing station .... ✗	❹...................Customer service
Highchairs/boosters .... ✓	❸............................ Stroller access

WWW.JOESAMERICAN.COM

PEABODY—ROUTE 128/114 (AT RT 114); 978.532.9500; M-TH 11:30-10:30, F-SA 11:30-11, SU 11:30-9

WOBURN—311 MISHAWUM RD (AT COMMERCE WY); 781.935.7200; M-TH 11:30-10:30, F-SA 11:30-11, SU 11:30-9

Johnny D's Uptown Restaurant ★★★☆☆
"...great Saturday and Sunday brunches... very kid-friendly... they provide toys for kids although they're a tad dog-eared... no kids' menu for brunch but kids' menu for dinner... welcoming atmosphere...**"**

Children's menu...................... ✓	$..Prices
Changing station .... ✗	❺...................Customer service
Highchairs/boosters .... ✗	❺............................ Stroller access

SOMERVILLE—17 HOLLAND ST (AT COLLEGE AVE); 617.776.2004; M-F 12:30-1, SA-SU 9-1

Johnny Rockets ★★★★★

"...burgers, fries and a shake served up in a 50's-style diner... we love the singing waiters—they're always good for a giggle... my daughter is enthralled with the juke box and straw dispenser... sit at the counter and watch the cooks prepare the food... simple, satisfying and always a hit with the little ones..."

Children's menu .... ✓ $$ .... Prices
Changing station .... ✗   ❹ .... Customer service
Highchairs/boosters .... ✓   ❸ .... Stroller access

WWW.JOHNNYROCKETS.COM

BURLINGTON—ONE BURLINGTON MALL (AT BURLINGTON MALL); 781.273.2727; M-SA 11-11; FREE PARKING

PEABODY—210 ANDOVER ST (AT NORTHSHORE SHOPPING CTR); 978.532.2999; M-TH 9-10, F-SA 9-11, SU 9-9

Mr Bartley's Burger Cottage ★★★★☆

"...happy to have babies there... they even moved us to a table away from cold door opening... loud and crowded... minimal space for strollers... casual place where you can get a good burger... fast service..."

Children's menu .... ✓ $$ .... Prices
Changing station .... ✗   ❸ .... Customer service
Highchairs/boosters .... ✓   ❷ .... Stroller access

CAMBRIDGE—1246 MASSACHUSETTS AVE (AT PLYMPTON ST); 617.354.6559; M-SA 11-9

Neillio's ★★★★☆

"...best for take out that's more on the healthy side... great homemade pasta to cook at home, as well as wonderful Italian dishes both cooked to order and in the freezer for later use... excellent resource for a new parent..."

Children's menu .... ✓ $$ .... Prices
Changing station .... ✗   ❹ .... Customer service
Highchairs/boosters .... ✓   ❺ .... Stroller access

WWW.NEILLIOS.COM

ARLINGTON—218 MASSACHUSETTS AVE (AT WINTER ST); 781.643.6644; DAILY 8-6:30; FREE PARKING

Ninety Nine Restaurant ★★★★☆

"...standard pub fare in a casual atmosphere... huge portions at reasonable prices... no worries bringing kids here— they can get noisy and messy and nobody cares... plenty of activity and the staff takes good care of you... chicken fingers, pasta, etc...."

Children's menu .... ✓ $$ .... Prices
Changing station .... ✓   ❹ .... Customer service
Highchairs/boosters .... ✓   ❸ .... Stroller access

WWW.99RESTAURANTS.COM

ANDOVER—464 LOWELL ST (AT BROWN ST); 978.475.8033; M-F 11:15-11, SA-SU 11:15-12AM

BILLERICA—160 LEXINGTON ST (AT MIDDLESEX TPK); 978.663.3999; M-W 11:15-10:30, TH-SA 11:15-11:30, SU 11:15-10

BILLERICA—672 BOSTON RD (AT PAYSON RD); 978.667.9789; M-W 11:15-10:30, TH-SA 11:15-11:30, SU 11:15-10

CAMBRIDGE—220 ALEWIFE BROOK PKWY (AT CONCORD AVE); 617.576.0999; M-W 11:15-10:30, TH-SA 11:15-11:30, SU 11:15-10

DANVERS—60 COMMONWEALTH AVE (AT LIBERTY TREE MALL); 978.762.8994; M-W 11:30-10:30, TH-SA 11:30-11, SU 11:30-10; MALL PARKING

HAVERHILL—786 RIVER ST (AT REVERE AVE); 978.372.8303; M-W 11-10:30, TH-SA 11-11:30, SU 11-9:30

LOWELL—850 CHELMSFORD ST (AT INDUSTRIAL AVE); 978.458.9199; M-W 11:15-10:30, TH-SA 11:15-11:30, SU 11:15-10

LYNNFIELD—317 SALEM ST (AT WALNUT ST); 781.599.8119; M-W 11:30-10:30, TH-SA 11:30-11:30, SU 11:15-9:30

NORTH ANDOVER—267 CHICKERING RD (AT FERNVIEW AVE); 978.683.9999; M-W 11:15-10:30, TH-SA 11:15-11:30, SU 11:15-10

REVERE—121 VFW PKWY (AT KIMBALL AVE); 781.289.9991; M-W 11:30-11, TH-SA 11:30-12, SU 11:15-10

SALEM—15 BRIDGE ST (AT HUBON ST); 978.740.8999; M-W 11:30-10:30, TH-SA 11:30-11:30, SU 11:30-9:30

SAUGUS—181 BROADWAY (AT PINE ST); 781.233.1999; M-W 11:15-10:30, TH-SA 11:15-11:30, SU 11:15-10

SOMERVILLE—20 CUMMINGS ST (AT THE MALL AT ASSEMBLY SQ); 617.629.0599; M-W 11:15-10:30, TH-SA 11:15-11:30, SU 11:15-10; MALL PARKING

STONEHAM—10 MAIN ST (AT NORTH ST); 781.279.0399; M-W 11:15-11, TH-SA 11:15-11:30, SU 11:15-10:30

WOBURN—291 MISHAWUM RD (AT COMMERCE WY); 781.935.7210; M-W 11:15-10:30, TH-SA 11:15-11:30, SU 11:15-10:30

Not Your Average Joe's ★★★★★

"...eclectic, creative selections with enough basics to satisfy the pickiest eater... the food is generally good, and they have a high tolerance for the noise that children sometimes make... the staff was ready and waiting with a highchair... no fuss about noise or mess... be prepared to wait a while on weekend nights... wonderful soups, pasta, brick-oven pizzas, fish, etc...."

Children's menu .... ✓ $$$ .... Prices
Changing station .... ✓   ❹ .... Customer service
Highchairs/boosters .... ✓   ❹ .... Stroller access
WWW.NOTYOURAVERAGEJOES.COM

ARLINGTON—645 MASSACHUSETTS AVE (AT WATER ST); 781.643.1666; M-TH 11:30-10, F-SA 11:30-11, SU 12-9

BEVERLY—45 ENON ST (AT HOOVER ST); 978.927.8950; M-TH 11:30-10, F-SA 11:30-11, SU 12-9

METHUEN—90 PLEASANT VALLEY ST (AT MILK ST); 978.974.0015; M-TH 11:30-10, F-SA 11:30-11, SU 12-9

NEWBURYPORT—1 MARKET SQ FIREHOUSE CTR (AT MERRIMAC ST); 978.462.3808; M-SA 11-10, SU 11-10

Panera Bread ★★★★½

"...soups, salads, sandwiches and delicious desserts... cafe food at great prices... the booths are big enough to put your car seat and store your stuff... fresh bread makes their sandwiches special... some locations have a have a community room which is a great place for a moms group to sit, park our strollers and breastfeed if need be..."

Children's menu .... ✗ $$ .... Prices
Changing station .... ✓   ❹ .... Customer service
Highchairs/boosters .... ✓   ❹ .... Stroller access
WWW.PANERABREAD.COM

BURLINGTON—24 CAMBRIDGE ST (AT BURLINGTON PLAZA); 781.272.1365; M-F 6-9, SA-SU 7-8

EVERETT—27 MYSTIC VIEW RD (AT GATEWAY CTR); 617.387.8135; M-F 6-9, SA 7-9, SU 7-8

SAUGUS—647 BROADWAY (AT NEWBURYPORT TPKE); 781.941.2220; M-F 6-9, TH-SA 6-10

Porter Exchange Restaurants ★★★★☆

"...great selection... amazing spot for authentic Asian cuisine... rather hectic which makes it okay for children .... several small boutique-type eateries—it's always teeming with kids and high chairs... good place to bring kids..."

Children's menu .... ✗ $$ .... Prices
Changing station...................... ✗   ❹ .... Customer service
Highchairs/boosters .... ✗   ❹ .... Stroller access

CAMBRIDGE—1 PORTER SQ (AT PORTER RD)

Rainforest Cafe ★★★½☆

"...like eating in the jungle... the decor keeps the kids entertained and the food ain't bad... kids either love it or are terrified at first and need to ease into the wild animal thing... I get at least 20 extra minutes of hang time with my friends because my daughter is so enchanted by the setting... waiters tend to be very accommodating... they always give me (with my three kiddos) an extra large table... watch the toy section chock full of 'but I want it' items..."

Children's menu .... ✓ $$$ .... Prices
Changing station...................... ✓   ❹ .... Customer service
Highchairs/boosters .... ✓   ❹ .... Stroller access

WWW.RAINFORESTCAFE.COM

BURLINGTON—75 MIDDLESEX TURNPIKE (AT BURLINGTON MALL); 781.272.7555; M-TH 11-10, F-SA 11-11, SU 11-7; MALL PARKING

Renee's Cafe ★★★☆☆

"...I love this breakfast place, but not with a baby... too small for a stroller... great breakfast place, very kid-friendly, nice high chairs, friendly staff... casual, fine for kids to make themselves heard..."

Children's menu .... ✗ $$ .... Prices
Changing station...................... ✗   ❹ .... Customer service
Highchairs/boosters .... ✗   ❸ .... Stroller access

SOMERVILLE—198 HOLLAND ST (AT BROADWAY); 617.623.2727; W-SU 7-1:30AM

Sylvan Street Grille ★★★★☆

"...good atmosphere, and decent food... go for Sunday brunch if you can... large menu, good prices... the waitstaff was very attentive and helpful—they warmed up baby food for us in kitchen... food was very good ..."

Children's menu .... ✗ $$ .... Prices
Changing station...................... ✗   ❹ .... Customer service
Highchairs/boosters .... ✗   ❹ .... Stroller access

WWW.SYLVANSTREETGRILLE.COM

PEABODY—12 SYLVAN ST (AT ANDOVER ST); 978.774.1724

TGI Friday's ★★★★☆

"...good old American bar food with a reasonable selection for the healthier set as well... I love that the kids' meal includes salad... my daughter requests the potato skins on a regular basis (which is good because they are also my favorite)... moderately priced... cheerful servers are used to the mess my kids leave behind... relaxed scene... I'd steer clear on a Friday night unless you don't mind waiting and watching the singles scene..."

Children's menu .... ✓ $$ .... Prices
Changing station...................... ✓   ❹ .... Customer service
Highchairs/boosters .... ✓   ❸ .... Stroller access

WWW.TGIFRIDAYS.COM

DANVERS—49 NEWBURY ST (AT NEWBURYPORT TPKE); 978.777.2420; M-SU 11-12:30

EVERETT—33 MYSTIC VIEW RD (AT REVERE BEACH PKWY); 617.387.5226

METHUEN—90 PLEASANT VALLEY RD (AT THE LOOP); 978.794.8443; DAILY 11-12:30; PARKING LOT

WOBURN—230 MISHAWUM RD (AT RT 95); 781.932.9550; DAILY 11-11; PARKING LOT

Toraya Restaurant ★★★★☆

"...excellent sushi, including good specials, and very kid-friendly staff... difficult to get a stroller inside at times... great sushi, casual atmosphere, kids welcome..."

Children's menu .... ✗	$$ .... Prices	
Changing station .... ✗	❺ .... Customer service	
Highchairs/boosters .... ✓	❸ .... Stroller access	

ARLINGTON—890 MASSACHUSETTS AVE (AT LOCKELAND AVE); 781.641.7477; SU T W TH 5-10, F-SU 5-11,

Uno Chicago Grill ★★★★☆

"...family-friendly, good stroller access... steaks, crisp salads, juicy burgers, sandwiches, flavorful pastas, chicken, seafood ... kids' menu, high chairs available..."

Children's menu .... ✗	$ .... Prices	
Changing station .... ✗	❹ .... Customer service	
Highchairs/boosters .... ✗	❺ .... Stroller access	

WWW.UNOS.COM

REVERE—399 SQUIRE RD (AT NORTHGATE SHOPPING CTR); 781.289.2330

Vinny T's Of Boston ★★★★★

"...delicious, family style Italian... inexpensive, good food... excellent place for a celebration-type meal... very large serving sizes... no kids' menu but there are many things that they can eat off of their parents' plates... brought my two girls (both under 2 and a half) in for lunch - the staff was great, very kid-friendly...they usually give you lots of extra spaghetti so you don't even have to order a kids meal..."

Children's menu .... ✓	$$$ .... Prices	
Changing station .... ✓	❹ .... Customer service	
Highchairs/boosters .... ✓	❹ .... Stroller access	

WWW.VINNYTSOFBOSTON.COM

DANVERS—100 INDEPENDENCE WAY (AT LIBERTY TREE MALL); 978.762.3500

Western Suburbs

★★★★★ "lila picks"

- ★ Cabot's Ice Cream
- ★ Deluxe Town Diner
- ★ John Brewer's Tavern
- ★ Johnny Rockets
- ★ Not Your Average Joe's
- ★ Vinny T's Of Boston
- ★ Zaftigs Delicatessen

Anna's Taqueria ★★★½☆

"...not entirely geared toward kids but it works, and the food is amazing and cheap... tasty burritos that everyone will love... welcoming low-key environment... small seating area, but fairly stroller-friendly..."

Children's menu	✗	$	Prices
Changing station	✗	❹	Customer service
Highchairs/boosters	✓	❹	Stroller access

BROOKLINE—1412 BEACON ST (AT SUMMIT AVE); 617.739.7300; DAILY 10-11:30

Applebee's Neighborhood Grill ★★★½☆

"...geared to family dining—they expect you to be loud and leave a mess... macaroni & cheese, hot dogs, and tasty grilled cheese... activity book and special kids cup are a bonus... service can be slow, but they will cover you with things to snack on... stay clear on Friday and Saturday nights... comfort food in a casual atmosphere... even though it's part of a very large chain you get the feeling it's a neighborhood-type place..."

Children's menu	✓	$$	Prices
Changing station	✓	❹	Customer service
Highchairs/boosters	✓	❸	Stroller access

WWW.APPLEBEES.COM

MILFORD—91 MEDWAY RD (AT BAY RD); 508.478.9523; M-TH 11-11, F-SA 11-12, SU 11-10

NEWTON—316 WASHINGTON ST (AT PEABODY ST); 617.244.1375; M-W 11-11, TH-SA 11-12, SU 11-9

WESTFORD—149 LITTLETON RD (AT NIXON RD); 978.692.7831; M-TH 11-11, F-SA 11-12, SU 11-11

Benjarong Restaurant ★★★☆☆

"...decent Thai food right near the Children's Museum... rate this one for its convenience and its prompt service..."

Children's menu	✗	$$	Prices
Changing station	✗	❸	Customer service
Highchairs/boosters	✗	❸	Stroller access

www.lilaguide.com

ACTON—214 MAIN ST (AT PROSPECT ST); 978.635.9580; DAILY 4:30-9

Bertucci's Brick Oven Pizzeria ★★★½☆

"...a laid-back Italian eatery with delicious Italian grub... pizza, pasta, something for everyone... get the olive oil for dipping, this makes waiting for the pizza a bearable experience with hungry tots... not an obviously kid-friendly restaurant, but they do a good job of accommodating parents with tots... great kids' menu... it can get busy, so go early... finding room for strollers can be challenging, but the staff is very accommodating...**"**

Children's menu	✓	$$	Prices
Changing station	✓	❹	Customer service
Highchairs/boosters	✓	❹	Stroller access

WWW.BERTUCCIS.COM

BROOKLINE—4 BROOKLINE PL (AT WASHINGTON ST); 617.731.2300; M-TH 11-10, F-SA 11-11, SU 12-10

CHESTNUT HILL—300 BOYLSTON ST (AT FLORENCE ST); 617.965.0022; M-TH 11-10, F-SA 11-11, SU 12-8

FRAMINGHAM—150 WORCESTER RD (AT CALDOR RD); 508.879.9161; M-TH 11-10, F-SA 11-11, SU 12-10

LEXINGTON—1777 MASSACHUSETTS AVE (AT WALTHAM ST); 781.860.9000; M-TH 11-10, F-SA 11-11, SU 12-10

MARLBOROUGH—388 BOSTON POST RD (AT VILLAGE DR); 508.460.0911; M-TH 11-10, F-SA 11-11, SU 12-10

MARLBOROUGH—601 DONALD LYNCH BLVD (AT SOLOMON POND MALL); 508.485.3636; M-TH 11-10, F-SA 11-11, SU 12-10

NEWTON—275 CENTRE ST (AT PEARL ST); 617.244.4900; M-TH 11-10, F-SA 11-12, SU 12-10

WALTHAM—475 WINTER ST (AT 2ND AVE); 781.684.0650; M-TH 11-10, F-SA 11-12, SU 12-10

WESTBOROUGH—161 TURNPIKE RD (NEAR CHAUNCY LAKE); 508.898.3074; M-TH 11-10, F-SA 11-12, SU 12-10

Blue Ribbon Bar-B-Q ★★★★☆

"...excellent barbecue for mom and dad... if your little one likes macaroni and cheese, they have some of the best around... laid-back atmosphere, take out and outdoor seating make it perfect for restless toddlers... generous portions...**"**

Children's menu	✓	$$	Prices
Changing station	✗	❹	Customer service
Highchairs/boosters	✓	❸	Stroller access

WWW.BLUERIBBONBBQ.COM

NEWTON—1375 WASHINGTON ST (AT CHERRY ST); 617.332.2583; M-SA 11:30-9, SU 12-8

Boca Grande Restaurant ★★★★½

"...cheap but tastes great... the basic, yet excellent, food is perfect for youngsters...**"**

Children's menu	✗	$	Prices
Changing station	✗	❺	Customer service
Highchairs/boosters	✓	❹	Stroller access

WWW.BOCAGRANDE.COM

BROOKLINE—1294 BEACON ST (AT HARVARD ST); 617.739.3900; DAILY 10:30-10:30

Brigham's Inc ★★★½☆

"...eating at an ice cream parlor—what could be better?.. wide selection of decent food... try to avoid the main lunch hour, that's when they are at their busiest and the service is slowest... an *inexpensive option that works great for moms and babies... service tends to be inconsistent...* "

Children's menu	✓	$$	Prices
Changing station	✗	❸	Customer service
Highchairs/boosters	✓	❸	Stroller access

WWW.BRIGHAMS.COM

BELMONT—2 TRAPELO RD (AT PINE ST); 617.484.9882; DAILY 10-10, SU 11-10

WALTHAM—90 RIVER ST (AT WILLOW ST); 781.893.9516; DAILY 8-8; FREE PARKING

WELLESLEY—268 WASHINGTON ST (AT WORCHESTER ST); 781.235.9749; DAILY 11-10

Bugaboo Creek Steak House ★★★★☆

"*...a definite must-go place for families with children... delicious food for grown-ups and a nice selection of food on the kids' menu... all kids' meals come with ice cream... all the hustle and bustle around us kept my son entertained while we waited for our meal... the singing tree (and moose) will either delight your child or scare the bejesus out of him... terrific service—the staff goes out of their way to cater to families... fun for birthdays—staff sings and brings out the birthday moose, which the honored one is supposed to kiss...*"

Children's menu	✓	$$$	Prices
Changing station	✓	❹	Customer service
Highchairs/boosters	✓	❹	Stroller access

WWW.BUGABOOCREEKSTEAKHOUSE.COM

FRAMINGHAM—345 COCHITUATE RD (AT FRAMINGHAM MALL); 508.370.9001; M-TH 11:30-10, F-SA 11:30-10:30, SU 12-9; MALL PARKING

MILFORD—124 MEDWAY RD (OFF RT 495); 508.478.2888; M-TH 11:30-10, F-SA 11:30-10:30, SU 12-9

WATERTOWN—617 ARSENAL ST (AT ARSENAL MALL); 617.924.9000; M-TH 11:30-10, F-SA 11:30-10:30, SU 12-9; MALL PARKING

Cabot's Ice Cream ★★★★★

"*...this old-fashioned ice cream parlor serves great breakfast (all day), lunches, dinners and ice cream galore... kids love to sit at the counter, and you often see kids' sports teams stopping by after a game... easy fit with a stroller... super casual atmosphere...*"

Children's menu	✗	$$	Prices
Changing station	✗	❹	Customer service
Highchairs/boosters	✗	❹	Stroller access

WWW.CABOTS.COM

NEWTONVILLE—743 WASHINGTON ST (AT COURT ST); 617.964.9200; T-SU 9-11, F-SA 9-11:45

California Pizza Kitchen ★★★★☆

"*...you can't go wrong with their fabulous pizza... always clean... the food's great, the kids' drinks all come with a lid... the staff is super friendly to kids.... crayons and coloring books keep little minds busy... most locations have a place for strollers at the front... no funny looks or attitude when breastfeeding... open atmosphere with friendly service... tables are well spaced so you don't feel like your kid is annoying the diners nearby (it's usually full of kids anyway)...*"

Children's menu	✓	$$	Prices
Changing station	✓	❹	Customer service
Highchairs/boosters	✓	❹	Stroller access

WWW.CPK.COM

NATICK—1245 WORCESTER RD (AT DEAN RD); 508.651.1506; M-TH 11-10, F-SA 11-11, SU 12-8

Casey's Diner ★★★★★
"...an institution... best hot dogs around..."

Children's menu	✗	$	Prices
Changing station	✗	❺	Customer service
Highchairs/boosters	✓	❶	Stroller access

NATICK—36 SOUTH AVE (AT HAYES ST); 508.655.3761; M-F 10:30-8:30, SA 10:30-4, SU 12-3

Cheesecake Factory, The ★★★★☆
"...although their cheesecake is good, we come here for the kid-friendly atmosphere and selection of good food... eclectic menu has something for everyone... they will bring your tot a plate of yogurt, cheese, bananas and bread free of charge... we love how flexible they are—they'll make whatever my kids want... lots of mommies here... always fun and always crazy... no real kids' menu, but the pizza is great to share... waits can be really long..."

Children's menu	✗	$$$	Prices
Changing station	✓	❹	Customer service
Highchairs/boosters	✓	❸	Stroller access

WWW.THECHEESECAKEFACTORY.COM

CHESTNUT HILL—300 BOYLSTON ST (AT FLORENCE ST); 617.964.3001; M-TH 11-11:30, F-SA 11:30-12:30, SU 10-11; PARKING AVAILABLE

Crossroads Cafe ★★★☆☆
"...lots of parking and stroller-accessible... no waiting area to speak of except the bar area... very busy Sunday night... went on a Saturday afternoon and did not have to wait..."

Children's menu	✓	$$	Prices
Changing station	✓	❸	Customer service
Highchairs/boosters	✓	❸	Stroller access

WWW.CROSSROADSCAFEACTON.COM

ACTON—405 NAGOG SQ (AT HWY 2A); 978.263.9733; M-TH 11:30-11, F 11:30-12, SA 12-12, SU 11-10

Dairy Joy ★★★★☆
"...although a bit pricey, this is THE summer place for dinner and ice cream... we go once a week and it is a real treat... the food is delicious, far better than you would ever expect... get there early, the lines can get outrageous (but usually move quickly)..."

Children's menu	✗	$$$	Prices
Changing station	✗	❹	Customer service
Highchairs/boosters	✗	❺	Stroller access

WESTON—331 N AVE (AT KINGS GRANT RD); 781.894.7144; DAILY 11-8

Deluxe Town Diner ★★★★★
"...an ideal spot for the whole family... they bring you great little chairs that hook on to the table... gave us oyster crackers and fruit when we sat down without our even asking... menu is extensive and appealing to kids of all ages... willing to make kids' portions out of anything on the menu... kid-friendly cups... sweet-potato pancakes are a big hit... prompt service... best to arrive early on the weekends..."

Children's menu	✓	$$	Prices
Changing station	✗	❺	Customer service
Highchairs/boosters	✓	❶	Stroller access

WWW.DELUXETOWNDINER.COM

WATERTOWN—627 MOUNT AUBURN ST (AT BIGELOW AVE); 617.926.8400; DAILY 6AM-10PM

Finagle A Bagel

★★★☆☆

"...fun community bagel shop with a weekly visit from the 'music man'... very kid-friendly—little tables and books for kids to entertain themselves while mom and dad get to eat... tasty bagel sandwiches... something for everyone to nibble on..."

Children's menu	✗	$$$	Prices
Changing station	✗	❸	Customer service
Highchairs/boosters	✗	❸	Stroller access

WWW.FINAGLEABAGEL.COM

WAYLAND—54 BOSTON POST RD (AT WHITE RD); 508.358.6282; M-SA 6-7, SU 6:30-6; STREET PARKING

Firefly's

★★★★★

"...a lot for infants and kids to look at... nice kids' menu... huge adult menu, with good prices... food is excellent—our 9-month-old had enough to look at to keep her busy... they also have call-ahead seating, so you don't have to wait as long with an impatient child... Sunday buffet is also good and inexpensive... a great barbeque restaurant..."

Children's menu	✓	$$$	Prices
Changing station	✓	❺	Customer service
Highchairs/boosters	✓	❹	Stroller access

WWW.FIREFLYSBBQ.COM

MARLBOROUGH—350 E MAIN ST (AT COOK LN); 508.357.8883; M-TH 4:30-10, F-SA 4:30-11, SU 11:30-10

Friendly's

★★★★☆

"...we love Friendly's because it's fast, fun and the food is pretty good... you may wait a bit for your service but given the promise of a sundae most kids will persevere... colorful menu and M&M pancakes... desert and a drink are included with some kids' meals... convenient if you have kids of varying ages—there's something good for everyone... burgers, sandwiches and more fries than you'll know what to do with..."

Children's menu	✓	$$	Prices
Changing station	✓	❸	Customer service
Highchairs/boosters	✓	❸	Stroller access

WWW.FRIENDLYS.COM

ACTON—387 MASSACHUSETTS AVE (AT MAIN ST); 978.263.0530; SU-TH 7-10, F-SA 7-11; FREE PARKING

BEDFORD—343A GREAT RD (AT SHAWSHEEN RD); 781.275.0780; SU-TH 7-10, F-SA 7--11; FREE PARKING

FRAMINGHAM—234 UNION AVE (AT LINCOLN ST); 508.875.1055; SU-TH 7-10, F-SA 7-11

FRAMINGHAM—27 TEMPLE ST (AT WORCESTER RD); 508.875.1542; SU-TH 7-10, F-SA 7-11

LEXINGTON—1060 WALTHAM ST (AT TRAPELO RD); 781.899.5887; SU-TH 7-10, F-SA 7-11

MEDFIELD—536 MAIN ST (AT N MEADOWS RD); 508.359.6143; SU-TH 7-10, F-SA 7-11

NATICK—1245 WORCESTER ST (AT NATICK MALL); 508.651.3962; SU-TH 7-10, F-SA 7-11

SUDBURY—457 BOSTON POST RD (AT NOBSCOT RD); 978.443.2033; SU-TH 7-10, F-SA 7-11

WATERTOWN—560 ARSENAL ST (AT ARSENAL MALL); 617.924.3068; SU-TH 7-10, F-SA 7-11; MALL PARKING

Joe's American Bar & Grill ★★★½☆

"...great bar food and friendly atmosphere—avoid peak times, as it gets very busy... they brought our food quickly and also helped us pack up quickly when the meltdown began... the waiter just smiled as our daughter tossed all of her food on the floor... no attitude, just helpful service... it's easy to find food here for the whole family..."

Children's menu	✗	$$$	Prices
Changing station	✗	❹	Customer service
Highchairs/boosters	✓	❸	Stroller access

WWW.JOESAMERICAN.COM

FRAMINGHAM—1 WORCESTER RD (AT SHOPPERS WORLD); 508.820.8389; M-TH 11-11, F-SA 11-12, SU 11-10

John Brewer's Tavern ★★★★★

"...New England-style pub food... on Mondays, kids eat free if you buy a drink... our waitress was very attentive to our child and did her best to ensure that our whole family had fun... a happy, casual eating place—everyone is happy by the time you leave..."

Children's menu	✓	$$	Prices
Changing station	✗	❺	Customer service
Highchairs/boosters	✓	❹	Stroller access

WWW.JOHNBREWERSTAVERN.COM

WALTHAM—39 MAIN ST (AT WARREN ST); 781.899.0549; M-SA 11:30-1, SU 12-12

Johnny Rockets ★★★★★

"...burgers, fries and a shake served up in a 50's-style diner... we love the singing waiters—they're always good for a giggle... my daughter is enthralled with the juke box and straw dispenser... sit at the counter and watch the cooks prepare the food... simple, satisfying and always a hit with the little ones..."

Children's menu	✓	$$	Prices
Changing station	✗	❹	Customer service
Highchairs/boosters	✓	❸	Stroller access

WWW.JOHNNYROCKETS.COM

NATICK—1245 WORCESTER RD (AT NATICK MALL); 508.651.3546; M-TH 9-10, F-SA 9-11, SU 9-9; MALL PARKING

Johnny's Luncheonette ★★★★☆

"...all-American comfort foods plus a soda fountain... a fun place to dine with toddlers... they brought my son's dinner out as soon as it was ready... crayons and paper for the kids... they understand if your kid makes a mess... go early on the weekends to beat the crowds... fast service gets you in and out quickly... noisy enough that you can't tell whose kids are being loud..."

Children's menu	✓	$$	Prices
Changing station	✗	❺	Customer service
Highchairs/boosters	✓	❸	Stroller access

NEWTON—30 LANGLEY RD (AT BEACON ST); 617.527.3223; SU-TH 8-9, F-SA 8-10

Ninety Nine Restaurant ★★★★½☆

"...standard pub fare in a casual atmosphere... huge portions at reasonable prices... no worries bringing kids here— they can get noisy and messy and nobody cares... plenty of activity and the staff takes good care of you... chicken fingers, pasta, etc...."

Children's menu	✓	$$	Prices
Changing station	✓	❹	Customer service
Highchairs/boosters	✓	❸	Stroller access

WWW.99RESTAURANTS.COM

HUDSON—255 WASHINGTON ST (AT BOLTON ST); 978.562.9918; M-W 11:30-10:30, TH-SA 11:30-11:30, SU 11:30-10

MILFORD—196B E MAIN ST (AT MEDWAY ST); 508.634.1999; M-W 11:30-10:30, TH-SA 11:30-11:30, SU 11:30-10

WALTHAM—110 SOUTH ST (AT ADAMS AVE); 781.893.4999; M-W 11:30-10:30, TH-SA 11:30-11:30, SU 11:30-10

Not Your Average Joe's ★★★★★

❝...eclectic, creative selections with enough basics to satisfy the pickiest eater... the food is generally good, and they have a high tolerance for the noise that children sometimes make... the staff was ready and waiting with a highchair... no fuss about noise or mess... be prepared to wait a while on weekend nights... wonderful soups, pasta, brick-oven pizzas, fish, etc.... ❞

Children's menu ✓	$$$	Prices
Changing station ✓	❹	Customer service
Highchairs/boosters ✓	❹	Stroller access

WWW.NOTYOURAVERAGEJOES.COM

WATERTOWN—55 MAIN ST (AT CHURCH ST); 617.926.9229; M-TH 11:30-10, F-SA 11:30-11, SU 12-9

Ruby Tuesday ★★★½☆

❝...nice variety of healthy choices on the kids' menu—turkey, spaghetti, chicken tenders... you can definitely find something healthy here... prices are on the high side but at least everyone can find something they like... service is fast and efficient... my daughter makes a mess and they never let me clean it up... your typical chain but it works—you'll be happy to see ample aisle space, storage for your stroller, and attentive staff... ❞

Children's menu ✓	$$	Prices
Changing station ✓	❹	Customer service
Highchairs/boosters ✓	❸	Stroller access

WWW.RUBYTUESDAY.COM

FRAMINGHAM—659 WORCESTER RD (AT RT 9); 508.820.1680; M-TH 11-11, F-SA 11-12, SU 11-10

MARLBOROUGH—771 BOSTON POST RD EAST (AT DICENZO BLVD); 508.480.0300; M-TH 11-10, F-SA 11-11, SU 9-9

WATERTOWN—485 ARSENAL ST (AT ARSENAL MALL); 617.926.6070; SU-TH 11-10, F-SA 11-12

WESTBOROUGH—32 LYMAN ST (AT TPKE RD); 508.389.9985; M-TH 11-11, F-SA 11-12, SU 11-10

TGI Friday's ★★★★☆

❝...good old American bar food with a reasonable selection for the healthier set as well... I love that the kids' meal includes salad... my daughter requests the potato skins on a regular basis (which is good because they are also my favorite)... moderately priced... cheerful servers are used to the mess my kids leave behind... relaxed scene... I'd steer clear on a Friday night unless you don't mind waiting and watching the singles scene... ❞

Children's menu ✓	$$	Prices
Changing station ✓	❹	Customer service
Highchairs/boosters ✓	❸	Stroller access

WWW.TGIFRIDAYS.COM

FRAMINGHAM—1 WORCESTER RD (AT RT 9); 508.875.7735; DAILY 11:30-12:30

MARLBOROUGH—601 DONALD LYNCH BLVD (AT SOLOMOND POND MALL); 508.303.0996; M-SA 11-12:30, SU 11-11:30

Vidalia's Truck Stop ★★★★☆

"*...affordable, local diner... great brunch... they show cartoons in the back of the restaurant (where they usually seat families)... my only complaint is that the wait for food is usually a bit long for young children...*"

Children's menu	✓	$$	Prices
Changing station	✗	❹	Customer service
Highchairs/boosters	✓	❷	Stroller access

WELLESLEY—13 CENTRAL ST (AT CREST RD); 781.431.0011; DAILY 8-8

Village Smokehouse ★★★☆☆

"*...great barbecue at good prices... small children's menu, and it's noisy enough in the evenings that kids fit right in...*"

Children's menu	✗	$$$	Prices
Changing station	✗	❹	Customer service
Highchairs/boosters	✓	❹	Stroller access

WWW.VILLAGESMOKEHOUSE.COM

BROOKLINE—6 HARVARD SQ (AT WASHINGTON ST); 617.566.3782; SU-W 4-10, TH 11:30-10, F 11:30-11, SA 12-11

Vinny T's Of Boston ★★★★★

"*...delicious, family style Italian... inexpensive, good food... excellent place for a celebration-type meal... very large serving sizes... no kids' menu but there are many things that they can eat off of their parents' plates... brought my two girls (both under 2 and a half) in for lunch - the staff was great, very kid-friendly...they usually give you lots of extra spaghetti so you don't even have to order a kids meal...*"

Children's menu	✓	$$$	Prices
Changing station	✓	❹	Customer service
Highchairs/boosters	✓	❹	Stroller access

WWW.VINNYTSOFBOSTON.COM

BROOKLINE—1700 BEACON ST (AT WILLSTON RD); 617.277.3400; M-TH 11:30-10:30, F-SA 11:30-11:30, SU 12-10

LEXINGTON—20 WALTHAM ST (AT MASS AVE); 781.820.5200; M-TH 11:30-10, F-SA 11:30-11, SU 12-10

NATICK—801 WORCESTER RD (AT THE NATICK CTR); 508.655.8787; M-TH 11:30-10, F-SA 11:30-11, SU 12-10

Watch City Brewing Co ★★★★☆

"*...Sunday brunch with kids' offerings and complete with a train set for them to play with... food is not great, however, there is a train table and toys in the middle of the room... you are actually able to have a conversation with the adults while kids play...*"

Children's menu	✓	$$	Prices
Changing station	✗	❹	Customer service
Highchairs/boosters	✓	❹	Stroller access

WWW.WATCHCITYBREW.COM/

WALTHAM—256 MOODY ST (AT PINE ST); 781.647.4000; M-T W 11:30-10, TH 11:30-10:30, F-SA 11:30-11, SU 4-9

Zaftigs Delicatessen ★★★★★

"*...great deli food... kid-friendly because it is so busy—no one can hear my baby cry through all the noise... just don't go at peak times because they are a super popular spot... the portions are enormous so you'll have plenty to take home...*"

Children's menu	✓	$$	Prices
Changing station	✗	❹	Customer service
Highchairs/boosters	✓	❹	Stroller access

WWW.ZAFTIGS.COM

BROOKLINE—335 HARVARD ST (AT PLEASANT ST); 617.975.0075; DAILY 8-10; STREET PARKING

Southern Suburbs

★★★★★

"lila picks"

- ★ Good Days Restaurant
- ★ Johnny Rockets
- ★ Not Your Average Joe's
- ★ Vinny T's Of Boston

Applebee's Neighborhood Grill ★★★★☆

"...geared to family dining—they expect you to be loud and leave a mess... macaroni & cheese, hot dogs, and tasty grilled cheese... activity book and special kids cup are a bonus... service can be slow, but they will cover you with things to snack on... stay clear on Friday and Saturday nights... comfort food in a casual atmosphere... even though it's part of a very large chain you get the feeling it's a neighborhood-type place...**"**

Children's menu	✓	$$	Prices
Changing station	✓	❹	Customer service
Highchairs/boosters	✓	❸	Stroller access

WWW.APPLEBEES.COM

STOUGHTON—525 WASHINGTON ST (AT CENTRAL ST); 781.341.9103

WEYMOUTH—35 PLEASANT ST (AT PLEASANT VALLEY SHOPPING MALL); 781.340.1332; M-SA 11-11; MALL PARKING

WEYMOUTH—765 BRIDGE ST (AT HARBORLIGHT MALL); 781.331.8550; SU-TH 11-11, F-SA 11-12; MALL PARKING

Bertucci's Brick Oven Pizzeria ★★★★☆

"...a laid back Italian eatery with delicious Italian grub... pizza, pasta, something for everyone... get the olive oil for dipping, this makes waiting for the pizza a bearable experience with hungry tots... not an obviously kid-friendly restaurant, but they do a good job of accommodating parents with tots... great kids' menu... it can get busy, so go early... finding room for strollers can be challenging, but the staff is very accommodating...**"**

Children's menu	✓	$$	Prices
Changing station	✓	❹	Customer service
Highchairs/boosters	✓	❹	Stroller access

WWW.BERTUCCIS.COM

BRAINTREE—412 FRANKLIN ST (OFF W ST); 781.849.3066; M-SA 11-10; FREE PARKING

BROCKTON—1285 BELMONT ST (OFF MILL ST); 508.584.3080

CANTON—95 WASHINGTON ST (AT THOMAS FLATLEY VLG MALL); 781.828.9910

HINGHAM—90 DERBY ST (AT RT 35); 781.740.4405

MANSFIELD—243 CHAUNCY ST (AT COPELAND DR); 508.339.3655

NEEDHAM—1257 HIGHLAND AVE (AT KINGSBURY ST); 781.449.3777

NORWOOD—1405 PROVIDENCE HWY (AT SUMNER ST); 781.762.4155

RANDOLPH—55 MAZZEO DR (NEAR CLINICAL WAY); 781.986.8333

Brigham's Inc ★★★½☆

"...eating at an ice cream parlor—what could be better?.. wide selection of decent food... try to avoid the main lunch hour, that's when they are at their busiest and the service is slowest... an inexpensive option that works great for moms and babies... service tends to be inconsistent..."

Children's menu	✓	$$	Prices
Changing station	✗	❸	Customer service
Highchairs/boosters	✓	❸	Stroller access

WWW.BRIGHAMS.COM

HINGHAM—37 MAIN ST (AT NORTH ST); 781.740.4687; DAILY 11-10

MATTAPAN—1621 BLUE HILL AVE (AT FAIRWAY ST); 617.298.6398; DAILY 8-8; FREE PARKING

WOLLASTON—13A BEALE ST (AT HANCOCK ST); 617.471.9750; DAILY 10-11

Bugaboo Creek Steak House ★★★★☆

"...a definite must-go place for families with children... delicious food for grown-ups and a nice selection of food on the kids' menu... all kids' meals come with ice cream... all the hustle and bustle around us kept my son entertained while we waited for our meal... the singing tree (and moose) will either delight your child or scare the bejesus out of him... terrific service—the staff goes out of their way to cater to families... fun for birthdays—staff sings and brings out the birthday moose, which the honored one is supposed to kiss..."

Children's menu	✓	$$$	Prices
Changing station	✓	❹	Customer service
Highchairs/boosters	✓	❹	Stroller access

WWW.BUGABOOCREEKSTEAKHOUSE.COM

BRAINTREE—551 JOHN MAHAR HWY (AT PLAIN ST); 781.848.0002

DEDHAM—850 PROVIDENCE HWY (AT WILSON AVE); 781.407.9890

Clyde's Roadhouse Bar & Grille ★★★★☆

"...good food and friendly atmosphere... very kid-friendly... tables covered in brown paper and crayons provided... kids' meals come with a plastic sheriff's badge..."

Children's menu	✓	$$	Prices
Changing station	✗	❹	Customer service
Highchairs/boosters	✓	❸	Stroller access

WALPOLE—642 PROVIDENCE HWY (AT HIGH PLAIN ST); 508.660.2206

Friendly's ★★★½☆

"...we love Friendly's because it's fast, fun and the food is pretty good... you may wait a bit for your service but given the promise of a sundae most kids will persevere... colorful menu and M&M pancakes... desert and a drink are included with some kids' meals... convenient if you have kids of varying ages—there's something good for everyone... burgers, sandwiches and more fries than you'll know what to do with..."

Children's menu	✓	$$	Prices
Changing station	✓	❸	Customer service
Highchairs/boosters	✓	❸	Stroller access

WWW.FRIENDLYS.COM

ATTLEBORO—10 WASHINGTON ST (AT CUMBERLAND AVE); 508.761.9104

ATTLEBORO—524 PLEASANT ST (AT LINDSEY ST); 508.226.3081; DAILY 11-9; FREE PARKING

BRIDGEWATER—70 BROAD ST, RTE 18 (AT MAIN ST); 508.697.3228

BROCKTON—708 BELMONT ST (AT ANGUS BEATON DR); 508.583.8652; DAILY 11-9; FREE PARKING

DEDHAM—757 PROVIDENCE HWY (AT ENTERPRISE DR); 781.329.1191; DAILY 11-9; FREE PARKING

HANOVER—1775 WASHINGTON ST (AT HIGHWAY 53); 781.826.6917

HOLBROOK—711 S FRANKLIN ST (AT LAUREL PARK); 781.767.0028; DAILY 11-9; FREE PARKING

NEEDHAM—173 CHESTNUT ST (AT OAK ST); 781.444.7661

NORWOOD—1469 PROVIDENCE HWY (AT UNION ST); 781.769.7583

QUINCY—213 INDEPENDENCE AVE (AT LURTON ST); 617.471.2522; DAILY 11-9; FREE PARKING

RANDOLPH—866 N MAIN ST (AT OAK ST); 781.963.1628; DAILY 11-9; FREE PARKING

RAYNHAM—427 ROUTE 44 (AT SOUTH ST W); 508.822.6966

SOUTH WEYMOUTH—1021 MAIN ST (AT GASLIGHT DR); 781.337.8877; DAILY 11-9; FREE PARKING

STOUGHTON—630 WASHINGTON ST (AT LINCOLN ST); 781.344.4198; DAILY 11-9; FREE PARKING

WEYMOUTH—415 WASHINGTON ST (AT FEDERAL ST); 781.337.6353

WOLLASTON—699 HANCOCK ST (AT WENTWORTH RD); 617.773.9550

WRENTHAM—1 PREMIUM BLVD (AT S ST); 508.384.7160

Frozen Freddies ★★★★★

"...great ice cream... only place where a kid's cone is one dollar..."

Children's menu	✗	$	Prices
Changing station	✗	❺	Customer service
Highchairs/boosters	✗	❶	Stroller access

HTTP://FROZENFREDDIES.COM

QUINCY—435 WASHINGTON ST (AT KITTREDGE AVE); 617.328.7772; M-SA 11:30-9, SU 12-9

Good Days Restaurant ★★★★★

"...styled along the theme of a 1950s diner... plenty of room for a stroller and highchair... old pictures line the walls and they have wonderful homemade sodas... food is great... menu is extensive... the price is right and it's the ideal destination for a mellow family dinner..."

Children's menu	✓	$$	Prices
Changing station	✗	❹	Customer service
Highchairs/boosters	✓	❺	Stroller access

WEST BRIDGEWATER—99 S MAIN ST (AT ASH ST); 508.584.0077; DAILY 7-10PM

Grand Buffet ★★★★☆

"...large Chinese buffet with food for even picky eaters.... fish tank... very friendly waitstaff..."

Children's menu	✗	$$	Prices
Changing station	✗	❹	Customer service
Highchairs/boosters	✓	❹	Stroller access

CANTON—100 WASHINGTON ST (AT THOMAS J FLATLEY VILLAGE MALL); 781.828.8188; SU-TH 11:30-9:30, F-SA 11:30-10:30; MALL PARKING

Joe's American Bar & Grill ★★★★☆

"...great bar food and friendly atmosphere—avoid peak times, as it gets very busy... they brought our food quickly and also helped us pack up quickly when the meltdown began... the waiter just smiled as our daughter tossed all of her food on the floor... no attitude, just helpful service... easy to find food for the whole family..."

Children's menu	✓	$$$	Prices
Changing station	✗	❹	Customer service
Highchairs/boosters	✓	❸	Stroller access

WWW.JOESAMERICAN.COM

BRAINTREE—250 GRANITE ST (AT NORTH ST); 781.848.0200; SU-TH 11-11, F-SA 11-12

DEDHAM—985 PROVIDENCE HWY (AT ARIADNE RD); 781.329.0800; SU-TH 11-11, F-SA 11-12

HANOVER—2087 WASHINGTON ST (AT WEBSTER ST); 781.878.1234; M-TH 11:30-10:30, F SA 11:30-11:30, SU 11-10:30

Johnny Rockets ★★★★★

"...burgers, fries and a shake served up in a 50's-style diner... we love the singing waiters—they're always good for a giggle... my daughter is enthralled with the juke box and straw dispenser... sit at the counter and watch the cooks prepare the food... simple, satisfying and always a hit with the little ones..."

Children's menu	✓	$$	Prices
Changing station	✗	❹	Customer service
Highchairs/boosters	✓	❸	Stroller access

WWW.JOHNNYROCKETS.COM

BRAINTREE—250 GRANITE (AT SOUTH SHORE PLAZA); 781.843.5250; M-F 11-9:30, SA 10:30-9:30, SU 11-7; FREE PARKING

My Sister & I Restaurant ★★★☆☆

"...local greasy spoon place that is kid-friendly offering a wide range of comfort foods... small surroundings, but worth the wait... strollers have to be left outside..."

Children's menu	✓	$$	Prices
Changing station	✗	❹	Customer service
Highchairs/boosters	✓	❷	Stroller access

BRIDGEWATER—42 CENTRAL SQ (AT BEDFORD ST); 508.697.9544; M-F 6AM-2AM, SA 7AM-2AM, SU 7AM-1AM

Newcomb Farms Restaurant ★★★★☆

"...all fresh, homemade food... the servers are friendly and responsive... the only downside is that it is a rather small restaurant and would not accommodate strollers... love their breakfasts... reasonably priced..."

Children's menu	✓	$$	Prices
Changing station	✗	❺	Customer service
Highchairs/boosters	✓	❸	Stroller access

WWW.BIRCHMIRE.COM/NEWCOMB.HTML

MILTON—1139 RANDOLPH AVE (AT HILLSIDE ST); 617.698.9547; M-TH 7-3:30PM, F-SU 7-8PM

Ninety Nine Restaurant ★★★½☆

"...standard pub fare in a casual atmosphere... huge portions at reasonable prices... no worries bringing kids here— they can get noisy and messy and nobody cares... plenty of activity and the staff takes good care of you... chicken fingers, pasta, etc...."

Children's menu	✓	$$	Prices
Changing station	✓	❹	Customer service
Highchairs/boosters	✓	❸	Stroller access

WWW.99RESTAURANTS.COM

BRAINTREE—SOUTH SHORE PLAZA (AT GRANITE ST); 781.849.9902; M-W 11:30-10:30, TH-SA 11:30-11:30, SU 11:30-10

BRIDGEWATER—233 BROAD ST (AT CRAPO ST); 508.279.2799; M-W 11:30-10:30, TH-SA 11:30-11:30, SU 11:30-10

CANTON—362 TURNPIKE ST (AT DEL POND DR); 781.821.8999; M-W 11:30-10:30, TH-SA 11:30-11:30, SU 11:30-10

EASTON—99 BELMONT ST (AT BRISTOL DR); 508.238.2999; M-W 11:30-10:30, TH-SA 11:30-11:30, SU 11:15-9:30

HINGHAM—428 LINCOLN ST (AT BEAL ST); 781.740.8599; SU-W 11:30-11, TH-SA 11:30-12

NORTH ATTLEBORO—1510 S WASHINGTON ST (AT CUMBERLAND AVE); 508.399.9990; M-W 11:30-11, TH-SA 11:30-12, SU 11-10

QUINCY—59 NEWPORT AVE (AT HOLBROOK RD); 617.472.5000; M-W 11:30-11, THU-SA 11:30-12, SU 11:15-10

ROCKLAND—2 ACCORD PARK (AT RTE 228); 781.871.4178; M-W 11:30-11, THU-SA 11:30-12, SU 11:30-10

WALPOLE—55 BOSTON PROVIDENCE TPKE (NEAR HWY 95); 508.668.6017; M-W 11:30-10:30, TH-SA 11:30-11:30, SU 11:30-9:30

WEYMOUTH—1094 MAIN ST (AT DERBY ST); 781.340.9000; M-W 11:30-10:30, TH-SA 11:30-11:30, SU 11:30-9:30

Not Your Average Joe's ★★★★★

"...eclectic, creative selections with enough basics to satisfy the pickiest eater... the food is generally good, and they have a high tolerance for the noise that children sometimes make... the staff was ready and waiting with a highchair... no fuss about noise or mess... be prepared to wait a while on weekend nights... wonderful soups, pasta, brick-oven pizzas, fish, etc...."

Children's menu	✓	$$$	Prices
Changing station	✓	❹	Customer service
Highchairs/boosters	✓	❹	Stroller access

WWW.NOTYOURAVERAGEJOES.COM

NEEDHAM—105 CHAPEL ST (AT GREAT PLAIN AVE); 781.453.9300; M-TH 11:30-10, F-SA 11:30-11, SU 12-9

RANDOLPH—16 MAZZEO DR (AT RT 139); 781.961.7200; M-TH 11-10, F-SA 11:30-11, SU 12-9

Piccadilly Pub

Children's menu	✓	✓	Changing station
Highchairs/boosters	✓		

WWW.PICCADILLYPUB.COM

ATTLEBORO—11 ROBERT TORNER BLVD N (AT SHAWS TRIBORO PLAZA); 508.643.2244; M-W 11-11, TH-SA 11-1, SU 12-9

RANDOLPH—1050 N MAIN ST (AT REED ST); 781.986.9981; M-T 11:30-10:30, W-SA 11:30-11, SU 11:30-9,

Ruby Tuesday ★★★★½☆

"...nice variety of healthy choices on the kids' menu—turkey, spaghetti, chicken tenders... you can definitely find something healthy here... prices are on the high side but at least everyone can find something they like... service is fast and efficient... my daughter makes a mess and they never let me clean it up... your typical chain but it works—you'll be happy to see ample aisle space, storage for your stroller, and attentive staff..."

Children's menu	✓	$$	Prices
Changing station	✓	❹	Customer service
Highchairs/boosters	✓	❸	Stroller access

WWW.RUBYTUESDAY.COM

ATTLEBORO—287 WASHINGTON ST (AT HIGHLAND AVE); 508.761.6620; SU-TH 11-11, F-SA 11-12

WRENTHAM—1 PREMIUM OUTLETS BLVD (AT NICKERSON LN); 508.384.5213; SU-TH 11-11, F-SA 11-12AM

Texas Road House ★★★★☆

"...welcome to Texas... they play a jukebox with country music that is overwhelming when you first walk in, but by the end of the meal I didn't even notice it... three cheers for the food and service... they give roasted peanuts (with shells) when you're seated, so the floor is covered with peanut shells... fun but a bit dangerous for the not so steady... NOT for peanut-allergic clientele..."

Children's menu	✓	$$$	Prices
Changing station	✓	❹	Customer service
Highchairs/boosters	✓	❹	Stroller access

WWW.TEXASROADHOUSE.COM

BROCKTON—124 WESTGATE DR (AT WESTGATE MALL AND PLAZA); 508.427.6244; M-TH 4-10:30, F 4-11, SA 11:30-11, SU 11:30-9:30; MALL PARKING

TGI Friday's ★★★★☆

"...good old American bar food with a reasonable selection for the healthier set as well... I love that the kids' meal includes salad... my daughter requests the potato skins on a regular basis (which is good because they are also my favorite)... moderately priced... cheerful servers are used to the mess my kids leave behind... relaxed scene... I'd steer clear on a Friday night unless you don't mind waiting and watching the singles scene..."

Children's menu	✓	$$	Prices
Changing station	✓	❹	Customer service
Highchairs/boosters	✓	❸	Stroller access

WWW.TGIFRIDAYS.COM

DEDHAM—750 PROVIDENCE HWY (AT ENTERPRISE DR); 781.251.0650; DAILY 11-12:45

NORTH ATTLEBORO—1385 S WASHINGTON ST N (OFF ALLEN AVE); 508.643.7488; DAILY 11-12:30; PARKING LOT

NORWELL—285 WASHINGTON ST (AT RT 53); 781.659.1583; SU-TH11:30-11, F-SA 11:30-12; PARKING LOT

NORWOOD—1345 PROVIDENCE HWY (AT SUMNER ST); 781.769.3397; DAILY 11:30-1

Town Spa Pizza ★★★★☆

"...terrific pizza and a very relaxed atmosphere... lots of TVs for the adults to catch a glimpse of the game while kids stuff themselves with yummy pizza... small pieces are perfect for toddlers..."

Children's menu	✗	$$	Prices
Changing station	✗	❹	Customer service
Highchairs/boosters	✓	❹	Stroller access

STOUGHTON—1119 WASHINGTON ST (AT PLAIN ST); 781.344.2030; M-SA 11-12, SU 12-12

Vinny T's Of Boston ★★★★★

"...delicious, family style Italian... inexpensive, good food... excellent place for a celebration-type meal... very large serving sizes... no kids' menu but there are many things that they can eat off of their parents' plates... brought my two girls (both under 2 and a half) in for lunch - the staff was great, very kid-friendly...they usually give you lots of extra spaghetti so you don't even have to order a kids meal..."

Children's menu	✓	$$$	Prices
Changing station	✓	❹	Customer service
Highchairs/boosters	✓	❹	Stroller access

WWW.VINNYTSOFBOSTON.COM

DEDHAM—233 ELM ST (AT ROBINWOOD RD); 781.320.8999; M-TH 11:30-10, F-SA 11:30-11, SU 12-10

Westbury Farms

★★☆☆

"...basic diner with inexpensive kids' meals .. pancakes for under $2 and just as good as Bickford's..."

Children's menu	✓	$	Prices
Changing station	✗	❸	Customer service
Highchairs/boosters	✓	❸	Stroller access

WWW.WESTBURYFARMS.COM

NORWOOD—997 PROVIDENCE HWY (AT DEAN ST); 781.769.9086; T-F 6-8, SA-M 6-3

doulas & lactation consultants

Editor's Note: Doulas and lactation consultants provide a wide range of services and are very difficult to classify, let alone rate. In fact the terms 'doula' and 'lactation consultant' have very specific industry definitions that are far more complex than we are able to cover in this brief guide. For this reason we have decided to list only those businesses and individuals who received overwhelmingly positive reviews, without listing the reviewers' comments.

Greater Boston Area

Anna Jaques Hospital (Birth Center)
Labor doula x   x .... Postpartum doula
Pre & post natal massage x   ✓ .... Lactation consultant
WWW.AJH.ORG
NEWBURYPORT—25 HIGHLAND AVE (AT LAFAYETTE ST); 978.463.1060; CALL FOR SCHEDULE

Association of Labor Assistants & Childbirth Educators (ALACE)
Labor doula .... ✓   x .... Postpartum doula
Pre & post natal massage x   x .... Lactation consultant
WWW.ALACE.ORG
BOSTON—617.441.2500

Best Fed Associates
Labor doula x   x .... Postpartum doula
Pre & post natal massage x   ✓ .... Lactation consultant
WWW.BESTFED.NET
WRENTHAM—185 CHESTNUT ST (AT ACORN RD); 508.384.3674; CALL FOR CONSULTATION

Brigham And Women's Hospital (Parent & Childbirth Education)
Labor doula x   x .... Postpartum doula
Pre & post natal massage x   ✓ .... Lactation consultant
WWW.BRIGHAMANDWOMENS.ORG
FENWAY/KENMORE—75 FRANCIS ST (AT BINNEY ST); 617.264.4747; CHECK SCHEDULE ONLINE

Cambridge Birth Center, The
Labor doula .... ✓   ✓ .... Postpartum doula
Pre & post natal massage x   ✓ .... Lactation consultant
WWW.CAMBRIDGEBIRTHCENTER.ORG
CAMBRIDGE—1493 CAMBRIDGE ST (AT HIGHLAND AVE); 617.665.2229; CHECK SCHEDULE ONLINE

Doulas of North America (DONA)
Labor doula .... ✓   ✓ .... Postpartum doula
Pre & post natal massage x   x .... Lactation consultant
WWW.DONA.ORG
BOSTON—888.788.3662

Isis Maternity
Labor doula x   ✓ .... Postpartum doula
Pre & post natal massage .... ✓   ✓ .... Lactation consultant
WWW.ISISMATERNITY.COM
BROOKLINE —2 BROOKLINE PL (AT BROOKLINE AVE); 781.429.1500; M W-TH 9-9, T F-SA 9-5; GARAGE AT BROOKLINE PLACE

NEEDHAM —110 2ND AVE (AT HIGHLAND AVE); 781.429.1500; M-TU 9-9, W 9-5, TH 9-9, F-SU 9-5; PARKING LOT

La Leche League

Labor doula .... ✗   ✗ .... Postpartum doula
Pre & post natal massage .... ✗   ✓ .... Lactation consultant

WWW.LALECHELEAGUE.ORG

BOSTON—VARIOUS LOCATIONS; 847.519.7730; CHECK SCHEDULE ONLINE; FREE PARKING

Saints Memorial Medical Center (Lactation Services)

Labor doula .... ✗   ✗ .... Postpartum doula
Pre & post natal massage .... ✗   ✓ .... Lactation consultant

WWW.SAINTS-MEMORIAL.ORG

LOWELL—1 HOSPITAL DR (AT NESMITH ST); 978.934.8474; CALL FOR SCHEDULE

Salem Hospital (Lactation Services)

Labor doula .... ✗   ✗ .... Postpartum doula
Pre & post natal massage .... ✗   ✓ .... Lactation consultant

WWW.NSMC.PARTNERS.ORG

SALEM—81 HIGHLAND AVE (AT COLBY ST); 888.217.6455; CALL FOR SCHEDULE

Tufts-New England Medical Center (Childbirth Education)

Labor doula .... ✗   ✗ .... Postpartum doula
Pre & post natal massage .... ✗   ✗ .... Lactation consultant

WWW.NEMC.ORG/OBGYN/MATERN.HTM

DOWNTOWN—750 WASHINGTON ST (AT KNEELAND ST); 617.636.0175; CALL FOR SCHEDULE

Winchester Hospital (Lactation Services)

Labor doula .... ✗   ✗ .... Postpartum doula
Pre & post natal massage .... ✗   ✓ .... Lactation consultant

WWW.WINCHESTERHOSPITAL.ORG

WINCHESTER—41 HIGHLAND AVE (AT ALBAN ST); 781.756.4788; CALL FOR APPT

exercise

City of Boston

★★★★★
"lila picks"

★ Bounceback Fitness ★ Stroller Strides
★ Stroller Fit

Beacon Light Yoga ★★★★½
"...a Kripalu-affiliated yoga studio... prenatal and mom and baby yoga... a little pricey, but it's a terrific way to relax and meet other expecting moms and moms with their babies..."

Prenatal	✓	$$$	Prices
Mommy & me	✓	❺	Decor
Child care available	✗	❺	Customer service

WWW.BEACONLIGHTYOGA.COM
ALLSTON/BRIGHTON—215 BRIGHTON AVE (AT HIGGINS ST); 617.562.0717; CHECK SCHEDULE ONLINE

Blissful Monkey Yoga Studio ★★★★☆
"...fun Mom/Baby yoga classes... great instructors..."

Prenatal	✓	$$	Prices
Mommy & me	✓	❹	Decor
Child care available	✗	❸	Customer service

WWW.BLISSFULMONKEY.COM
JAMAICA PLAIN—663 CENTRE ST (AT GREEN ST); 617.522.4411; CHECK SCHEDULE ONLINE

Boston Center For Adult Education ★★★★★
"...the prenatal yoga class is just amazing!.. only offered on Tuesdays... an hour and a half of relaxation and rejuvenation... the guide is very kind and peaceful... low-key environment and convenient location... reasonably priced... nice place to meet soon-to-be-moms... relax, stretch your bones and connect with your baby and your body... fyi—you have to climb to the fourth floor for classes and the toilet is on the second floor..."

Prenatal	✓	$$$	Prices
Mommy & me	✗	❺	Decor
Child care available	✗	❸	Customer service

WWW.BCAE.ORG
BACK BAY—5 COMMONWEALTH AVE (AT ARLINGTON ST); 617.267.4430; CHECK SCHEDULE ONLINE; GARAGES

Bounceback Fitness ★★★★★
"...offers a comprehensive fitness routine, including cardio and strength training... specifically for new moms who want to get back in shape quickly... challenging and rewarding workout... classes for all levels... onsite baby-sitting is very handy for the busy mom!..."

Prenatal	✗	$$ .... Prices
Mommy & me	✓	❺ .... Decor
Child care available	✓	❺ .... Customer service

WWW.BOUNCEBACKFITNESS.COM

BOSTON—VARIOUS LOCATIONS; 617.968.2979; CHECK SCHEDULE ONLINE; PARKING LOT

Fitness Etcetera For Women ★★★★☆

"...new facility and great babysitting... great machines and instructors..."

Prenatal	✗	$$$$ .... Prices
Mommy & me	✗	❹ .... Decor
Child care available	✓	❹ .... Customer service

WWW.FITNESSETCETERA.COM

WEST ROXBURY—1208 VFW PKWY (AT GARDNER ST); 617.325.0030; M-TH 5:30-9, F 5:30-8, SA-SU 7:30-7

Healthworks Fitness Center ★★★★½

"...tons of classes in a friendly environment... great for women of all fitness levels... I had a fabulous personal trainer... mommy and me class is a fun way to meet other new moms... the prenatal yoga class offers the right level of intensity... a wonderful place to relax each week... a fairly kid-friendly health club, with childcare and yoga for pre- and postnatal women..."

Prenatal	✓	$$$ .... Prices
Mommy & me	✓	❹ .... Decor
Child care available	✓	❹ .... Customer service

WWW.HEALTHWORKSFITNESS.COM

BACK BAY—441 STUART ST (AT TRINITY PL); 617.859.7700; CHECK SCHEDULE ONLINE; VALIDATED GARAGE AT THE CLARION

Stroller Fit ★★★★★

"...a great workout for parents and the kids are entertained the whole time... a great way to ease back into exercise after your baby's birth... the instructor is knowledgeable about fitness and keeping babies happy... motivating, supportive, and fun for kids and moms... sometimes they even set up a play group for after class... not just a good workout, but also a great chance to meet other moms and kids..."

Prenatal	✗	$$ .... Prices
Mommy & me	✓	❺ .... Decor
Child care available	✗	❺ .... Customer service

WWW.STROLLERFIT.COM

BOSTON—VARIOUS LOCATIONS; 617.429.6369

Stroller Strides ★★★★★

"...fantastic fun and very effective for losing those post-baby pounds... this is the greatest way to stay in shape as a mom—you have your baby in the stroller with you the whole time... the instructors are very professional, knowledgeable and motivating... beautiful, outdoor locations... classes consist of power walking combined with body toning exercises using exercise tubing and strollers... a great way to bond with my baby and other moms..."

Prenatal	✗	$$$ .... Prices
Mommy & me	✓	❺ .... Decor
Child care available	✗	❸ .... Customer service

WWW.STROLLERSTRIDES.NET

JAMAICA PLAIN—VARIOUS LOCATIONS; 617.823.4219; CHECK SCHEDULE ONLINE

WEST ROXBURY—VARIOUS LOCATIONS; 617.823.4219; CHECK SCHEDULE ONLINE

Wellspace   ★★★★☆

"...Celeste runs an excellent prenatal yoga class here... prenatal yoga, massage, and acupuncture... acupuncture helped me get my baby to turn head down... the massages were great during my last trimester... wonderful services ..."

Prenatal	✓	$$ .... Prices
Mommy & me	✗	❺ .... Decor
Child care available	✗	❺ .... Customer service

WWW.WELLSPACE.COM

SOUTH BOSTON—326 A ST (AT MELCHER ST); 617.876.2660; CHECK SCHEDULE ONLINE

Northern Suburbs

★★★★★
"lila picks"

- ★ Stroller Strides
- ★ Yoga In Harvard Square
- ★ Yoga Mandala

Arlington Center, The ★★★★⯪

"...there is a lovely prenatal yoga class here on Friday nights... it was a great way to meet local pregnant women and to make friends... owner is very helpful...**"**

Prenatal	✓	$$	Prices
Mommy & me	✓	❹	Decor
Child care available	✗	❺	Customer service

WWW.ARLINGTONCENTER.ORG

ARLINGTON—369 MASSACHUSETTS AVE (AT PALMER ST); 781.316.0282; CHECK SCHEDULE ONLINE

Baby Boot Camp ★★★★⯪

"...a great, low-cost, outdoor mom and baby workout... I've met some really fun moms and babies at these classes... not only fun, but more importantly I got results... the first class is free so there's no excuse not to give it a try... instructors are well-trained physical therapists that really know their stuff... class sizes are limited... it's like a personal trainer and motivational system all in one... I do their exercises even when I'm on my own with my baby...**"**

Prenatal	✗	$$$	Prices
Mommy & me	✓	❸	Decor
Child care available	✗	❸	Customer service

WWW.BABYBOOTCAMP.COM

NORTH ANDOVER—VARIOUS LOCATIONS; 617.755.4149; CHECK SCHEDULE ONLINE

SWAMPSCOTT—VARIOUS LOCATIONS; 781.334.6479; CHECK SCHEDULE ONLINE

WAKEFIELD—VARIOUS LOCATIONS; 781.334.6479; CHECK SCHEDULE ONLINE

Boston Sports Club ★★★☆☆

"...they have some trainers with pre-and postnatal experience, good to get you motivated... day care available some hours...**"**

Prenatal	✓	$$$	Prices
Mommy & me	✓	❸	Decor
Child care available	✓	❸	Customer service

WWW.BOSTONSPORTSCLUB.COM

CAMBRIDGE—625 MASSACHUSETTS AVE (AT MAGAZINE ST); 617.876.5550; M-TH 5:30-10, F 5:30-9, SA-SU 8-8; STREET PARKING

Harvard Vanguard Medical Center Yoga ★★★★★

"...this prenatal yoga class was amazing and so helpful during labor!.. I went for a total of six months during my pregnancy and had a four-hour labor! (not sure if that's the only reason, but the focus on breath work during the class came in really handy)... this class also fits those that aren't much into the 'new agey' type yoga classes that are often offered..."

Prenatal	✓	$$$	Prices
Mommy & me	✗	❸	Decor
Child care available	✗	❺	Customer service

WWW.VANGUARDMED.ORG

SOMERVILLE—40 HOLLAND ST (AT WINTER ST); 877.439.5465; CHECK SCHEDULE ONLINE; GARAGE

Healthworks Fitness Center ★★★★☆

"...tons of classes in a friendly environment... great for women of all fitness levels... I had a fabulous personal trainer... mommy and me class is a fun way to meet other new moms... the prenatal yoga class offers the right level of intensity... a wonderful place to relax each week... a fairly kid-friendly health club, with childcare and yoga for pre- and postnatal women..."

Prenatal	✓	$$$	Prices
Mommy & me	✓	❹	Decor
Child care available	✓	❹	Customer service

WWW.HEALTHWORKSFITNESS.COM

CAMBRIDGE—36 WHITE ST (AT PORTER SQUARE SHOPPING CTR); 617.497.4454; CHECK SCHEDULE ONLINE

Jazzercise ★★★★☆

"...the class meets Tuesdays and Thursdays at 7 and Saturdays at 9... the teacher is enthusiastic and fit... this is a great, fun way to take off baby weight in a non threatening, non 'look at me' environment... Jacki Griffin, the teacher, is wonderful..."

Prenatal	✗	$$	Prices
Mommy & me	✗	❹	Decor
Child care available	✗	❺	Customer service

WWW.JAZZERCISE.COM

ARLINGTON—40 TUFTS ST (AT RALEIGH ST); 781.646.5721; CHECK SCHEDULE ONLINE

Jenkyns, Patricia ★★★★☆

"...Trish Jenkyns teaches a postpartum exercise class at the Unitarian Church in Arlington Center on Mass Ave... she also does massage and other P.T. type stuff... best of all, she's a warm, caring and knowledgeable health professional..."

Prenatal	✗	$$$	Prices
Mommy & me	✗	❸	Decor
Child care available	✗	❺	Customer service

ARLINGTON—180 MASSACHUSETTS AVE (AT CHANDLER ST)

Karma Yoga Studio ★★★☆☆

"...gentle yoga workout geared to pregnant moms... no previous yoga experience is required... caring and calming instructor... fun mommy and me class... attractive studio... beware of stairs if you have a big stroller..."

Prenatal	✓	$$	Prices
Mommy & me	✓	❺	Decor
Child care available	✗	❸	Customer service

WWW.KARMAYOGASTUDIO.COM

CAMBRIDGE—1132 MASSACHUSETTS AVE (AT CAMBRIDGE COMMON); 617.547.9642; CHECK SCHEDULE ONLINE

Melrose-Wakefield Hospital (Family Education) ★★★☆☆

"...terrific... family education, CPR, and First Aid instructors and other credentialed educators make me feel like I'm in really good hands... wonderful classes that offer prenatal yoga, infant care, childbirth education, and more..."

Prenatal	✓	$$$	Prices
Mommy & me	✗	❸	Decor
Child care available	✗	❸	Customer service

WWW.HALLMARKHEALTH.COM

MELROSE—585 LEBANON ST (AT PORTER ST); 781.338.7561; CALL FOR SCHEDULE

Mystic River Yoga ★★★★☆

"...prenatal, chidren's and family yoga... prenatal yoga classes fill up here... knowledgeable staff... clean, well lit studio... peaceful and relaxing classes... really enjoyed having the time to just breathe, be near other moms, get support... I always left the studio feeling lighter and more centered, even with my bulging belly..."

Prenatal	✓	$$$	Prices
Mommy & me	✓	❹	Decor
Child care available	✗	❹	Customer service

WWW.MYSTICRIVERYOGA.COM

MEDFORD—196 BOSTON AVE (AT STOUGHTON ST); 781.396.0808; CHECK SCHEDULE ONLINE; PARKING LOT

Saints Memorial Medical Center (Family Birth Unit)

Prenatal	✓	✗	Mommy & me
Child care available	✗		

WWW.SAINTS-MEMORIAL.ORG

LOWELL—1 HOSPITAL DR (AT NESMITH ST); 978.934.8504; CALL FOR SCHEDULE

Shakti Yoga & Healing Art ★★★★☆

"...wonderful studio, and I feel very supported by the instructors... offerings include Itsy-Bitsy Baby Yoga.... as well as classes for tots crawling through 2 yrs... breastfeeding supportive environment..."

Prenatal	✓	$	Prices
Mommy & me	✓	❺	Decor
Child care available	✗	❸	Customer service

WWW.SHAKTIMOVES.COM

NORTH CHELMSFORD—11 SCHOOL ST (AT JORDAN ST); 978.251.1001; CHECK SCHEDULE ONLINE

Stroller Strides ★★★★★

"...fantastic fun and very effective for losing those post-baby pounds... this is the greatest way to stay in shape as a mom—you have your baby in the stroller with you the whole time... the instructors are very professional, knowledgeable and motivating... beautiful, outdoor locations... classes consist of power walking combined with body toning exercises using exercise tubing and strollers... a great way to bond with my baby and other moms..."

Prenatal	✗	$$$	Prices
Mommy & me	✓	❸	Decor

Child care available .... ✗   ❸ .... Customer service

WWW.STROLLERSTRIDES.NET

BURLINGTON—VARIOUS LOCATIONS; 781.799.2925; CHECK SCHEDULE ONLINE

WAKEFIELD—VARIOUS LOCATIONS; 888.569.1637; CHECK SCHEDULE ONLINE

XerStroll ★★★☆☆

"...very enjoyable!..."

Prenatal	✓	$$$	Prices
Mommy & me	✓	❸	Decor
Child care available	✗	❸	Customer service

HTTP://STROLLING.HOME.COMCAST.NET

WAKEFIELD—781.910.6614

Yoga East ★★★☆☆

"...wonderful resource for pregnant women looking to stay active and loose... reasonable prices... overall quality of the classes were well worth the cost..."

Prenatal	✓	$$$	Prices
Mommy & me	✗	❹	Decor
Child care available	✗	❹	Customer service

WWW.YOGAEAST.NET

WAKEFIELD—20 DEL CARMINE ST (AT WATERS ST); 781.224.0722; CHECK SCHEDULE ONLINE

Yoga In Harvard Square ★★★★★

"...fun prenatal yoga classes... fabulous yoga instructor is gentle and personable without being too New Age... taught me helpful visualizations to keep me calm and collected... extremely relaxing... a place to build great camaraderie with other moms... wonderful teacher with loads of experience..."

Prenatal	✓	$$$	Prices
Mommy & me	✓	❹	Decor
Child care available	✗	❹	Customer service

WWW.YOGAINHARVARDSQUARE.COM

CAMBRIDGE—66 WINTHROP ST (AT HARVARD ST); 617.864.9642; CHECK SCHEDULE ONLINE

Yoga Mandala ★★★★★

"...prenatal and mommy and Buddha baby yoga... fantastic classes... great bonding experience with your new baby... a nice place to meet other new moms... you can buy a session and make up classes if you miss one... the instructor has children and is very knowledgeable about a woman's body during childbirth..."

Prenatal	✓	$$$	Prices
Mommy & me	✓	❺	Decor
Child care available	✗	❺	Customer service

WWW.YOGAMANDALA.COM

WINCHESTER—6 MOUNT VERNON ST (AT CHURCH ST); 781.368.9339; CHECK SCHEDULE ONLINE

Western Suburbs

"lila picks" ★★★★★

- ★ Bounceback Fitness
- ★ Stroller Strides
- ★ Living Yoga

Bounceback Fitness ★★★★★
"...offers a comprehensive fitness routine, including cardio and strength training... specifically for new moms who want to get back in shape quickly... challenging and rewarding workout... classes for all levels... onsite baby-sitting is very handy for the busy mom!..."

Prenatal	✗	$$	Prices
Mommy & me	✗	❹	Decor
Child care available	✓	❺	Customer service

WWW.BOUNCEBACKFITNESS.COM

CHESTNUT HILL—PINE MANOR COLLEGE (AT S HUNTINGTON AVE); 617.968.2979; CHECK SCHEDULE ONLINE; FREE PARKING

Earthsong Yoga Center (Itsy Bitsy Yoga) ★★★★☆
"...fun for the babies—able to meet other moms..."

Prenatal	✓	$$$	Prices
Mommy & me	✓	❸	Decor
Child care available	✗	❸	Customer service

WWW.BABY-YOGA.COM

MARLBOROUGH—186 MAIN ST (AT FLORENCE ST); 508.405.1885; CHECK SCHEDULE ONLINE

Fitness Etcetera For Women ★★★☆☆
"...cool to be in a gym full of women... sensitive to the special needs of pregnant ladies... comfortable... lots of 'gentle' classes where pregnant women were welcome..."

Prenatal	✗	$$$	Prices
Mommy & me	✗	❸	Decor
Child care available	✗	❹	Customer service

WWW.FITNESSETCETERA.COM

NATICK—1400 WORCESTER RD (AT SHERWOOD PLAZA); 508.875.2290; CHECK SCHEDULE ONLINE; PARKING LOT

Green Planet ★★★★★
"...wonderful yoga classes for new mothers and their babies..."

Prenatal	✓	$	Prices
Mommy & me	✓	❺	Decor
Child care available	✗	❸	Customer service

WWW.THEGREENPLANET.COM

NEWTON—22 LINCOLN ST (AT WALNUT ST); 617.332.7841; M-F 10-6, SA 10-5; PARKING LOT

Healthworks Fitness Center ★★★★⯪

❝...tons of classes in a friendly environment... great for women of all fitness levels... I had a fabulous personal trainer... mommy and me class is a fun way to meet other new moms... the prenatal yoga class offers the right level of intensity... a wonderful place to relax each week... a fairly kid-friendly health club, with childcare and yoga for pre- and postnatal women...❞

Prenatal	✓	$$$	Prices
Mommy & me	✓	❹	Decor
Child care available	✓	❹	Customer service

WWW.HEALTHWORKSFITNESS.COM

BROOKLINE—920 COMMONWEALTH AVE (AT ST PAUL ST); 617.731.3030; CHECK SCHEDULE ONLINE

Isis Maternity ★★★★☆

❝...terrific prenatal yoga... good mommy yoga class... instructors are wonderful and will correct your form as needed... a great variety of classes, a great way to get out of the house post-baby... pricey, but very good... classes can be canceled at short notice...❞

Prenatal	✓	$$$	Prices
Mommy & me	✓	❹	Decor
Child care available	✗	❹	Customer service

WWW.ISISMATERNITY.COM

BROOKLINE —2 BROOKLINE PL (AT BROOKLINE AVE); 781.429.1500; M W-TH 9-9, T F-SA 9-5; GARAGE AT BROOKLINE PLACE

Laughing Dog Yoga ★★★★☆

❝...Helen runs an excellent program... good program to help babies sleep and relieve gas...❞

Prenatal	✓	$$$	Prices
Mommy & me	✓	❸	Decor
Child care available	✗	❸	Customer service

WWW.LDYOGA.COM

WELLESLEY—159 LINDEN ST (AT EVERETT ST); 781.239.0992

Living Yoga ★★★★★

❝...prenatal and mommy and me classes... enjoyed every minute... came out feeling relaxed and connected... the baby classes were super for getting out of the house and back into the groove... great, down-to- earth instructor sets a friendly tone for the class... the postures can be challenging, but beginners feel comfortable... the best part of my week!..❞

Prenatal	✓	$$	Prices
Mommy & me	✓	❺	Decor
Child care available	✗	❺	Customer service

WATERTOWN—613 MOUNT AUBURN ST (AT IRMA AVE); 617.306.3511; CHECK SCHEDULE ONLINE

Newton Wellesley Hospital (Wellness Center & Childbirth Education) ★★★★☆

❝...I loved the postpartum aerobics, you bring your non-mobile infant in his carrier or on a mat, and set him near you while you get yourself back in shape!.. this was a lot of fun, and a good way to meet other new moms... you must stop attending when your baby becomes *mobile... the hypnobirthing classes were incredible... Kathy was great...* **"**

Prenatal...............................	✓	$$ .... Prices	
Mommy & me........................	✓	❹ .... Decor	
Child care available...............	✗	❹ .... Customer service	

WWW.NWH.ORG

NEWTON—2014 WASHINGTON ST (AT WALSINGHAM ST); 617.243.6649; CALL FOR SCHEDULE; PARKING LOT

Serenity Yoga & Wellness ★★★★☆

"...wonderful place to practice yoga... from prenatal, postnatal to regular..... massage too!... **"**

Prenatal...............................	✓	$ .... Prices	
Mommy & me........................	✗	❹ .... Decor	
Child care available...............	✗	❸ .... Customer service	

WWW.SERENITYYOGA.COM

BEDFORD—18 NORTH RD (AT HIGHWAY 225); 781.275.4092; CHECK SCHEDULE ONLINE

Stroller Strides ★★★★★

"...fantastic fun and very effective for losing those post-baby pounds... this is the greatest way to stay in shape as a mom—you have your baby in the stroller with you the whole time... the instructors are very professional, knowledgeable and motivating... beautiful, outdoor locations... classes consist of power walking combined with body toning exercises using exercise tubing and strollers... a great way to bond with my baby and other moms... **"**

Prenatal...............................	✗	$$$ .... Prices	
Mommy & me........................	✓	❺ .... Decor	
Child care available...............	✗	❸ .... Customer service	

WWW.STROLLERSTRIDES.NET

BROOKLINE—VARIOUS LOCATIONS; 617.823.4219; CHECK SCHEDULE ONLINE

FRAMINGHAM—VARIOUS LOCATIONS; 888.514.2455; CHECK SCHEDULE ONLINE

MARLBOROUGH—VARIOUS LOCATIONS; 888.514.2455; CHECK SCHEDULE ONLINE

NATICK—VARIOUS LOCATIONS; 888.514.2455; CHECK SCHEDULE ONLINE

Wow! ★★★★☆

"...this is a well stocked gym with excellent babysitting availability for working parents... great aerobics classes... **"**

Prenatal...............................	✗	$$ .... Prices	
Mommy & me........................	✗	❹ .... Decor	
Child care available...............	✓	❸ .... Customer service	

WWW.WORKOUTWORLD.COM

WALTHAM—41 SEYON ST (AT GROVE ST); 866.677.2222

YMCA ★★★★☆

"...the variety of fitness programs offered is astounding... class types and quality vary from facility to facility, but it's a must for new moms to check out... most facilities offer some kind of kids' activities or child care so you can time your workouts around the classes... aerobics, yoga, pool—offers Pilates now... my favorite classes are the mom & baby yoga... the best bang for your buck... they have it all—great programs that meet the needs of a diverse range of families... **"**

Prenatal...............................	✓	$$$ .... Prices	
Mommy & me........................	✓	❹ .... Decor	
Child care available...............	✓	❹ .... Customer service	

WWW.YMCABOSTON.ORG

BRIGHTON—615 WASHINGTON ST (AT BRECK AVE); 617.782.3535; CALL FOR SCHEDULE

FRAMINGHAM—280 OLD CONNECTICUT PATH (AT HARDY ST); 508.879.4420; CALL FOR SCHEDULE; FREE PARKING

NEWTON—276 CHURCH ST (AT RICHARDSON ST); 617.244.6050; CALL FOR SCHEDULE

WALTHAM—725 LEXINGTON ST (AT COLLEGE FARM RD); 781.894.5295; CALL FOR SCHEDULE

Southern Suburbs

Isis Maternity ★★★★☆

"...terrific prenatal yoga... good mommy yoga class... instructors are wonderful and will correct your form as needed... a great variety of classes, a great way to get out of the house post-baby... pricey, but very good... classes can be canceled at short notice..."

Prenatal	✓	$$$	Prices
Mommy & me	✓	❺	Decor
Child care available	✗	❺	Customer service

WWW.ISISMATERNITY.COM

NEEDHAM —110 2ND AVE (AT HIGHLAND AVE); 781.429.1500; M-TU 9-9, W 9-5, TH 9-9, F-SU 9-5; PARKING LOT

Massage Works ★★★★★

"...great prenatal massage... wonderful staff..."

Prenatal	✓	$$$$	Prices
Mommy & me	✗	❹	Decor
Child care available	✗	❹	Customer service

WWW.MASSAGEWORKS.COM

BRAINTREE—335 WASHINGTON ST (AT ELM ST); 781.356.1700; M-F 1-9 SA SU 10-6; PARKING LOT

Wow! ★★★☆☆

"...hey, you can't beat the price—overlook the rest and just work out... the babysitting service was not adequate and as a result my son won't go back..."

Prenatal	✗	$$	Prices
Mommy & me	✗	❷	Decor
Child care available	✗	❸	Customer service

WWW.WORKOUTWORLD.COM

NORWOOD—942 PROVIDENCE HWY (AT DEAN ST); 781.762.6999; CHECK SCHEDULE ONLINE

YMCA ★★★★☆

"...the variety of fitness programs offered is astounding... class types and quality vary from facility to facility, but it's a must for new moms to check out... most facilities offer some kind of kids' activities or childcare so you can time your workouts around the classes... aerobics, yoga, pool—our Y even offers Pilates now... my favorite classes are the mom & baby yoga... the best bang for your buck... they have it all—great programs that meet the needs of a diverse range of families..."

Prenatal	✓	$$	Prices
Mommy & me	✓	❷	Decor
Child care available	✓	❷	Customer service

WWW.YMCABOSTON.ORG

NEEDHAM—863 GREAT PLAIN AVE (AT WARREN ST); 781.444.6400; CALL FOR SCHEDULE

parent education & support

Greater Boston Area

★★★★★ "lila picks"

- ★ Baby Matters
- ★ Beverly Hospital (Parent Education Department)
- ★ Brigham And Women's Hospital (Parent & Childbirth Education)
- ★ Cambridge Birth Center, The
- ★ Isis Maternity
- ★ Massachusetts General Hospital (Mother-Child Center)
- ★ North Suburban Family Network
- ★ South Shore Hospital (Women's Family Health)
- ★ Warmlines Parent Resources

Anna Jaques Hospital (Women's Health Care)

Childbirth classes	✗	✓	Breastfeeding support
Parent group/club	✓	✓	Child care info

WWW.AJH.ORG

NEWBURYPORT—25 HIGHLAND AVE (AT LAFAYETTE ST); 978.556.0100; CALL FOR SCHEDULE

Baby Matters ★★★★★

"...supportive, positive and helpful staff that provides a ton of practical information to new parents... informative without providing too much detail... variety of classes—including a sibling class for children about to have a new baby brother or sister... pre and postnatal classes are worthwhile... thought the weekend course was just the right length...**"**

Childbirth classes	✓	$$	Prices
Parent group/club	✓	❹	Class selection
Breastfeeding support	✓	❹	Staff knowledge
Child care info	✓	❹	Customer service

WWW.BABY-MATTERS.COM

BACK BAY—330 BROOKLINE AVE (AT BETH ISRAEL DEACONESS MEDICAL CTR); 978.535.4503; CHECK SCHEDULE ONLINE

BRAINTREE—10 FORBES RD (AT BETH ISRAEL DEACONESS HEALTH CARE); 978.535.4503; CHECK SCHEDULE ONLINE

LEXINGTON—482 BEDFORD ST (AT BETH ISRAEL DEACONESS HEALTH CARE); 978.535.4503; CHECK SCHEDULE ONLINE

NEEDHAM—272 CHESTNUT ST (AT VILLAGE SQ); 978.535.4503; CHECK SCHEDULE ONLINE

Beverly Hospital (Parent Education Department) ★★★★★

❝...we were thrilled with the instruction at this center... wonderful knowledgeable staff eager to answer questions... I am an avid subscriber to many parenting resources and I always left feeling I was getting the best info... most health insurances will partially reimburse for parenting classes... ❞

Childbirth classes	✓	$$	Prices
Parent group/club	✓	❸	Class selection
Breastfeeding support	✓	❹	Staff knowledge
Child care info	✗	❹	Customer service

WWW.BEVERLYHOSPITAL.ORG

BEVERLY—85 HERRICK ST (AT SOBIER RD); 978.927.9103; CHECK SCHEDULE ONLINE; HOSPITAL PARKING LOT

Boston Medical Center (Breastfeeding Center)

Childbirth classes	✗	✓	Breastfeeding support
Parent group/club	✗	✗	Child care info

WWW.BMC.ORG

DOWNTOWN—850 HARRISON AVE (AT NORTHAMPTON ST); 617.414.6455; CALL FOR SCHEDULE

Bradley Method, The ★★★★☆

❝...12 week classes that cover all of the basics of giving birth... run by individual instructors nationwide... classes differ based on the quality and experience of the instructor... they cover everything from nutrition and physical conditioning to spousal support and medication... wonderful series that can be very educational... their web site has listings of instructors on a regional basis... ❞

Childbirth classes	✓	$$$	Prices
Parent group/club	✗	❸	Class selection
Breastfeeding support	✗	❸	Staff knowledge
Child care info	✗	❸	Customer service

WWW.BRADLEYBIRTH.COM

BOSTON—VARIOUS LOCATIONS; 800.422.4784; CHECK SCHEDULE & LOCATIONS ONLINE

Brigham And Women's Hospital (Parent & Childbirth Education) ★★★★★

❝...their classes are offered through Isis Maternity and are just the best... lots of information... they also offer teen parenting classes and fatherhood workshops... the teacher was wonderful and we enjoyed the classes tremendously... great instructors—they really offer a great resource to the community... ❞

Childbirth classes	✓	$$	Prices
Parent group/club	✓	❹	Class selection
Breastfeeding support	✓	❺	Staff knowledge
Child care info	✗	❺	Customer service

WWW.BRIGHAMANDWOMENS.ORG

FENWAY/KENMORE—75 FRANCIS ST (AT BINNEY ST); 617.264.4747; CHECK SCHEDULE ONLINE

parent education & support

Cambridge Birth Center, The ★★★★★

"...look no further for breastfeeding and mom's support... incredible place to get prenatal care through delivery... could not have had a better experience throughout my entire pregnancy... respect parents' choices and beliefs and promote a gentle approach to birthing..."

Childbirth classes	✓	$	Prices
Parent group/club	✗	❹	Class selection
Breastfeeding support	✓	❺	Staff knowledge
Child care info	✗	❺	Customer service

WWW.CAMBRIDGEBIRTHCENTER.ORG

CAMBRIDGE—1493 CAMBRIDGE ST (AT HIGHLAND AVE); 617.665.2229; CHECK SCHEDULE ONLINE

Cambridge Center For Adult Education

Childbirth classes	✗	✓	Breastfeeding support
Parent group/club	✗	✓	Child care info

WWW.CCAE.ORG

CAMBRIDGE—42 BRATTLE ST (AT FARWELL ST); 617.547.6789; CHECK SCHEDULE ONLINE

City of Cambridge Center For Families

Childbirth classes	✗	✗	Breastfeeding support
Parent group/club	✓	✗	Child care info

WWW.CAMBRIDGEMA.GOV

CAMBRIDGE—70 RINDGE AVE (AT RINDGEFIELD ST); 617.349.3002; CHECK SCHEDULE ONLINE

Emerson Hospital (Tender Beginnings) ★★★★☆

"...practical, useful and well-organized prenatal class... the infant care class and breastfeeding class should have been longer—they were both two hours and at times things felt rushed... wide assortment of pre and postnatal classes..."

Childbirth classes	✓	$$	Prices
Parent group/club	✓	❹	Class selection
Breastfeeding support	✓	❹	Staff knowledge
Child care info	✗	❹	Customer service

WWW.EMERSONHOSPITAL.ORG

CONCORD—133 ORNAC (AT RTE 2); 978.287.3268; CHECK SCHEDULE ONLINE

Families First Parenting Programs ★★★☆☆

"...interesting, well priced programs... primarily postnatal resources..."

Childbirth classes	✗	$$$	Prices
Parent group/club	✓	❸	Class selection
Breastfeeding support	✗	❹	Staff knowledge
Child care info	✗	❸	Customer service

WWW.FAMILIES-FIRST.ORG

CAMBRIDGE—99 BISHOP RICHARD ALLEN DR (AT ESSEX ST); 617.868.7687; CHECK SCHEDULE ONLINE; STREET PARKING

First Connections

Childbirth classes	✗	✗	Breastfeeding support
Parent group/club	✓	✗	Child care info

CONCORD—111 OLD RD (AT OLD MARLBORO RD); 978.287.0221; CALL FOR SCHEDULE

Isis Maternity ★★★★★

"...what an amazing resource for new parents... knowledgeable staff and a great place to meet other parents to get support... excellent new mom and dad classes... informative and fun for parents and babies... this is definitely the best place to go for childbirth education—the staff is terrific... a welcoming, comfortable environment with a wide variety of class offerings... the lactation consultation services were excellent as is the selection of merchandise in the store..."

Childbirth classes	✓	$$$	Prices
Parent group/club	✓	❺	Class selection
Breastfeeding support	✓	❺	Staff knowledge
Child care info	✗	❺	Customer service

WWW.ISISMATERNITY.COM

BROOKLINE —2 BROOKLINE PL (AT BROOKLINE AVE); 781.429.1500; M W-TH 9-9, T F-SA 9-5; GARAGE AT BROOKLINE PLACE

NEEDHAM —110 2ND AVE (AT HIGHLAND AVE); 781.429.1500; M-TU 9-9, W 9-5, TH 9-9, F-SU 9-5; PARKING LOT

Jewish Family & Children's Services ★★★★☆

"...new mother's groups are free, very informative, comforting and led by volunteers... new moms are joining all the time and once the kids get bigger, you have a ready made playgroup... it's entirely non-denominational... wonderful way for new moms to get out of the house in those early weeks..."

Childbirth classes	✓	$$	Prices
Parent group/club	✓	❸	Class selection
Breastfeeding support	✓	❹	Staff knowledge
Child care info	✗	❹	Customer service

WWW.JFCSBOSTON.ORG

DOWNTOWN—31 NEW CHARDON ST (AT HAWKINS ST); 617.227.6641; CHECK SCHEDULE ONLINE

Lamaze International ★★★★☆

"...thousands of women each year are educated about the birth process by Lamaze educators... their web site offers a list of local instructors... they follow a basic curriculum, but invariably class quality will depend on the individual instructor... in many ways they've set the standard for birth education classes..."

Childbirth classes	✓	$$$	Prices
Parent group/club	✗	❸	Class selection
Breastfeeding support	✗	❸	Staff knowledge
Child care info	✗	❸	Customer service

WWW.LAMAZE.ORG

BOSTON—VARIOUS LOCATIONS; 800.368.4404; CHECK SCHEDULE AND LOCATIONS ONLINE

Lawrence General Hospital (Lactation Support)

Childbirth classes	✗	✓	Breastfeeding support
Parent group/club	✓	✓	Child care info

WWW.LAWRENCEGENERAL.ORG

LAWRENCE—1 GENERAL ST (AT PROSPECT ST); 978.683.4000; CHECK SCHEDULE ONLINE

Massachusetts General Hospital (Mother-Child Center) ★★★★★

"...cannot say enough wonderful things about the classes we took at MGH... the all-day childbirth class option is particularly great—concise, well presented, enthusiastic... breastfeeding and infant care classes were terrific... $15 per class—lots of topics and nurses teach the classes... staff is friendly and encourages questions... available after class for personal issues... the registration process could be improved, but the classes are very worthwhile..."

Childbirth classes	✓	$$		Prices
Parent group/club	✓	❺		Class selection
Breastfeeding support	✓	❺		Staff knowledge
Child care info	✗	❹		Customer service

WWW.MASSGENERAL.ORG/FAMILYEDUCATION

BEACON HILL/WEST END—55 FRUIT ST (AT GROVE ST); 617.726.4312; CHECK SCHEDULE ONLINE

Maternal Outreach

Childbirth classes	✗	✗		Breastfeeding support
Parent group/club	✓	✓		Child care info

WWW.MATERNALOUTREACH.COM

BACK BAY—416 MASSACHUSETTS AVE (AT COLUMBUS AVE); 617.267.7999

Medford Family Network ★★★★★

"...this new moms group was a savior... I met friends that taught me so much and encouraged me during the rough first months... hook into this fully funded family support center—you won't be disappointed... classes, play groups—I can't say enough good things about MFN..."

Childbirth classes	✓	$		Prices
Parent group/club	✓	❺		Class selection
Breastfeeding support	✗	❺		Staff knowledge
Child care info	✗	❺		Customer service

WWW.MEDFORD.K12.MA.US/MFAMNET/FAMHOM.HTM

MEDFORD—215 HARVARD ST (AT BENTON RD); 781.393.2106; CALL FOR SCHEDULE

Melrose-Wakefield Hospital (Family Education) ★★★★½☆

"...knowledgeable and caring instructors... well presented content... what a relief to have a preview of the world to come... my husband and I could have used more practice, but at least we knew what we were supposed to be doing..."

Childbirth classes	✓	$$		Prices
Parent group/club	✗	❹		Class selection
Breastfeeding support	✓	❹		Staff knowledge
Child care info	✓	❺		Customer service

WWW.HALLMARKHEALTH.COM

MELROSE—585 LEBANON ST (AT PORTER ST); 781.338.7561; CALL FOR SCHEDULE

Merrimack Valley Mothers of Twins

Childbirth classes	✗	✗		Breastfeeding support
Parent group/club	✓	✗		Child care info

WWW.MERRIMACKVALLEYMOTA.ORG

METHUEN—VARIOUS LOCATIONS; 978.685.0265

Metrowest Medical Center (Women's Resource Center) ★★★★☆

"...the education I received here proved to be invaluable... I left the class feeling less nervous and actually positively anticipating the birth of our first child... wide variety of programs, available evenings and weekends... **"**

Childbirth classes ✓	$$$	Prices
Parent group/club ✓	❹	Class selection
Breastfeeding support ✓	❹	Staff knowledge
Child care info ✗	❹	Customer service

WWW.MASS.GOV/DPH/FCH/GENETICS/RESOURCES.HTM

FRAMINGHAM—115 LINCOLN ST (AT EVERGREEN ST); 508.383.1580; CALL FOR SCHEDULE

Mocha Moms ★★★★★

"...a wonderfully supportive group of women—the kind of place you'll make lifelong friends for both mother and child... a comfortable forum for bouncing ideas off of other moms with same-age children... easy to get involved and not too demanding... the annual membership dues seem a small price to pay for the many activities, play groups, field trips, Moms Nights Out and book club meetings... local chapters in cities nationwide... **"**

Childbirth classes ✗	$$$	Prices
Parent group/club ✓	❸	Class selection
Breastfeeding support ✗	❸	Staff knowledge
Child care info ✗	❸	Customer service

WWW.MOCHAMOMS.ORG

BOSTON—VARIOUS LOCATIONS

Mom's Lunch Boston ★★★★☆

"...a nice way to meet other like-minded moms (especially moms who believe that not every meal with a newborn has to be eaten standing up while holding your baby!)... different speakers talk about various subjects, and the camaraderie is fun... you pay for a meal and hang out with other moms... the founder is very friendly and an excellent source of information regarding parenting in Boston... **"**

Childbirth classes ✗	$$$	Prices
Parent group/club ✓	❹	Class selection
Breastfeeding support ✗	❹	Staff knowledge
Child care info ✗	❺	Customer service

WWW.MOMSLUNCHBOSTON.COM

BOSTON—VARIOUS LOCATIONS; 617.553.0540; T-TH 11:30-2

MOMS Club ★★★★☆

"...an international nonprofit with lots of local chapters and literally tens of thousands of members... designed to introduce you to new mothers with same-age kids wherever you live... they organize all sorts of activities and provide support for new mothers with babies... very inexpensive for all the activities you get... book clubs, moms night out, play group connections... generally a very diverse group of women... **"**

Childbirth classes ✗	$$$	Prices
Parent group/club ✓	❸	Class selection
Breastfeeding support ✗	❸	Staff knowledge
Child care info ✗	❸	Customer service

WWW.MOMSCLUB.ORG

CITY OF BOSTON—VARIOUS LOCATIONS

Mothers and More ★★★★½☆

"...a very neat support system for moms who are deciding to stay at home... a great way to get together with other moms in your area for organized activities... book clubs, play groups, even a 'mom's only' night out... local chapters offer more or less activities depending on the involvement of local moms..."

Childbirth classes	✗	$$$	Prices
Parent group/club	✓	❸	Class selection
Breastfeeding support	✗	❸	Staff knowledge
Child care info	✗	❸	Customer service

WWW.MOTHERSANDMORE.COM

BOSTON—VARIOUS LOCATIONS; CHECK SCHEDULE & LOCATIONS ONLINE

Mount Auburn Hospital (Parent Childbirth Education Office) ★★★★½☆

"...instructors were extremely informative and provided wonderful handouts and resource lists... my group is still meeting six months later on our own... our teacher, a nurse and lactation specialist, was a great resource for the many new moms who were struggling with breastfeeding... valet parking was also much appreciated, especially for those who'd had C-sections... goes over all the basics..."

Childbirth classes	✓	$$	Prices
Parent group/club	✓	❹	Class selection
Breastfeeding support	✓	❹	Staff knowledge
Child care info	✗	❹	Customer service

WWW.MTAUBURN.CAREGROUP.ORG

CAMBRIDGE—330 MT AUBURN ST (AT CHANNING ST); 617.499.5121; CALL FOR SCHEDULE

North River Collaborative

Childbirth classes	✗	✗	Breastfeeding support
Parent group/club	✓	✗	Child care info

WWW.NORTHRIVERCOLLABORATIVE.ORG/

ROCKLAND—198 SPRING STR (AT MAGNOLIA DR); 781.681.9736

North Suburban Family Network ★★★★★

"...I love NSFN—all activities for children are free and most of the classes for parents are inexpensive... clean premises and friendly staff... the women that run the programs and teach the classes are fantastic... some of the classes require a registration fee, but they are all a great value... they run a really nice operation here..."

Childbirth classes	✓	$	Prices
Parent group/club	✓	❺	Class selection
Breastfeeding support	✓	❺	Staff knowledge
Child care info	✓	❺	Customer service

MELROSE—16 FRANKLIN ST (AT MAIN ST); 781.662.2722; CALL FOR SCHEDULE; PARKING AT BEEBE SCHOOL

Norwood Hospital (Me & My Baby)

Childbirth classes	✗	✗	Breastfeeding support
Parent group/club	✓	✗	Child care info

WWW.CARITASNORWOOD.ORG/HOME/

NORWOOD—800 WASHINGTON ST (AT CENTRAL ST); 781.278.6402; CALL FOR SCHEDULE; PARKING BEHIND BLDG

OrgagaGanics ★★★★☆

"...organic baby food delivered to your door... as a working mom I felt great that my child was eating homemade nutritious food... so much better than the baby food you buy at the supermarket... a quick an painless way to make sure your baby is eating the best food possible right from the start... absolutely worth the money..."

Childbirth classes	✗	$$$	Prices
Parent group/club	✗	❹	Class selection
Breastfeeding support	✗	❺	Staff knowledge
Child care info	✗	❺	Customer service

WWW.ORGAGA.COM

WELLESLEY—877.674.2422; CALL FOR DELIVERY SCHEDULE

Quincy Family Network (Community Care for Kids)

Childbirth classes	✗	✗	Breastfeeding support
Parent group/club	✓	✗	Child care info

WWW.QCAP.ORG

QUINCY—16 FRANKLIN ST (AT SCHOOL ST); 617.479.8181

Saints Memorial Medical Center (Family Birth Unit)

Childbirth classes	✗	✓	Breastfeeding support
Parent group/club	✗	✓	Child care info

WWW.SAINTS-MEMORIAL.ORG

LOWELL—1 HOSPITAL DR (AT NESMITH ST); 978.934.8504; CALL FOR SCHEDULE

Salem Hospital (Birth Place)

Childbirth classes	✗	✓	Breastfeeding support
Parent group/club	✗	✗	Child care info

WWW.NSMC.PARTNERS.ORG

SALEM—81 HIGHLAND AVE (AT COLBY ST); 978.739.6908; CALL FOR SCHEDULE

South Shore Hospital (Women's Family Health) ★★★★★

"...for a small hospital they offer a wide variety of classes and have an accommodating schedule for expectant parents who work irregular hours... everything from childbirth classes to free epidural and car seat info sessions... I feel much less anxious about bringing my first baby home now that I have taken the classes... new mommies group where I met many new friends... we still meet once a week after one year..."

Childbirth classes	✓	$$	Prices
Parent group/club	✗	❹	Class selection
Breastfeeding support	✗	❺	Staff knowledge
Child care info	✗	❹	Customer service

WWW.SOUTHSHOREHOSPITAL.ORG

SOUTH WEYMOUTH—55 FOGG RD (AT MAIN ST); 781.340.8332; CALL FOR SCHEDULE; FREE PARKING

Tufts-New England Medical Center (Childbirth Education)

Childbirth classes	✗	✓	Breastfeeding support
Parent group/club	✗	✗	Child care info

WWW.NEMC.ORG/OBGYN/MATERN.HTM

DOWNTOWN—750 WASHINGTON ST (AT KNEELAND ST); 617.636.4214; CALL FOR SCHEDULE

Warmlines Parent Resources ★★★★★

"...the best support for first-time moms... a wonderful way to meet other new moms and share the ups and downs of child birth... their facilities are really nice, but the best part is their staff—always helpful and engaged... wonderful community resource—especially for new moms and dads..."

Childbirth classes	✗	$$	Prices
Parent group/club	✓	❹	Class selection
Breastfeeding support	✗	❺	Staff knowledge
Child care info	✓	❺	Customer service

WWW.WARMLINES.ORG

NEWTON—225 NEVADA ST (AT LINWOOD AVE); 617.244.6843; CHECK SCHEDULE ONLINE

Watertown Family Network

Childbirth classes	✗	✗	Breastfeeding support
Parent group/club	✓	✗	Child care info

WWW.WATERTOWN.K12.MA.US/WFN

WATERTOWN—460 MAIN ST (AT PRESCOTT ST); 617.926.1661

pediatricians

Editor's Note: Pediatricians provide a tremendous breadth of services and are very difficult to classify and rate in a brief guide. For this reason we list only those practices for which we received overwhelmingly positive reviews. We hope this list of pediatricians will help you in your search.

City of Boston

Longwood Pediatrics
WWW.LONGWOODPEDS.YOURMD.COM/
BOSTON—319 LONGWOOD AVE (AT BLACKTEN CIR); 617.277.7320; M-F 8:30-5

Roslindale Pediatrics Associates
JAMAICA PLAIN—1153 CENTRE ST (AT ALANDALE RD); 617.522.3100; M-F 8-8:30 F 8-5

South Boston Community Health Center
WWW.BMC.ORG
BOSTON—850 HARRISON AVE (AT F ST); 617.414.5946; M-TH 8-8, F 8-5

Southern Jamaica Plain Health Center
JAMAICA PLAIN—640 CENTRE ST (AT GREEN ST); 617.983.4100; M-TH 8:6:15, F 8:30-5

Northern Suburbs

Alewife Brook Community Pediatrics
ARLINGTON—29 MASSACHUSETTS AVE (AT LAFAYETTE ST); 781.643.4507; M W F 8:30-5:30 T, TH 8:30-8

Arlington Pediatrics Associates PC
ARLINGTON—5 WATER ST (AT MASSACHUSETTS AVE); 781.641.5800; M-F 8-5, SA-SU HOL 9-12 BY APPT; STREET PARKING

Brook Alewife Community Pediatrics
ARLINGTON—29 MASSACHUSETTS AVE (AT BOULEVARD RD); 781.643.4507; M W 8:30-5, T TH 8:30-5:30, F 8:30-5:30

Cambridge Family Health
WWW.CHALLIANCE.ORG/LOCATIONS/CAM_FAM_HEALTH.HTM

CAMBRIDGE—2067 MASSACHUSETTS AVE (AT WALDEN ST); 617.575.5550; M-TH 8:45-5 F 9:15-5; PARKING BEHIND BLDG

CAMBRIDGE—237 HAMPSHIRE ST (AT INMAN SQUARE); 617.575.5570; M-TH 8:45-5 F9:15-5

Cambridge Pediatrics
WWW.CHALLIANCE.ORG

CAMBRIDGE—1493 CAMBRIDGE ST (AT HIGHLAND AVE); 617.665.1264; M-TH 8:30-6:30, F 8:30-5; GARAGE AT 1493 CAMBRIDGE ST

Cape Ann Pediatricians
GLOUCESTER—302 WASHINGTON ST (AT FERRY ST); 978.283.5079; M-F 9-5 SA 9-12

Children's Medical Office of North Andover
WWW.CHMED.COM

NORTH ANDOVER—477 ANDOVER ST (AT ELM ST); 978.975.3355; M-F 7-5

Dowd Medical Associates
READING—107 WOBURN ST (AT VINE ST); 781.944.4250; M-F 9-5

Garden City Pediatrics
WWW.GARDENCITYPEDIATRICS.COM

BEVERLY—83 HERRICK ST (AT HEATHER ST); 978.927.4980; M-F 8:15-5, SA-SU HOL 8:15-12

Gilchrist, Michael MD
CHELMSFORD—4 MEETING HOUSE RD (AT FLETCHER ST); 978.250.4081; M-F 8-5

Harvard Vanguard Medical Associates
WWW.HARVARDVANGUARD.ORG/DEFAULT.HTM

CAMBRIDGE—1611 CAMBRIDGE ST (AT ELERY ST); 617.661.5450; M-F 8-7:30

CHELMSFORD—228 BILLERICA RD (AT APOLLO DR); 978.250.6010; M-F 8-7:30

MEDFORD—26 CITY HALL MALL (AT RT 60); 781.306.5437; M-F 7:30-7

PEABODY—1 ESSEX CENTER DR (AT ESSEX GREEN DR); 978.977.4300; M-F 8-6

SOMERVILLE—40 HOLLAND ST (AT WINTER ST); 617.629.3000; M-F 8-6

Malden Family Health Center
WWW.FAMILYDOCTOR.ORG/MALDENFHC

MALDEN—100 HOSPITAL RD (AT MURRAY HILL RD); 781.338.7478; M-F 8-8 SA 9-4 SU 10-2

Mgh Revere Health Care Center
WWW.MASSGENERAL.ORG

REVERE—300 OCEAN AVE (AT SHIRLEY AVE); 781.485.6000; M-TH 8:30-8 F 8:30-5 SA 8:30-12

Peabody Pediatric Healthcare Associates
PEABODY—10 CENTENNIAL DR (AT SUMMIT AVE); 978.535.1110; M-F 9-5,6:30-9 SA-SU 9-5

Pediatricians, Inc.
WWW.PEDIATRICIANSINC.COM

WINCHESTER—955 MAIN ST (AT HEMINGWAY ST); 781.729.4262; M-F 9-5

Somerville Pediatric Services
SOMERVILLE—300 BROADWAY (AT BELMONT ST); 617.623.5437; M-F 8:30-5

Woburn Pediatric Associates
WWW.WOBURNPEDI.COM

WOBURN—7 ALFRED ST (AT 128 & MAIN ST); 781.933.6236; M-F 8-8, SA 9-1, SU 9-1; PARKING LOT

Western Suburbs

Acton Medical Associates
WWW.ACTONMEDICAL.COM
ACTON—321 MAIN ST (AT HWY 42); 978.263.0680; M-F 8:30-5

Center Pediatrics
NEWTON—1400 CENTRE (AT CRYSTAL LAKE); 617.244.9929; M-F 9-5

Centre Pediatric Associates
BROOKLINE—1 BROOKLINE PL (AT WASHINGTON ST); 617.735.8585; M-F 9-5

Charles River Medical Associates
WWW.CHARLESRIVERMED.COM
NATICK—233 W CENTRAL ST (AT NEWFIELD DR); 508.653.2133; M-F 9-5

Family Rhythms Inc
WWW.FAMILYRHYTHMS.NET
NATICK—218 N MAIN ST (RTE 27 NEAR RTE 9); 508.647.4955; M-TH 9-4:30, F 9-12; PARKING IN FRONT OF BLDG

Framingham Pediatrics
WWW.FRAMINGHAMPEDIATRICS.COM
FRAMINGHAM—125 NEWBURY ST (AT WHITTIER ST); 508.879.5764; M-TH 9-7, F 9-5

Holliston Pediatric Group
MILFORD—321 FORTUNE BLVD (AT E MAIN ST); 508.478.5996; M-F 8:30-5

Howard King Pediatrcis
NEWTON—2000 WASHINGTON ST (AT LONGFELLOW RD); 617.244.0021; CALL FOR APPT

Lexington Pediatrics
LEXINGTON—19 MUZZEY ST (AT RAYMOND ST); 781.862.4110; M-F 8-5

Patriot Pediatrics
WWW.PATRIOTPEDIATRICS.COM
BEDFORD—74 LOOMIS ST (AT RTE 225); 781.674.2900; M-TH 9:30-8:30, F 9:30-5, SA-SU 10-2 (ALL BY APPT ONLY) SICK WALK-INS M-F 8:30-9:30 ACUTE VISITS ONLY

Pediatric Associates of Wellesley
WESTON—134 SOUTH AVE (AT NEWTON ST); 781.736.0040; M-TH 7-8 F 7-5 SA-SU 8-12

Pediatrics At Newton-Wellesley
WWW.PEDIATRICSATNEWTONWELLESLEY.COM
NEWTON—2000 WASHINGTON ST (AT LONGFELLOW RD); 617.969.8989; M-F 8-5

Pediatrics West
WESTFORD—133 LITTLETON RD (AT NIXON RD); 978.577.0437; M-F 7-7

Saillant, Meredith MD
BROOKLINE—1180 BEACON ST (AT POWELL ST); 617.232.2915; M W F 9-5, T TH 9-7; STREET PARKING

Southboro Medical Group
FRAMINGHAM—761 WORCESTER RD (AT CURVE ST); 508.460.3100; M-F 8:30-5

Weston Pediatric Physicians
WWW.WESTONPEDIATRICS.COM
WESTON—486 BOSTON POST RD (AT CONCORD RD); 781.899.4456

Southern Suburbs

Bulotsky, Alan MD
BROCKTON—201 QUINCY ST (AT CENTRE ST); 508.584.1890; M-F 8-5:30, SA-SU 8-11:30; PARKING LOT

Dedham Medical Associates
WWW.DEDHAMMEDICAL.COM
DEDHAM—1 LYONS ST (AT GREENDALE AVE); 781.329.1400; M-F 8:30-5
NORWOOD—25 RIVER RIDGE DR (AT PROVIDENCE HWY); 781.329.1400; M-F 8:30-5

Hourigan, Philip MD
STOUGHTON—907 SUMNER ST (AT CHASE RUN); 781.344.3791; M-F 8:30-12:15 & 1:15-5

Jolles, Jon MD
HANOVER—51 MILLS ST (AT HIGHWAY 139); 781.826.2131; M-F 9-5

Needham Pediatrics
NEEDHAM—111 LINCOLN ST (AT KIMBALL ST); 781.444.7186; M-F 8-5 SA 8:30-1

Pediatric Associates Inc of Brockton
WWW.BEANSPROUT.NET
WEST BRIDGEWATER—291 E CENTER ST (AT EAST ST); 508.584.1210; M-F 8:30-5, SA 8:30-2, SU 8:30-12; PARKING LOT

Pediatric Healthcare
BROCKTON—830 OAK ST (AT RESERVOIR ST); 508.586.7334; M-TH 8:30-7, F 8:30-5, SA 8:30-12, SU 10-12; PARKING LOT

Westwood Mansfield Pediatrics
WWW.WMPEDS.YOURMD.COM
MANSFIELD—10 CREEDEN ST (AT CENTRAL ST); 508.339.9944; M-F 9-5

pediatricans

breast pump sales & rentals

Greater Boston Area

★★★★★
"lila picks"

★ Cambridge Medical Supply
★ Isis Maternity

Acton Pharmacy
WWW.ACTONPHARMACY.COM
ACTON—563 MASSACHUSETTS AVE (AT CENTRAL ST); 978.263.3901; M-F 8:30-8:30, SA 8:30-6, SU 8:30-4; FREE PARKING

Babies R Us ★★★½☆
"...Medela pumps, Boppy pillows and lots of other breastfeeding supplies... staff knowledge varies from store to store, but everyone was friendly and helpful... clean and well-stocked... not a huge selection, but what they've got is great and very competitively priced..."
Customer Service .... ❹ $$$ .... Prices
WWW.BABIESRUS.COM
BRAINTREE—450 GROSSMAN DR (AT UNION ST); 781.356.0475; M-SA 9:30-9:30, SU 11-7; PARKING IN FRONT OF BLDG
EVERETT—12 MYSTIC VIEW RD (AT GATEWAY SHOPPING CTR); 617.381.1537; M-SA 9:30-9:30, SU 11-7; MALL PARKING
FRAMINGHAM—1 WORCESTER RD (AT SHOPPPERS WORLD PLZ); 508.872.9358; M-SA 9:30-9:30, SU 11-7; PARKING IN FRONT OF BLDG
NORTH ATTLEBORO—1255 S WASHINGTON ST (AT EMERALD SQ MALL); 508.699.8218; M-SA 9:30-9:30, SU 11-7; PARKING IN FRONT OF BLDG
PEABODY—300 ANDOVER ST (AT PROSPECT ST); 978.532.0400; M-SA 9:30-9:30, SU 11-7; PARKING IN FRONT OF BLDG

Best Fed Associates ★★★★★
"...they will come to your house to give you the ultimate in breastfeeding support... they sell and rent Medela pumps... knowledgeable about the different models and will help you choose the best pump for your needs..."
Customer Service .... ❺ $$$$$ .... Prices
WWW.BESTFED.NET
WRENTHAM—185 CHESTNUT ST (AT ACORN RD); 508.384.3674; CALL FOR CONSULTATION

Brigham And Women's Hospital
WWW.BRIGHAMANDWOMENS.ORG/
FENWAY/KENMORE—75 FRANCIS ST (AT BINNEY ST); 617.732.7092; CALL FOR APPT

Cambridge Medical Supply ★★★★★

"...staff was extremely responsive whenever I called... prompt service... products readily available... gave me helpful information about health insurance companies' reimbursement policies... delivered a breast pump to me at the hospital less than 24 hours after I called... rentals available... free delivery and they pick up broken pumps... hassle free... extremely helpful people on the other end of the phone... they were fabulous..."

Customer Service....................... ❺ $$ .... Prices

CAMBRIDGE—218 MONSIGNOR O'BRIEN HWY (AT WINTER ST); 617.876.3810; M-F 9-5

Compass Healthcare ★★★★★

"...well trained and friendly staff—very knowledgable and supportive..."

Customer Service....................... ❺ $$$ .... Prices

FENWAY/KENMORE—375 LONGWOOD AVE (AT BROOKLINE AVE); 617.566.6772; M-F 8-5

Harvard Vanguard Medical Associates ★★★☆☆

"...the best midwives and lactation consultants around... I'm a better parent thanks to them... be sure you don't rent longer than you need—if you sign a contract, you don't get a refund for returning it early (even if it's months early)..."

Customer Service....................... ❹ $$$ .... Prices

WWW.HARVARDVANGUARD.ORG

WATERTOWN—485 ARSENAL ST (AT ARSENAL COURT DR); 617.972.5500; M TH 8-7, T-W F 8-5; FREE PARKING

Inman Pharmacy

WWW.INMANPHARMACY.COM

CAMBRIDGE—1414 CAMBRIDGE ST (AT INMAN SQ); 617.876.4868; M-F 8:30-8, SA 9-5:30, SU 9-2:30

Isis Maternity ★★★★★

"...they offer a great selection of breast pumps and rental plans... the staff is wonderful at helping you understand how to use the pumps... the best place for all things related to nursing—definitely come here first... nursing bras, pumps, slings and more...friendly, helpful and above all knowledgeable staff..."

Customer Service....................... ❺ $$$ .... Prices

WWW.ISISMATERNITY.COM

BROOKLINE —2 BROOKLINE PL (AT BROOKLINE AVE); 781.429.1500; M W-TH 9-9, T F-SA 9-5; GARAGE AT BROOKLINE PLACE

NEEDHAM —110 2ND AVE (AT HIGHLAND AVE); 781.429.1500; M-TU 9-9, W 9-5, TH 9-9, F-SU 9-5; PARKING LOT

Lactation Care ★★★★☆

"...sell and rent breast pumps for a fair price... they will even prorate the fee if you wind up renting for less time than originally expected... lactation consultants are caring and experienced... Medela pumps and accessories... I called in the morning and had my pump rental by the afternoon... available to answer questions..."

Customer Service....................... ❺ $$$ .... Prices

WWW.LACTATIONCARE.COM

NEWTON—25 FISHER AVE (AT KINGMAN RD); 617.244.5593; M-F 9-5:30, SA 9-1; STREET PARKING

www.lilaguide.com

Lactation Liaison
WWW.LACTATIONLIAISON.COM

GROTON—615 BOSTON RD (AT OLD LANTERN LN); 978.448.0654; CALL FOR APPT; PARKING BEHIND BLDG

Letourneau's Pharmacy ★★★★☆
"...they rent and sell breast pumps... they will also deliver your pump to your home... super helpful with choosing the right pump and learning how to use it...**"**
Customer Service .... ❺ $$$... Prices
WWW.LETOURNEAUS.NET

ANDOVER—349 N MAIN ST (AT POOR ST); 978.475.7779; M-F 8-6, SA 9-1; FREE PARKING

Melrose-Wakefield Hospital (Breastfeeding Support Center) ★★★★☆
"...Medela brand pumps for sale and rental... helpful in-house lactation consultants, and lactation support group which meets on Firdays... they also sell tubing and bras... a great resource...**"**
Customer Service .... ❹ $$... Prices
WWW.HALLMARKHEALTH.ORG/SERVICES_MATERNITY_LACTATION.PHP
MELROSE—585 LEBANON ST (AT MAIN ST); 781.979.6455; M-F 8:30-4, SA 10-2

Right Start, The ★★★☆☆
"...a small selection of pumps for sale... their prices are on the higher side, and the pump selection is pretty limited... they carry the Medela Pump-in-Style... they only carry the best... good quality and customer service might make it totally worthwhile...**"**
Customer Service .... ❺ $$$$....................................... Prices
WWW.RIGHTSTART.COM

NATICK—104 WORCESTER ST (AT OAK ST); 508.650.1271; M-SA 10-10, SU 11-7; MALL PARKING

Skenderian Apothecary ★★★★☆
"...great place for Medela products... they rent the Classic and Lactina models and sell the Medela Pump In Style... helpful staff with excellent availability of pumps... answered all my breastfeeding and pump questions...**"**
Customer Service .... ❺ $$$... Prices
WWW.SKENDERIANAPOTHECARY.COM

CAMBRIDGE—1613 CAMBRIDGE ST (AT ROBERTS RD); 617.354.5600; M-F 8-8, SA-SU 9-5

South Shore Hospital (Women's Family Health) ★★★★☆
"...expert lactation consultants... good selection of the basics, like bras, books and rental/sale pumps... a lifesaver for the frustrated and exhausted new mom... wonderful resource...**"**
Customer Service .... ❹ $$$... Prices
WWW.SOUTHSHOREHOSPITAL.ORG

SOUTH WEYMOUTH—55 FOGG RD (AT MAIN ST); 781.340.8332; CALL FOR SCHEDULE; FREE PARKING

Sullivan's Medical Supply ★★★☆☆
"...friendly staff helps with rentals or purchase of Medela products... $50 per month for rental plus $50 for purchase of the personal kit...**"**
Customer Service .... ❸ $$$... Prices

WWW.SULLIVANSPHARMACY.COM

ROSLINDALE—1 CORINTH ST (AT BELGRADE AVE); 617.325.0013; M-F 8-7, SA 8-4, SU 9-1

breast pump sales & rentals

Online

amazon.com ★★★★☆
"...I'm always amazed by the amount of stuff Amazon sells—including a pretty good selection of pumps... Medela, Avent, Isis, Ameda... prices range from great to average... pretty easy shopping experience... free shipping on bigger orders..."

babycenter.com ★★★★½
"...they carry all the major brands... prices are competitive, but keep in mind you'll need to pay for shipping too... the comments from parents are incredibly helpful... excellent customer service... easy shopping experience..."

birthexperience.com ★★★½☆
"...Medela and Avent products... great deal with the Canadian currency conversion... get free shipping with big orders... easy site to navigate..."

breast-pumps.com

breastmilk.com

ebay.com ★★★★½
"...you can get Medela pumps brand new in packaging with the warranty for $100 less than retail... able to buy immediately instead of having to bid and wait... wide variety... be sure to check for shipping price... great place to find deals, but research the seller before you bid..."

express-yourself.net

healthchecksystems.com

lactationconnection.com ★★★½☆
"...Ameda and Whisper Wear products... nice selection and competitive prices... quick delivery of any nursing or lactation product you can imagine... the selection of mom and baby related items is fantastic..."

medela.com ★★★★☆
"...well worth the money... fast, courteous and responsive... great site for a full listing of Medela products and links to purchase online... quality of customer service by phone varies... licensed lactation specialist answers e-mail via email at no charge and with quick turnaround..."

mybreastpump.com ★★★☆☆
"...a great online one-stop-shop for all things breast feeding... you can purchase hospital grade pumps from them... fast service for all your breastfeeding needs..."

diaper delivery services

Greater Boston Area

Changing Habits Diaper Service ★★★★☆

"...this 100 percent cotton cloth diaper service is reliable and affordable... better for the environment and cheaper than disposables... I especially like that the diapers you use are 'your' diapers, i.e. the ones you use are the same ones you get back the following week... they provide service to communities in Franklin, Hampshire and Middlesex counties... personalized attention when you call with questions...**"**

Customer Service .... ❸ $$$ .... Prices
Service AreaFranklin, Hampshire and Middlesex counties
WWW.CHANGINGHABITS.COM

DEERFIELD—588 GREENFIELD RD (AT BROUGHAMS POND RD); 413.665.0202; M-F 9-5; CALL FOR DELIVERY

Dede's Dide's Diaper Service ★★★☆☆

"...they make using cloth diapers on my 5-month-old baby very easy... seems that cloth diapering is becoming a lost art... couldn't even find diaper pails for cloth diapers in the stores—Dede's to the rescue!...**"**

Customer Service .... ❸ $$$ .... Prices
Service Areaservice the North Shore, call for info

PEABODY—0 HILLCREST AVE (AT OUTLOOK AVE); 978.532.5901

haircuts

Greater Boston Area

★★★★★

"lila picks"

★ Snip-its Haircuts For Kids
★ Styles 'N Smiles

Head To Toes ★★★★☆
"...owned by a parent who 'gets it'... fast service, kid friendly, a painless experience!!..."
Customer Service .... ❺ $$........................... Prices
WWW.HEADTOTOESSALON.COM
FOXBOROUGH—11 MECHANIC ST (AT COCASSET ST); 508.543.1112; M-W 9-8, TH 12-8, F 9-7, SA 9-3

Cuttery, The ★★★★☆
"...very gentle, excellent place... great prices..."
Customer Service .... ❺ $$$.......................... Prices
DOWNTOWN—100 CHARLES ST (AT PICKNEY ST); 617.227.0119; T-SA 9-6

Fantastic Sams ★★★★☆
"...good prices on kids' haircuts (includes a wash if needed, unlike other drop-in salons)... they take the time to talk with the kids, who are treated as the customer (the parent is included too)... haircuts have been excellent every time we've gone... they often run specials... nothing fancy but they do the trick..."
Customer Service .... ❹ $$........................... Prices
WWW.FANTASTICSAMS.COM
WOBURN—84 WASHINGTON ST (AT MONTVALE AVE); 781.939.9959; CALL FOR APPT

Great Cuts ★★★☆☆
"...great value, but the quality of the cuts varies considerably—sometimes it's great, sometimes not so great... stick with a stylist you know... no appointment necessary... a chain that offers cheap and quick cuts for both adults and kids ..."
Customer Service .... ❹ $$........................... Prices
WWW.GREATCUTS.NET
BROOKLINE—1381 BEACON ST (AT PARK ST); 617.232.0444; M-F 9-8, SA 9-6, SU 10-5
CAMBRIDGE—1 ELIOT ST (AT MT AUBURN ST); 617.576.3920; M-SA 9-7; FREE PARKING
DANVERS—139 ENDICOTT ST (AT ENDICOTT PLZ); 978.777.6444; M-SA 9-7; FREE PARKING
MEDFORD—463 SALEM ST (AT SPRING ST EXT); 781.391.0773; M-F 9-8, SA 9-6, SU 10-5

QUINCY—65 NEWPORT AVE (AT HOBROOK RD); 617.328.9191; M-F 9-8, SA 9-6, SU 10-8

REVERE—151 VFW PKWY (AT KIMBELL AVE); 781.284.6353; M-SA 9-7; FREE PARKING

SAUGUS—171 BROADWAY (AT PINE ST); 781.231.1539; M-SA 9-7; FREE PARKING

WALTHAM—723 MAIN ST (AT SPRING ST); 978.777.6444; CALL FOR APPT

WATERTOWN—137 MOUNT AUBURN ST (AT PARKER ST); 617.923.6200; M-F 9-8, SA 9-6, SU 10-5

WOBURN—352 CAMBRIDGE RD (AT REHABILITATION WAY); 781.932.0777; M-SA 9-7; FREE PARKING

Haircuts Ltd ★★★☆☆

"...walk-in haircut place... lollipops for the kids... reasonable prices..."

Customer Service.................. ❸ $$ .... Prices

NATICK—829 WORCESTER RD (AT NATICK CTR); 508.651.9122; M-F 9-8:45, SA 8:30-5:45, SU 12-4:45

Mario's Salon ★★★★★

"...wonderful salon... I keep going back... great cuts, great prices and friendly service..."

Customer Service.................. ❹ $$$ .... Prices

SOMERVILLE—75 HOLLAND ST (AT IRVING ST); 617.666.8210; M-F 8-7:30, SA 8-4:30

Philip's Total Care Salon ★★★☆☆

"...great experience... always quick, inexpensive and friendly..."

Customer Service.................. ❺ $$ .... Prices

WWW.PHILIPSSALON.COM

NORTH END—34 CHARTER ST (AT HENCHMAN ST); 617.523.8356; M 12-7, T TH F 9-7, W 9-9, SA 8-5

Snip-its Haircuts For Kids ★★★★★

"...the entertainment is unbeatable... kids' hair cut without all the stress... the only place we ever go... quick, painless and relatively cheap... they really know kids and how to keep them entertained while snipping away... they do a fabulous job... long waits (can be an hour or more) and they don't take appointments unless you join a VIP club... bubbles, videos, games and lollipops kept my daughter busy throughout the cut... patient stylists who know all the tricks to put your little one at ease... pricey but worth it for a stylist used to squirming kids..."

Customer Service.................. ❹ $$$ .... Prices

WWW.SNIPITS.COM

BURLINGTON—101 MIDDLESEX TPKE (AT MALL RD); 781.221.9939; M-SA 9-6, SU 10-5; PARKING LOT AT MALL

CANTON—95 WASHINGTON ST (AT DUNBAR ST); 781.821.1900; M-SA 9-6, SU 10-5

CHESTNUT HILL—25 BOYLSTON ST (AT THE MALL AT CHESTNUT HILL); 617.566.7647; M-SA 9-6, SU 10-5; PARKING LOT AT MALL

FRAMINGHAM—1 WORCESTER RD (AT SHOPPERS WORLD); 508.370.0006; M-SA 9-6, SU 10-5

PEABODY—300 ANDOVER ST (AT PALMER AVE); 978.532.1400; M-SA 9-6, SU 10-5

Styles 'n Smiles ★★★★★

"...TVs, lollipops, cookies and prizes for kids make it fun... still a little pricey... very clean... same-day appointments with virtually no wait... stylists are very patient... decent to excellent haircuts in a laid-back, child-friendly environment... make sure to make an appointment to avoid waiting... great place..."

Customer Service .... ❹ $$.. Prices

FRAMINGHAM—969 CONCORD ST (AT GERALD RD); 508.628.3688; T-F 9:30-6, SA 9-5

Supercuts ★★★★☆

"...results definitely vary from location to location... they did their best to amuse my son and an okay job with his hair... cheap and easy, with decent results... some locations have toys for kids to play with... walk-ins welcome, but make an appointment if you are going on the weekend... ask for the cutter who's best with kids... great cut for the price... fast and easy..."

Customer Service .... ❹ $$.. Prices

WWW.SUPERCUTS.COM

CAMBRIDGE—2150 MASSACHUSETTS AVE (AT MILTON ST); 617.492.0067; M-F 9-9, SA 9-7, SU 10-5

DANVERS—136 ANDOVER ST (AT GARDEN ST); 978.750.4441; M-F 9-9, SA 8:30-6, SU 11-5

FRAMINGHAM—405 WORCESTER RD (AT COCHILUATE RD); 508.879.0931; M-F 9-9, SA 9-6, SU 10-5

NEEDHAM—1299 HIGHLAND AVE (AT MAY ST); 781.455.9990; M-F 9-9, SA 8-6, SU 10-5

NEWBURYPORT—45 STOREY AVE (AT LOW ST); 978.462.9262; M-F 8-9, SA 9-6, SU 11-5

NEWTON—2058 COMMONWEALTH AVE (AT LEXINGTON ST); 617.928.0660; M-F 9-9, SA 8-6, SU 10-5

WALTHAM—1077 LEXINGTON ST (AT TRAPELO RD); 781.647.8360; CALL FOR APPT

Village Barber ★★★★★

"...these old-fashioned barbers are friendly, funny and worth every penny... a tear-free haircut... tons of toys and a playful atmosphere... this is the only place where my son doesn't cry... worth the drive and the money..."

Customer Service .... ❺ $$.. Prices

WESTON—483 BOSTON POST RD (AT COLPITTS RD); 781.893.9229; T-F 8-5, SA 8-2

nanny & babysitter referrals

Greater Boston Area

★★★★★ "lila picks"

- ★ Boston Nanny Centre
- ★ In Search Of Nanny Inc
- ★ Parents In A Pinch

Boston Nanny Centre ★★★★★

"...will fax you extensive portfolios of nannies... I used them for my last nanny, and it has worked out very well... the staff is very helpful in trying to match up families and nannies... a bit expensive... full-time, part-time and live-in referrals... I was disappointed that they do not hire nannies who want to take their own children with them..."

Baby nurses	✗	$$$$	Prices
Nannies	✓	❹	Candidate selection
Au pairs	✗	❹	Staff knowledge
Babysitters	✗	❹	Customer service
Service Area	All of Mass.		

WWW.BOSTONNANNY.COM
NEWTON—135 SELWYN RD (AT PARK DR); 617.527.0114; M-F 9-5

Boston's Best Baby Sitters/Nannies ★★★★½

"...a highly professional group that provides top-notch babysitter-locating services... they're great at finding emergency (last minute) care... you can also take infant CPR classes from them... wonderful and very reliable..."

Baby nurses	✗	$$$	Prices
Nannies	✓	❸	Candidate selection
Au pairs	✗	❸	Staff knowledge
Babysitters	✓	❸	Customer service

WWW.BBABYSITTERS.COM
BOSTON—617.268.7148; DAILY 8-8

Harvard Student Agencies Inc ★★★★☆

"...many friends have found fun, available babysitters through this service... ideal for weekend nights or the odd chunk of time that fits within a student's schedule... limited selection... free listings..."

Baby nurses	✗	$$	Prices
Nannies	✓	❷	Candidate selection
Au pairs	✗	❸	Staff knowledge
Babysitters	✓	❸	Customer service
Service Area	Greater Boston Area		

WWW.HSA.NET
CAMBRIDGE—53 CHURCH ST (AT BATTLE ST); 617.495.3033; M-F 10-6

In Search Of Nanny Inc ★★★★★

"...wonderful... a great way to find a really well-qualified nanny... they truly care about matching the right nanny with the right family... they follow-up and check in to make sure things are going well... professionally run... terrific service... very intuitive..."

Baby nurses.................................. ✗	$$$ .... Prices
Nannies.. ✓	❹ ....Candidate selection
Au pairs.. ✗	❹ .... Staff knowledge
Babysitters.................................. ✓	❹ .... Customer service

Service Area... Eastern Massachusetts
WWW.INSEARCHOFNANNY.COM

BEVERLY—30 RANTOUL ST (AT SCHOOL ST); 978.921.1735; M-TH 9-5, F 9-3; STREET PARKING

MA Office Of Child Care Services (OCCS) ★★★★☆

"...great web site, with tons of free information and links... searchable by town, zip code or type of childcare needed... listings include daycare centers, family daycare facilities and individual childcare providers... helped me figure out if I could get financial assistance... valuable local resource... a must-use site to verify state licensing..."

Baby nurses.................................. ✓	$$ .... Prices
Nannies.. ✓	❹ ....Candidate selection
Au pairs.. ✗	❹ .... Staff knowledge
Babysitters.................................. ✗	❸ .... Customer service

Service Area........................ statewide
WWW.EEC.STATE.MA.US

DOWNTOWN—600 WASHINGTON ST (AT HAYWARD PL); 617.988.6600

Nanny On The Net, A ★★★★☆

"...a national agency that places experienced (at least three years) nannies... easy to use and efficient... detailed background checks... all prospects are trained in CPR... legal, financial, and practical help for first-time 'employer' families... about $75 for the application fee and then additional placement fees when you succeed in finding a nanny..."

Baby nurses.................................. ✓	$$$ .... Prices
Nannies.. ✓	❹ ....Candidate selection
Au pairs.. ✗	❹ .... Staff knowledge
Babysitters.................................. ✗	❸ .... Customer service

Service Area....... Greater Boston Area
WWW.ANANNYONTHENET.COM

BOSTON—978.290.1578; M-F 9-5

Needham Youth Commission ★★★☆☆

"...for $5 you can get a list of all the kids in town who have signed up to provide various services, including babysitting... listings are even broken down by regions... this a great way to find mother's helpers who can be groomed into full-blown babysitters..."

Baby nurses.................................. ✗	$ .... Prices
Nannies.. ✗	❹ ....Candidate selection
Au pairs.. ✗	❸ .... Staff knowledge
Babysitters.................................. ✓	❸ .... Customer service

WWW.TOWN.NEEDHAM.MA.US/YOUTH

NEEDHAM—1471 HIGHLAND AVE (AT GREAT PLAINS AVE); 781.455.7518; M-F 8:30-5

Parents In A Pinch ★★★★★

"...very reliable, good experience... a bit pricey, but great for last-minute baby-sitting... friendly, caring, knowledgeable, and most importantly, well-screened baby-sitters..."

Baby nurses	✗	$$$$	Prices
Nannies	✓	❹	Candidate selection
Au pairs	✗	❹	Staff knowledge
Babysitters	✓	❹	Customer service
Service Area	statewide		

WWW.PARENTSINAPINCH.COM

BROOKLINE—45 BARTLETT CRES (AT WASHINGTON ST); 617.739.5437; M-F 8-5

Summer Placement Consultants

Baby nurses	✗	✓	Nannies
Au pairs	✓	✓	Babysitters

WWW.SUMMERPLACEMENTS.COM

MANCHESTER-BY-THE-SEA—POST OFFICE BOX 516; 978.526.1444

Online

★★★★★ "lila picks"

★ craigslist.org

4nannies.com
Baby nurses	✗	✓	Nannies
Au pairs	✗	✗	Babysitters

Service Area............... nationwide
WWW.4NANNIES.COM

aupaircare.com
Baby nurses	✗	✗	Nannies
Au pairs	✓	✗	Babysitters

Service Area............... International
WWW.AUPAIRCARE.COM

aupairinamerica.com
Baby nurses	✗	✗	Nannies
Au pairs	✓	✗	Babysitters

Service Area............... International
WWW.AUPAIRINAMERICA.COM

babysitters.com
Baby nurses	✗	✗	Nannies
Au pairs	✗	✓	Babysitters

Service Area............... nationwide
WWW.BABYSITTERS.COM

craigslist.org ★★★★★

"...you can find just about anything on craigslist... good starting point, especially if you don't want to spend a lot of money and are willing to do your own screening... we received at least 50 responses to our 'nanny wanted' ad... helped me find very qualified baby-sitters... includes all major cities in the US..."

Baby nurses	✓	✓	Nannies
Au pairs	✗	✓	Babysitters

WWW.CRAIGSLIST.ORG

enannysource.com
Baby nurses	✗	✓	Nannies
Au pairs	✗	✗	Babysitters

Service Area............... nationwide
WWW.ENANNYSOURCE.COM

findcarenow.com
Baby nurses	✗	✗	Nannies
Au pairs	✗	✓	Babysitters

Service Area............... nationwide
WWW.FINDCARENOW.COM

nanny & babysitter referrals

get-a-sitter.com

Baby nurses .... ✗	✗ .... Nannies
Au pairs .... ✗	✓ .... Babysitters
Service Area .... nationwide	
WWW.GET-A-SITTER.COM	

householdstaffing.com

Baby nurses .... ✓	✓ .... Nannies
Au pairs .... ✗	✗ .... Babysitters
WWW.HOUSEHOLDSTAFFING.COM	

interexchange.org

Baby nurses .... ✗	✗ .... Nannies
Au pairs .... ✓	✗ .... Babysitters
Service Area .... International	
WWW.INTEREXCHANGE.ORG	

nannies4hire.com

Baby nurses .... ✗	✓ .... Nannies
Au pairs .... ✗	✗ .... Babysitters
WWW.NANNIES4HIRE.COM	

nannylocators.com ★★★½☆

"...many listings of local nannies available... I have found that the listings are not always up to date... $100 subscriber fee to respond and contact nannies that have posted... different regions have varying amounts of listings available..."

Baby nurses .... ✗	✓ .... Nannies
Au pairs .... ✗	✗ .... Babysitters
Service Area .... Nationwide	
WWW.NANNYLOCATORS.COM	

sittercity.com ★★★★☆

"...wonderful online resource... an online baby-sitter database filled with mostly college and graduate students looking for baby-sitting and nanny jobs... candidates are not prescreened so you must check references... fee to access the database is $35 plus $5 per month... tends to be more useful for baby-sitters than regular daytime nannies..."

Baby nurses .... ✗	✗ .... Nannies
Au pairs .... ✗	✓ .... Babysitters
Service Area .... nationwide	
WWW.SITTERCITY.COM	

student-sitters.com

Baby nurses .... ✗	✗ .... Nannies
Au pairs .... ✗	✓ .... Babysitters
WWW.STUDENT-SITTERS.COM	

photographers

Greater Boston Area

★★★★★

"lila picks"

- ★ Judith Sargent Photography
- ★ Keirnan Conroy Klosek Photography
- ★ Kiddie Kandids
- ★ Maternal Glory Photography
- ★ Portrait Simple

Ann Elias Dreiker Photography ★★★☆☆
"...she is great with infants as well as older children... she really captured the essence of my children... a great photographer..."
Customer service.................... ❸ $$$...................................... Prices
NORTH EASTON—8 KERRY LN (AT RAMBLEWOOD DR); 508.238.7796

Dari Michele Photography ★★★★★
"...fantastic with kids, reasonably priced, amazing photos... works to your schedule, and will come to your home or meet you at the beach—Dari is wonderful..."
Customer service.................... ❺ $$$...................................... Prices
WWW.DARIMICHELE.COM
BACK BAY—125 NEWBURY ST (AT CLARENDON ST); 617.236.8700

David Fox Photography ★★★★★
"...wonderful talent... will travel to different locations... highly recommended..."
Customer service.................... ❺ $$$$$.................................. Prices
Service AreaMetro Western Greater Boston Area
WWW.DAVIDFOXPHOTOGRAPHER.COM
FRAMINGHAM—59 FOUNTAIN ST (AT MELLEN ST); 508.820.1130; CALL FOR APPT

Foto Factory ★★★★☆
"...no-hassle photos with excellent services... one-on-one sittings with minimum wait... better than Sears/JC Penney... pick your own pictures and packages... black and white or color..."
Customer service.................... ❹ $$.. Prices
Service AreaHaverhill, Marrimack Valley, Greater Boston
WWW.THEFOTOFACTORY.NET
HAVERHILL—19 ESSEX ST (AT WASHINGTON ST); 978.374.3774; CALL FOR APPT; PARKING AT 27 ESSEX ST

Hadi's Studio ★★★★☆

"...beautiful black-and-white photos of newborns... reasonably priced... love the shot of my baby with wings... special Santa picture events... she is very talented, and worth the wait..."

Customer service ❹ $$$ Prices
WWW.HADISTUDIO.COM
WAKEFIELD—249 N AVE (AT ALBION ST); 781.245.4688; CALL FOR APPT

Hilton Photography ★★★★☆

"...professional, flexible staff... spent plenty of time with the kids to get the picture just right... open to your ideas; great working with kids... pictures are a little pricey, but I have had several sets done here and have never been disappointed... don't be afraid to be assertive about what you want..."

Customer service ❺ $$$ Prices
WWW.HILTONPHOTOGRAPHY.COM
FRAMINGHAM—969 CONCORD ST (AT FOSTER DR); 508.875.6164; M-T TH-F 10-6, W 12-8

JCPenney Portrait Studio ★★★★☆

"...don't expect works of art, but they are great for a quick wallet photo... photographers and staff range from great to not so good... a quick portrait with standard props and backdrops... definitely join the portrait club and use coupons... waits are especially long around the holidays, so consider taking your Christmas pictures early... the e-picture option is a time saver... wait time for prints can be up to a month... look for coupons and you'll never have to pay full price..."

Customer service ❹ $$ Prices
WWW.JCPENNEYPORTRAITS.COM
MARLBOROUGH—573 DONALD LYNCH BLVD (AT SOLOMON POND MALL); 508.303.0150; M-SA 10-6:30, SU 11-4:30; MALL PARKING

Judith Sargent Photography ★★★★★

"...Judith Sargent has been photographing children and families for more than 15 years... she came to our house and took the most beautiful black and white photographs of us and our baby... great at provoking wonderful expressions... a professional that's worth every penny..."

Customer service ❺ $$$ Prices
Service Area: Boston area and available for travel
WWW.JCSPHOTOGRAPHY.COM
BOSTON—617.852.8827; CALL FOR APPT

Keirnan Conroy Klosek Photography ★★★★★

"...pictures with Keirnan is going to be a yearly tradition in our family... we had so many photos to choose from... creative without looking posed or staged... photojournalistic style... seeks out and finds the special smiles and expressions of her subjects, young and old... she has a real way with children..."

Customer service ❺ $$$ Prices
Service Area: On location and available for travel with the metro Boston area
WWW.KEIRNANCREATIVE.COM
BROOKLINE—617.461.6643; CALL FOR APPT

Kiddie Kandids ★★★★★

"...good quality photos for all occasions... they made a big effort to get a smile out of my grumpy son... you don't need to make a reservation, just pop in and have the pictures taken... no sitting fee...

photographers take the extra time necessary to get a great shot and they have the cutest props... lots of items to buy with your pictures on them—cups, bags, mouse pads... buy the CD of pictures rather than buying the prints... pictures are available right after the sitting... **"**

Customer service.......................... ❹ $$$... Prices

WWW.KIDDIEKANDIDS.COM

BRAINTREE—450 GROSSMAN DR (AT CENTRAL AVE); 781.380.3506; M-SA 9:30-8:30, SU 11-6

NORTH ATTLEBORO—1255 S WASHINGTON ST (AT ALLEN AVE); 508.699.2346; M-SA 9:30-8, SU 11-6

PEABODY—300 ANDOVER ST (AT RALPH RD); 978.538.1339; M-SA 9:30-8:30, SU 11-6

Kimberly Slater Photography ★★★★☆

"*...Kim does beautiful work and created treasured portraits of our children that we will enjoy for many years to come... on location as well as studio shoots...* **"**

Customer service.......................... ❸ $$$... Prices

Service Area: Greater Boston Area

WWW.KIMBERLYSLATER.COM

CHESTNUT HILL—617.713.0900; CALL FOR APPT

Maternal Glory Photography ★★★★★

"*...Elissa is a great photographer... she came to my home and made my baby and me feel at ease... the shots she captured of us are very special... I will cherish the photos always... I highly recommend her; our pictures are amazing and she is so easy to work with—pure magic... beautiful black-and-white photos that will become treasures... artwork... friendly and makes you feel comfortable during the photo shoot... not overpriced, but not cheap either... she strives to document the maternal connection and succeeds with every shot...* **"**

Customer service.......................... ❺ $$$... Prices

Service Area: Boston, Metro West, North and South Shores

WWW.MATERNALGLORY.COM

MEDFORD—781.396.2535; CALL FOR APPT

Picture People ★★★½☆

"*...this well-known photography chain offers good package deals that get even better with coupons... generally friendly staff despite the often 'uncooperative' little customers... they don't produce super fancy, artistic shots, but you get your pictures in under an hour... reasonable quality for a fast portrait... kind of hit-or-miss quality and customer service...* **"**

Customer service.......................... ❹ $$$... Prices

WWW.PICTUREPEOPLE.COM

BRAINTREE—250 GRANITE ST (AT NORTH ST); 781.843.7001; M-SA 10-10, SU 11-7

BURLINGTON—75 MIDDLESEX TPKE (AT OLD CONCORD RD); 781.270.9443; M-SA 10-10, SU 11-7

DANVERS—100 INDEPENDENCE WY (AT LIBERTY MALL); 978.774.8933; M-SA 10-9:30, SU 11-6; MALL PARKING

HANOVER—1775 WASHINGTON ST (AT HANOVER MALL); 781.826.9788; M-SA 10-9:30, SU 11-6; MALL PARKING

KINGSTON—INDEPENDENCE MALL WAY B110 (AT RT 3); 781.582.1524; M-SA 10-9:30, SU 11-6; MALL PARKING

MARLBOROUGH—580 DONALD LYNCH BLVD (AT SOLOMON POND); 508.486.9336; M-SA 10-9:30, SU 11-7

NORTH ATTLEBORO—360 EMERALD SQUARE (AT S WASHINGTON ST); 508.643.2577; M-SA 10:930, SU 11-6; MALL PARKING

SAUGUS—1277 BROADWAY (AT SQUARE ONE MALL); 781.231.2533; M-SA 10-10, SU 11-6; MALL PARKING

Portrait Simple ★★★★★

"...we love the quick service and competitive prices... we get all our son's pictures done here... gorgeous portraits... much higher quality photos than what you get at the big chains ..."

Customer service ❹ $$$ Prices

WWW.PORTRAITSIMPLE.COM

NATICK—1245 WORCESTER ST (AT NATICK MALL); 508.655.5600; M-SA 10-10, SU 11-6; MALL PARKING

Sears Portrait Studio ★★★☆☆

"...the price is right, but the service and quality are variable... make an appointment to cut down on the wait time... bring your coupons for even better prices... perfect for getting a nice wallet size portrait without spending a fortune... I wish the wait time for prints wasn't so long (two weeks)... the quality and service-orientation of the photographers really vary a lot—some are great, some aren't..."

Customer service ❸ $$ Prices

WWW.SEARSPORTRAIT.COM

BRAINTREE—250 GRANITE ST (AT BRAINTREE HILL PARK); 781.356.6090; M-SA 10-9, SU 11-7

BROCKTON—200 WESTGATE DR (AT REYNOLDS MEMORIAL HWY); 508.897.4269; MALL PARKING

BURLINGTON—1100 BURLINGTON MALL (AT HERITAGE WAY); 781.221.4970; M-SA 9-8:30, SU 11-6; MALL PARKING

CAMBRIDGE—100 CAMBRIDGESIDE PL (AT EDWIN H LAND BLVD); 617.252.3560; M-SA 10-8:30, SU 11-6

DEDHAM—300 PROVIDENCE HWY (AT DEDHAM MALL); 781.320.5140; M W TH-F 10-8:30, SA 10-6; MALL PARKING

HANOVER—1775 WASHINGTON ST (AT HANOVER MALL); 781.829.4125; MALL PARKING

MARLBOROUGH—521 DONALD LYNCH BLVD (AT SOLOMON POND MALL); 508.357.6269; M-F 10-8, 10-6, SA 10-6, SU 11-6; MALL PARKING

NATICK—1235 WORCESTER RD (AT DEAN RD); 508.650.2827; M-SA 10-8, SU 11-6, APPTS RECOMMENDED

NORTH ATTLEBORO—999 S WASHINGTON ST (AT EMERALD SQUARE MALL); 508.699.5148; M-F 9:30-8:30, SA 9-8:30, SU 11-6; MALL PARKING

PEABODY—210 ANDOVER ST UNIT E (AT PROSPECT ST); 978.977.7620; M-SA 9:30-7:30, SU 11-5

SAUGUS—1325 BROADWAY (AT SQUARE ONE MALL); 781.231.4587; M-SA 9:30-8, SU 11-6; PARKING IN FRONT OF BLDG

Target Portrait Studio ★★★☆☆

"...no sitting fee, reasonable prices (especially with the frequent buyers club), a shopping trip for me and the digital preview system for immediate gratification... pretty hit or miss with the photographer—some are patient and others are not... lots of backgrounds to choose from... even with an appointment we often have to wait... we've gotten some great pictures, enough to share with the entire extended family..."

Customer service ❹ $$ Prices

WWW.TARGET.COM

WOBURN—101 COMMERCE WY (AT ATLANTIC AVE); 781.904.0002; M-SA 8-10, SU 8-9; PARKING IN FRONT

Online

clubphoto.com
WWW.CLUBPHOTO.COM

dotphoto.com
WWW.DOTPHOTO.COM

flickr.com
WWW.FLICKR.COM

kodakgallery.com ★★★★½

"...the popular ofoto.com is now under it's wings... very easy to use desktop software to upload your pictures on their site... prints, books, mugs and other photo gifts are reasonably priced and are always shipped promptly... I like that there is no limit to how many pictures and albums you can have on their site..."
WWW.KODAKGALLERY.COM

photoworks.com
WWW.PHOTOWORKS.COM

shutterfly.com ★★★★½

"...I've spent hundreds of dollars with them—it's so easy and the quality of the pictures is great... they use really nice quality photo paper... what a lifesaver—since I store all of my pictures with them I didn't lose any when my computer crashed... most special occasions are taken care of with a personal photo calendar, book or other item with the cutest pictures of our kids... reasonable prices..."
WWW.SHUTTERFLY.COM

snapfish.com ★★★★☆

"...great photo quality and never a problem with storage limits... we love their photo books and flip books—easy to make and fun to give... good service and a good price... we have family that lives all over the country and yet everyone still gets to see and order pictures of our new baby..."
WWW.SNAPFISH.COM

indexes

alphabetical

by city/neighborhood

alphabetical

9 Months 84
A Pea In The Pod 78
Abigail's Children's Boutique...............36
Acton Medical Associates 205
Acton Pharmacy 210
Alewife Brook Community
    Pediatrics 203
Amelia's Kitchen 147
Ames Playground 129
Ann Elias Dreiker Photography 228
Anna Jaques Hospital (Birth Center) ...174
Anna Jaques Hospital (Women's
    Health Care) 192
Anna's Taqueria 157
Applebee's Neighborhood Grill 147, 157, 166
April Cornell 14, 21, 36, 52
Arena Farms 109
Arlington Center, The.........................181
Arlington Pediatrics Associates PC 203
Arlington Restaurant & Diner 148
Arnold Arboretum..............................126
Arnold's Gymnastics Academy 118
Artbeat 102
Association of Labor Assistants &
    Childbirth Educators (ALACE)..........174
Atkinson Pool.....................................109
Auburndale Playground (The Cove) 133
Babies R Us 21, 37, 52, 210
Baby Belle 14
Baby Boot Camp 181
Baby Depot At Burlington Coat
    Factory 22, 37, 53, 80, 84, 89
Baby Furniture Warehouse Store 22, 53
Baby Matters............................. 192, 193
Baby Place, The 37
BabyGap/GapKids 15, 22, 23, 38, 53
Babystyle.......................... 23, 38, 80, 85
Baker School Playground 133
Bambini Design 38
Barber Bros 39
Barefoot Books.....................................23
Barking Crab 140
Barn 39
Barnes & Noble ... 98, 102, 109, 110, 118
Barneys New York 39
Beacon Light Yoga 178
Beanstalk Consignment........................54
Bella..40
Bellini..40
Benjarong Restaurant 158
Bennigan's Grill & Tavern 140
Bertucci's Brick Oven Pizzeria ... 140, 141, 148, 158, 166, 167
Best Fed Associates 174, 210
Beverly Hospital (Parent Education
    Department) 193
Blissful Monkey Yoga Studio 178

Blue Hills Trailside Museum................ 119
Blue Ribbon Bar-B-Q 148, 158
Boca Grande Restaurant 158
Bombay Kids.. 54
Bonkers Fun House 103
Bonpoint 15
Border Cafe 149
Borders Books............. 98, 103, 110, 119
Boston Athenaeum............................... 99
Boston Baby........................... 23, 40, 54
Boston Center For Adult Education 178
Boston Children's Museum 99
Boston Common 126
Boston Medical Center (Breastfeeding
    Center)... 193
Boston Nanny Centre.......................... 222
Boston Nature Center and Wildlife
    Sanctuary 119
Boston Sports Club 181
Boston Sports Clubs........................... 110
Boston's Best Baby Sitters/Nannies 222
Bounceback Fitness.................... 179, 185
Boy Scout Park 129
Brackett School Playground 129
Bradley Method, The 193
Brattle Theatre 103
Brewer/Burroughs Tot Lot 126
Brigham And Women's Hospital 210
Brigham And Women's Hospital
    (Parent & Childbirth Education)174, 193
Brigham's 141
Brigham's Inc 149, 159, 167
Brook Alewife Community Pdtrcs....... 203
Brown Sugar Cafe 141
Brujito's Play Cafe.............................. 103
Bugaboo Creek Steak House..... 149, 159, 167
Build-A-Bear Workshop 104, 119
Bulotsky, Alan MD 207
Burlington Mall................................... 149
Butterfly Place At Papillon 111
Cabot's Ice Cream 159
Cafe Barada.. 150
California Pizza Kitchen 141, 150, 160
Callahan State Park............................. 133
Callery Park 129
Calliope 24
Cambridge Birth Center, The 174, 194
Cambridge Center For Adult
    Education 194
Cambridge Common 130
Cambridge Family Health................... 203
Cambridge Medical Supply 211
Cambridge Pediatrics 203
Cape Ann Pediatricians 203
Carol Ann's 55
Carter's 40, 55
Caryl Park 137

index alphabetical

Casa De Moda Clothing Dance & Gifts 24
Casey Park 134
Casey's Diner 160
Castle Island & Fort Independence 126
Center Pediatrics 205
Centre Pediatric Associates 205
Centre Street Cafe 141
Chamberi Shoes 24
Changing Habits Diaper Service 216
Charles River Medical Associates 205
Charley's 142
Charlie's Sandwich Shoppe 142
Cheddars Pizzeria 150
Cheesecake Factory, The 150, 160
Children's Medical Office of North Andover 203
Children's Museum 120
Children's Orchard 25, 41, 55
Children's Place, The ... 15, 25, 41, 55, 56
Christopher Columbus Waterfront Park 127
Chuck E Cheese's 104, 111, 120
City of Cambridge Center For Families 194
Clayroom 99, 104, 111, 120
Clyde's Roadhouse Bar & Grille 167
Cochituate State Park 134
Cold Spring Park 134
Compass Healthcare 211
Concord Toy Shoppe 42
Coolidge Corner Theatre 111
Copley Flair 15, 16
Costco 25, 42, 56
Creative Movement Arts Center 120
Crossroads Cafe 160
Curious George Goes To Wordsworth 26
Cuttery, The 218
Dairy Joy 160
Dana Park 130
Danehy Park 130
Dari Michele Photography 228
David Fox Photography 228
De Cordova Museum & Sculpture Park 112
Dede's Dide's Diaper Service 216
Dedham Medical Associates 207
Defazio Tot Lot 137
Deluxe Town Diner 161
Destination Maternity 85
Discovery Museums, The 112
Doulas Of North America (DONA) 174
Dowd Medical 203
Dowd Medical Associates 203
Doyles Cafe 142
Drumlin Farm Wildlife Sanctuary 112
DW Field Park 137
Earthsong Yoga Center (Itsy Bitsy Yoga) 185
Emerson Hospital (Tender Beginnings) 194
Fairbanks Community Center Playground 134
Families First Parenting Programs 194
Family Music Makers 99, 105, 112, 120
Family Rhythms Inc 205
Fantastic Sams 218
Fillipello Park 134
Finagle A Bagel 161
Firefly's 161
First Connections 195
Fitness Etcetera For Women 185
Foot Stock 42
Foto Factory 228
Framingham Pediatrics 205
Francis William Bird Park 137
Franklin Park Zoo 99
Frida Bee 26
Friendly's 142, 151, 161, 167, 168
Friendly's at Hanover Mall 168
Friendship Park 137
Friendship Park Playground 130
Frozen Freddies 168
Fuddruckers 151
Full Moon 152
Gap Maternity 81, 85, 89
Garden City Pediatrics 203
Garden In The Woods 113
Garden Of Eden 142
Georges Island 127
Gilchrist, Michael MD 203
Ginn Field 130
Good Days Restaurant 168
Goodhearts 26
Grand Buffet 168
Great Brook Farm State Park 134
Great Cuts 218, 219
Green Planet 42, 113, 186
Gym Fit 113
Gymboree 16, 27, 43, 56
Gymboree Play & Music 105, 113, 121
Gymnastics Academy Of Boston 105
H & M 16, 78
Habitat Education Center and Wildlife Sanctuary 113
Hadi's Studio-Art-Photography 229
Haircuts Ltd 219
Hancock Park 130
Hard Rock Cafe 143
Harvard Student Agencies Inc 222
Harvard Vanguard Medical Associates 204, 211
Harvard Vanguard Medical Center Yoga 182
Haskell Tot Lot Playground 135
Haus 27
Head To Toes 218
Healthworks Fitness Center 179, 182, 186
Henry Bear's Park 27, 43
Hill House 100
Hilton Photography 229
Holliston Pediatric Group 205

www.lilaguide.com

Hourigan, Philip MD 207
Howard King Pediatrcis 205
Hudson Public Library 113
In Search Of Nanny Inc 223
Inman Pharmacy..................................211
Isis Maternity............ 43, 57, 85, 90, 114,
    121, 174, 175, 186, 189, 195,
    211
It Rains Fishes 152
Jacadi..16, 44
Jamaica Pond 127
Janie And Jack.......................................44
Jasper White's Summer Shack ... 143, 152
Jazzercise 182
JCPenney..57, 90
JCPenney Portrait Studio 229
Jenkyns, Patricia 182
Jewish Community Center 105, 114, 121
Jewish Family & Children's Services 195
Joe Fish Seafood Restaurant 152
Joe Moakley Park 127
Joe's American Bar & Grill 143, 152,
    162, 169
John Brewer's Tavern 162
Johnny D's Uptown Restaurant 153
Johnny Rockets 153, 162, 169
Johnny's Luncheonette........................162
Jolles, Jon MD......................................207
Jordan's Furniture..................... 28, 44, 57
JP Boing's Toy Shop...............................17
Judith Sargent Photography 229
Karma Yoga Studio 183
Kaya Restaurant 143
KB Toys 28, 44, 45, 57, 58
Keirnan Conroy Klosek
    Photography....................................229
Kenzie Kids 45
Kid To Kid 45
Kid's Foot Locker 45, 58
Kiddie Kandids 230
Kids Club Fun Land 121
Kids En Vogue..28
Kids Place, The 114
Kids Playground 105
Kids R Kids 17
Kidz Planet Gymnastics........................121
Kimberly Slater Photography 230
King & I...144
Kingsley Park.......................................130
Klassy Kids 28
Kohl's.................... 29, 46, 58, 81, 86, 90
La Leche League..................................175
Lactation Care......................................211
Lactation Liaison..................................212
Lady Grace 81, 86, 90
Lake Quannapowitt..............................131
Lamaze International...........................195
Larz Anderson Park 135
Laughing Dog Yoga 186
Lawrence General Hospital
    (Lactation Support) 195
Learning Tree Store 29

Lester Harry's................................. 17, 29
Letourneau's Pharmacy....................... 212
Lexington Pediatrics 205
Little Gym, The 106, 122
Living Yoga 186
Longhorn Steakhouse 144
Longwood Pediatrics........................... 202
Lynch Park 131
MA Office Of Child Care Services
    (OCCS)... 223
Macy's................... 18, 30, 46, 59, 79, 81,
    82, 86, 91
Made By Me Paint Your Own Pottery. 106
Magic Beans 46
Malden Family Health Center............. 204
Marblehead Toy Shop, The 30
Marcie & Me............................... 114, 122
Mario's Salon...................................... 219
Mary Baker Eddy Library 100
Mass General Gift Shop 18
Massachusetts General Hospital
    (Mother-Child Center).................... 196
Massage Works 189
Maternal Glory Photography.............. 230
Maternal Outreach 196
Maxima Art Center 47
Maxima Gift Center 30
McCormick & Schmicks 144
Medford Family Network 196
Melrose Common 131
Melrose-Wakefield Hospital
    (Breastfeeding Support Center) 212
Melrose-Wakefield Hospital (Family
    Education)............................... 183, 196
Memorial-Spaulding Elementary
    School Playground......................... 135
Merrimack Valley Mothers of Twins ... 196
Metrowest Medical Center (Women's
    Resource Center)............................ 197
Mgh Revere Health Care Center 204
Michelson's Shoes 47, 59
Millennium Park................................. 127
Mimi Maternity 82, 86, 91
Minute Man Trail 131
Mocha Moms 197
Mom's Lunch Boston 197
Mommy Chic Maternity 87
MOMS Club 197
Motherhood Maternity 79, 82, 87, 91
Mothers and More............................. 198
Mount Auburn Hospital (Parent
    Childbirth Education Office) 198
Mr Bartley's Burger Cottage............... 153
Mud Puddle Toys 31
Mulberry Road 18
Museum Of Science 100
Music For Aardvarks And Other
    Mammals....................................... 100
Music Together.......... 101, 106, 115, 122
My Gym Children's Fitness Center 107,
    115, 123
My Sister & I Restaurant..................... 169

index alphabetical

Myrtle Street Playground 127
Mystic River Yoga 183
Nanny On The Net, A 223
Nara Park & Swim Area 135
Needham Pediatrics 207
Needham Youth Commission 223
Neillio's 153
New England Aquarium 101
Newcomb Farms Restaurant 169
Newton Wellesley Hospital
  (Wellness Center & Childbirth
  Education) 187
Ninety Nine Restaurant 153, 154, 163, 170
No Name Restaurant 144
North River Collaborative 198
North Shore Children's Museum 107
North Suburban Family Network 198
Norwood Hospital (Me & My Baby) 198
Not Your Average Joe's 154, 163, 170
Nutshell 59
Oilily 18
Old Navy 19, 31, 47, 59, 60, 79, 82, 83, 92
One Stop Fun Inc 115
OrgagaGanics 199
OshKosh B'Gosh 60
Panera Bread 154, 155
Parents In A Pinch 224
Parents' Pride 60
Parish Cafe 144
Patriot Pediatrics 205
Payless Shoe Source 19, 31
Peabody Pediatric Healthcare
  Associates 204
Pediatric Associates Inc of Brockton 207
Pediatric Associates of Wellesley 205
Pediatric Healthcare 207
Pediatricians, Inc. 204
Pediatrics At Newton-wellesley 205
Pediatrics West 206
Penguin Park 131
Percy Rideout Playground 135
Periwinkles 48
Perpetual Motion 107
Perrin Park 135
Perry Park 137
Petit Bateau 19
Philip's Total Care Salon 219
Piccadilly Pub 170
Picco Pizza & Ice Cream Co 145
Picture People 230, 231
Pink Dolly 83
Planet Gymnastics 116
Pope John Paul II Park 128
Port O'Call Exchange 31
Porter Exchange Restaurants 155
Portrait Simple 231
Pottery Barn Kids 32, 48
Priceless Kids 32, 48, 60, 61
Puppet Showplace Theatre 116
Quincy Family Network
  (Community Care for Kids) 199
Rainbow Kids 61
Rainforest Cafe 155
Raymond Park 131
Red Wagon 20
Reel Moms (Loews Theatres) 101, 107
Renee's Cafe 155
Right Start, The 48, 212
Ringgold Park (Hanson Street Play
  Area) 128
Robbins Farm/Skyline Park 132
Roseann's 61
Roslindale Pediatrics Associates 202
Ruby Tuesday 163, 171
Rugged Bear 32, 49, 61
Saillant, Meredith MD 206
Saints Memorial Medical Center
  (Family Birth Unit) 183, 199
Saints Memorial Medical Center
  (Lactation Services) 175
Salem Hospital (Birth Place) 199
Salem Hospital (Lactation Services) 175
Salem Willows Park 107
Sears 33, 49, 62, 83, 87, 92
Sears Portrait Studio 231
Serenity Yoga & Wellness 187
Shakti Yoga & Healing Art 183
Shedd Park 132
Sheep Pasture 123
Shoe Market Kids 62
Showcase Cinema (Baby Pictures) 123
Simonds Park 132
Skenderian Apothecary 212
Smith Farm 123
Snip-its Haircuts For Kids 219
Somerville Pediatric Svc 204
Sonsie Restaurant 145
South Boston Community Health
  Center 202
South Shore Hospital (Women's
  Family Health) 199, 212
Southboro Medical Group 206
Southern Jamaica Plain Health Center 202
Spy Pond Playground 132
Stellabella Toys 33
Stone Zoo 108
Stoughton St Park 132
Strasburg Children 62
Stride Rite Shoes 33, 50, 63
Stroller Fit 179
Stroller Strides 179, 180, 184, 187
Styles 'n Smiles 220
Sullivan Park 132
Sullivan's Medical Supply 213
Summer Placement Consultants 224
Supercuts 220
Swan Boats at the Public Garden 101
Sweet William 63
Sylvan Street Grille 155
Talbots Kids 20, 34, 50, 63
Target 20, 34, 50, 64, 79, 83, 88, 92
Target Portrait Studio 231

Texas Road House	171
TGI Friday's	145, 156, 163, 171
Thorton's Restaurant	145
Tia's On The Waterfront	145
Titus Sparrow Park	128
Toraya Restaurant	156
Town Spa Pizza	171
Toy Box	64
Toys R Us	20, 34, 35, 51, 64
Tremont 647	146
Tufts Library Park	138
Tufts-New England Medical Center (Childbirth Education)	175, 199
Tumble Kids USA	108, 116
Uno Chicago Grill	156
Vidalia's Truck Stop	164
Village Baby	51
Village Barber	220
Village Smokehouse	164
Village Toy Shop	64
Vinny T's Of Boston	146, 156, 164, 172
Walden Pond	136
Wards Berry Farm	124
Warmlines Parent Resources	116, 200
Warren-Manning State Forest	132
Watch City Brewing Co	164
Watertown Family Network	117, 200
Wellspace	180
Westbury Farms	172
Weston Pediatric Physicians	206
Westwood Mansfield Pediatrics	207
Whimsy	51
Winchester Hospital (Lactation Services)	175
Winthrop Square Park	136
Woburn Pediatric Associates	204
Wow!	187, 189
XerStroll	184
YMCA	108, 117, 124, 188, 190
Yoga East	184
Yoga In Harvard Square	184
Yoga Mandala	184
Zaftigs Delicatessen	165

by city/neighborhood

Acton
Acton Medical Associates 205
Acton Pharmacy 210
Benjarong Restaurant 158
Crossroads Cafe 160
Discovery Museums, The 112
Friendly's 161
Gymboree Play & Music 113
Music Together 115
Nara Park & Swim Area 135
Planet Gymnastics 116
Priceless Kids 48
Rugged Bear 49

Allston/Brighton
Beacon Light Yoga 178

Amesbury
Friendly's 150

Andover
Bertucci's Brick Oven Pizzeria 148
Friendly's 150
Letourneau's Pharmacy 212
Music Together 106
Ninety Nine Restaurant 153
Penguin Park 131
Rugged Bear 32

Arlington
Alewife Brook Community Pediatrics 203
Arlington Center, The 181
Arlington Pediatrics Associates PC 203
Arlington Restaurant & Diner 148
Artbeat 102
Blue Ribbon Bar-B-Q 148
Brackett School Playground 129
Brigham's Inc 149
Brook Alewife Community Pdtrcs 203
Friendly's 151
Henry Bear's Park 27
Jazzercise 182
Jenkyns, Patricia 182
Maxima Gift Center 30
Minute Man Trail 131
Music Together 106
Neillio's 153
Not Your Average Joe's 154
Pink Dolly 84
Robbins Farm/Skyline Park 132
Spy Pond Playground 132
Toraya Restaurant 156

Attleboro
Chuck E Cheese's 120
Friendly's 167
Music Together 122

Piccadilly Pub 170
Ruby Tuesday 170

Auburndale
Auburndale Playground (The Cove) 133
Clayroom 111
Music Together 115

Avon
Costco 56
Jordan's Furniture 57

Back Bay
9 Months 78
A Pea In The Pod 78
Baby Matters 192
BabyGap/GapKids 15
Barnes & Noble 98
Bertucci's Brick Oven Pizzeria . 140, 141
Bonpoint 15
Boston Center For Adult Education 178
Brown Sugar Cafe 141
California Pizza Kitchen 141
Charley's 142
Copley Flair 15
Dari Michele Photography 228
Family Music Makers 99
Gymboree 16
Hard Rock Cafe 143
Healthworks Fitness Center 179
Jacadi 16
Jasper White's Summer Shack 143
Joe's American Bar & Grill 143
Kaya Restaurant 143
Lester Harry's 17
Longhorn Steakhouse 144
Mary Baker Eddy Library 100
Maternal Outreach 196
Mulberry Road 18
Oilily 18
Parish Cafe 144
Petit Bateau 19
Picco Pizza & Ice Cream Co 145
Sonsie Restaurant 145
Swan Boats at the Public Garden ... 101
Talbots Kids 20
TGI Friday's 145
Thorton's Restaurant 145
Titus Sparrow Park 128
Vinny T's Of Boston 146

Beacon Hill/West End
King & I 144
Mass General Gift Shop 18
Massachusetts General Hospital (Mother-Child Center) 196
Museum Of Science 100
Myrtle Street Playground 128
Red Wagon 20

www.lilaguide.com

Bedford
- Friendly's 161
- Music Together 115
- Patriot Pediatrics 205
- Rugged Bear 49
- Serenity Yoga & Wellness 187

Bellingham
- BabyGap/GapKids 38
- Barnes & Noble 109
- Old Navy 47

Belmont
- Bella 40
- Brigham's Inc 159
- Habitat Education Center and Wildlife Sanctuary 113
- Music Together 115

Beverly
- Bertucci's Brick Oven Pizzeria 148
- Beverly Hospital (Parent Education Department) 193
- Casa De Moda Clothing Dance & Gifts 24
- Garden City Pediatrics 203
- In Search Of Nanny Inc 223
- Lynch Park 131
- Not Your Average Joe's 154
- Rugged Bear 32

Billerica
- Baby Depot At Burlington Coat Factory 22, 81
- Children's Orchard 25
- Friendly's 151
- Ninety Nine Restaurant 153
- Warren-Manning State Forest 132

Boston
- Association of Labor Assistants & Childbirth Educators (ALACE) 174
- Borders Books 98
- Boston's Best Baby Sitters/Nannies 222
- Bounceback Fitness 179
- Bradley Method, The 193
- Doulas of North America (DONA) 174
- Georges Island 127
- Hill House 100
- Judith Sargent Photography 229
- La Leche League 175
- Lamaze International 195
- Longwood Pediatrics 202
- Mocha Moms 197
- Mom's Lunch Boston 197
- Mothers and More 198
- Music For Aardvarks And Other Mammals 100
- Nanny On The Net, A 223
- Ringgold Park (Hanson Street Play Area) 128
- South Boston Community Health Center 202
- Stroller Fit 179

Boxford
- Boy Scout Park 129

Braintree
- Babies R Us 52, 210
- Baby Depot At Burlington Coat Factory 53, 89
- Baby Furniture Warehouse Store 53
- Baby Matters 192
- BabyGap/GapKids 53
- Barnes & Noble 118
- Bertucci's Brick Oven Pizzeria 166
- Borders Books 119
- Boston Baby 54
- Bugaboo Creek Steak House 167
- Build-A-Bear Workshop 119
- Children's Place, The 55
- Gap Maternity 89
- Gymboree 56
- Joe's American Bar & Grill 169
- Johnny Rockets 169
- KB Toys 57, 58
- Kid's Foot Locker 58
- Kiddie Kandids 230
- Lady Grace 90
- Macy's 59, 91
- Massage Works 189
- Mimi Maternity 91
- Music Together 122
- Ninety Nine Restaurant 169
- Picture People 230
- Sears 62, 92
- Sears Portrait Studio 231
- Stride Rite Shoes 63
- Talbots Kids 63

Bridgewater
- Friendly's 167
- Music Together 122
- My Sister & I Restaurant 169
- Ninety Nine Restaurant 169

Brighton
- Jewish Community Center 114
- YMCA 117, 188

Brockton
- Bertucci's Brick Oven Pizzeria 166
- Bulotsky, Alan MD 207
- Children's Place, The 56
- DW Field Park 137
- Friendly's 168
- KB Toys 58
- Macy's 59, 91
- Old Navy 59, 92
- Pediatric Healthcare 207
- Rainbow Kids 61
- Sears 62, 92

240

participate in our survey at

Sears Portrait Studio	231
Texas Road House	171
Toys R Us	64

Brookline

Anna's Taqueria	157
BabyGap/GapKids	38
Baker School Playground	133
Bambini Design	38
Barnes & Noble	110
Bertucci's Brick Oven Pizzeria	158
Boca Grande Restaurant	158
Centre Pediatric Associates	205
Children's Place, The	41
Clayroom	111
Coolidge Corner Theatre	111
Family Music Makers	112
Great Cuts	218
Healthworks Fitness Center	186
Henry Bear's Park	43
Isis Maternity	43, 86, 114, 174, 186, 195, 211
Keirnan Conroy Klosek Photography	229
Lady Grace	86
Larz Anderson Park	135
Magic Beans	46
Music Together	115
Parents In A Pinch	224
Puppet Showplace Theatre	116
Saillant, Meredith MD	206
Stride Rite Shoes	50
Stroller Strides	187
Village Baby	51
Village Smokehouse	164
Vinny T's Of Boston	164
Winthrop Square Park	136
Zaftigs Delicatessen	165

Burlington

BabyGap/GapKids	22
Babystyle	23, 81
Barnes & Noble	102
Brigham's Inc	149
Build-A-Bear Workshop	104
Burlington Mall	149
Children's Place, The	25
Chuck E Cheese's	104
Gymboree	27
Gymboree Play & Music	105
Johnny Rockets	153
KB Toys	28
Kohl's	29, 82
Macy's	30, 82
Mimi Maternity	83
Motherhood Maternity	83
Old Navy	31
Panera Bread	154
Picture People	230
Pottery Barn Kids	32
Rainforest Cafe	155
Sears	33, 84
Sears Portrait Studio	231
Simonds Park	132
Snip-its Haircuts For Kids	219
Stride Rite Shoes	33
Stroller Strides	184
Talbots Kids	34

Cambridge

April Cornell	21
BabyGap/GapKids	22
Barefoot Books	23
Bertucci's Brick Oven Pizzeria	148
Border Cafe	149
Borders Books	103
Boston Sports Club	181
Brattle Theatre	103
Cafe Barada	150
California Pizza Kitchen	150
Calliope	24
Cambridge Birth Center, The	174, 194
Cambridge Center For Adult Education	194
Cambridge Common	130
Cambridge Family Health	203
Cambridge Medical Supply	211
Cambridge Pediatrics	203
Cheddars Pizzeria	150
Cheesecake Factory, The	150
Children's Place, The	25
City of Cambridge Center For Families	194
Curious George Goes To Wordsworth	26
Dana Park	130
Danehy Park	130
Families First Parenting Programs	194
Family Music Makers	105
Frida Bee	26
Full Moon	151
Gap Maternity	82
Great Cuts	218
Gymnastics Academy Of Boston	105
Hancock Park	130
Harvard Student Agencies Inc	222
Harvard Vanguard Medical Associates	203
Healthworks Fitness Center	182
Henry Bear's Park	27
Inman Pharmacy	211
Jasper White's Summer Shack	152
Karma Yoga Studio	183
KB Toys	28
Kingsley Park	130
Made By Me Paint Your Own Pottery	106
Motherhood Maternity	83
Mount Auburn Hospital (Parent Childbirth Education Office)	198
Mr Bartley's Burger Cottage	153
Music Together	106
Ninety Nine Restaurant	153
Old Navy	31, 83

Payless Shoe Source 31
Porter Exchange Restaurants 155
Raymond Park 131
Sears 33, 84
Sears Portrait Studio 231
Skenderian Apothecary 212
Stellabella Toys 33
Supercuts 220
Toys R Us 34
YMCA 108
Yoga In Harvard Square 184

Canton

Bertucci's Brick Oven Pizzeria 166
Grand Buffet 168
Gymboree Play & Music 121
Music Together 122
Ninety Nine Restaurant 170
Snip-its Haircuts For Kids 219

Carlisle

Great Brook Farm State Park 134
Music Together 115

Chelmsford

Bertucci's Brick Oven Pizzeria 148
Friendly's 151
Friendship Park Playground 130
Gilchrist, Michael MD 203
Harvard Vanguard Medical
  Associates 204
KB Toys 28
Kohl's 29, 82
Music Together 106

Chestnut Hill

BabyGap/GapKids 38
Babystyle 38, 85
Barnes & Noble 110
Barneys New York 39
Bertucci's Brick Oven Pizzeria 158
Borders Books 110
Bounceback Fitness 185
Cheesecake Factory, The 160
Children's Orchard 41
Gymboree 43
Janie And Jack 44
Kenzie Kids 45
Kimberly Slater Photography 230
Music Together 115
Pottery Barn Kids 48
Rugged Bear 49
Snip-its Haircuts For Kids 219

Cohasset

Shoe Market Kids 62

Concord

Arena Farms 109
Concord Toy Shoppe 42
Emerson Hospital (Tender
  Beginnings) 194

First Connections 195
Foot Stock 42
Music Together 115
Percy Rideout Playground 135
Walden Pond 136

Danvers

Applebee's Neighborhood Grill 147
Boston Baby 23
Children's Orchard 25
Chuck E Cheese's 104
Costco 25
Great Cuts 218
Kohl's 29, 82
Little Gym, The 106
Music Together 106
Ninety Nine Restaurant 153
Old Navy 31
Picture People 230
Supercuts 220
Target 34, 84
TGI Friday's 156
Vinny T's Of Boston 156

Dedham

Bugaboo Creek Steak House 167
Costco 56
Dedham Medical Associates 207
Friendly's 168
Joe's American Bar & Grill 169
Music Together 122
My Gym Children's Fitness Center .. 123
Old Navy 59, 92
Sears 62, 92
Sears Portrait Studio 231
TGI Friday's 171
Toys R Us 64
Vinny T's Of Boston 171

Deerfield

Changing Habits Diaper Service 216

Dorchester

Old Navy 19, 79
Target 20, 80
Castle Island & Fort Independence .. 127
Franklin Park Zoo 99
Pope John Paul II Park 128
Toys R Us 20

Dover

Caryl Park 137

Downtown

April Cornell 14
BabyGap/GapKids 15
Barnes & Noble 98
Bennigan's Grill & Tavern 140
Bertucci's Brick Oven Pizzeria 141
Boston Athenaeum 99
Boston Children's Museum 99
Boston Common 126

242   participate in our survey at

Boston Medical Center
(Breastfeeding Center) 193
Brigham's 141
Children's Place, The 15
Copley Flair 16
Cuttery, The 218
H & M 16, 79
Jewish Family & Children's
Services 195
MA Office Of Child Care Services
(OCCS) 223
Macy's 18, 79
McCormick & Schmicks 144
Motherhood Maternity 79
New England Aquarium 101
Payless Shoe Source 19
Reel Moms (Loews Theatres) 101
Tufts-New England Medical
Center (Childbirth Education). 175, 199

East Boston

Payless Shoe Source 19

East Bridgewater

Music Together 122
Smith Farm 123

East Walpole

Francis William Bird Park 137
KB Toys 58
Kohl's 58, 90

Easton

Clayroom 120
Ninety Nine Restaurant 170

Everett

Babies R Us 21, 210
Chuck E Cheese's 104
Costco 25
Old Navy 31, 83
Panera Bread 154
Target 34, 84
TGI Friday's 156

Fenway/Kenmore

Bertucci's Brick Oven Pizzeria 141
Brigham And Women's Hospital 210
Brigham And Women's Hospital
(Parent & Childbirth Education) 174, 193
Compass Healthcare 211

Foxborough

Head To Toes 218

Framingham

Babies R Us 37, 210
Barnes & Noble 110
Bertucci's Brick Oven Pizzeria 158
Borders Books 110
Bugaboo Creek Steak House 159
Callahan State Park 133

Children's Orchard 41
David Fox Photography 228
Framingham Pediatrics 205
Friendly's 161
Garden In The Woods 113
Gymboree Play & Music 113
Hilton Photography 229
Jewish Community Center 114
Joe's American Bar & Grill 162
Kohl's 46, 86
Macy's 46, 87
Metrowest Medical Center
(Women's Resource Center) 197
Music Together 115
My Gym Children's Fitness Center .. 115
Old Navy 47
Ruby Tuesday 163
Snip-its Haircuts For Kids 219
Southboro Medical Group 206
Stroller Strides 187
Styles 'n Smiles 220
Supercuts 220
Target 50, 88
TGI Friday's 163
Toys R Us 51
Whimsy 51
YMCA 117, 188

Gloucester

Cape Ann Pediatricians 203
Friendly's 151
Port O'Call Exchange 31

Groton

Lactation Liaison 212
Music Together 106

Hanover

Borders Books 119
Children's Place, The 56
Friendly's 168
Joe's American Bar & Grill 169
Jolles, Jon MD 207
KB Toys 58
Kid's Foot Locker 58
Motherhood Maternity 91
Old Navy 60
Picture People 230
Rugged Bear 61
Sears Portrait Studio 231
Toy Box 64

Haverhill

Foto Factory 228
Friendly's 151
Ninety Nine Restaurant 154

Hingham

Barnes & Noble 118
Beanstalk Consignment 54
Bertucci's Brick Oven Pizzeria 166
Bombay Kids 54

Brigham's Inc 167
Carol Ann's 55
Kohl's 58, 90
Music Together 122
Ninety Nine Restaurant 170
Old Navy 60
Sweet William 63
Talbots Kids 63

Holbrook
Friendly's 168

Hudson
Hudson Public Library 113
Ninety Nine Restaurant 163

Jamaica Plain
Arnold Arboretum 126
Blissful Monkey Yoga Studio 178
Brewer/Burroughs Tot Lot 126
Centre Street Cafe 141
Clayroom 99
Doyles Cafe 142
Jamaica Pond 127
JP Boing's Toy Shop 17
Music Together 101
Roslindale Pediatrics Associates 202
Southern Jamaica Plain Health
Center 202
Stroller Strides 179

Kingston
BabyGap/GapKids 53
Borders Books 119
Build-A-Bear Workshop 119
Kid's Foot Locker 58
Motherhood Maternity 91
My Gym Children's Fitness
Center 123
Old Navy 60, 92
Picture People 230
Sears 62, 92
Target 64, 92

Lawrence
Friendly's 151
Lawrence General Hospital
(Lactation Support) 195

Lexington
Baby Matters 193
Bertucci's Brick Oven Pizzeria 158
Boston Sports Clubs 110
Friendly's 161
Lexington Pediatrics 205
Michelson's Shoes 47
Vinny T's Of Boston 164

Lincoln
De Cordova Museum & Sculpture
Park 112
Drumlin Farm Wildlife Sanctuary 112

Lowell
Callery Park 129
Chuck E Cheese's 104
Haus 27
Music Together 106
Ninety Nine Restaurant 154
Perpetual Motion 107
Saints Memorial Medical Center
(Family Birth Unit) 183, 199
Saints Memorial Medical Center
(Lactation Services) 175
Shedd Park 132

Lynn
Ames Playground 129

Lynnfield
Ninety Nine Restaurant 154

Malden
Applebee's Neighborhood Grill 147
Lady Grace 82
Malden Family Health Center 204

Manchester-by-the-Sea
Summer Placement Consultants 224

Mansfield
Arnold's Gymnastics Academy 118
Bertucci's Brick Oven Pizzeria 166
Westwood Mansfield Pediatrics 207

Marblehead
Jewish Community Center 105
Lester Harry's 29
Marblehead Toy Shop, The 30
Mud Puddle Toys 31
Music Together 106

Marlborough
Bertucci's Brick Oven Pizzeria 158
Borders Books 110
Children's Place, The 41
Earthsong Yoga Center (Itsy Bitsy
Yoga) 185
Firefly's 161
JCPenney Portrait Studio 229
KB Toys 44
Motherhood Maternity 88
Music Together 115
Picture People 230
Ruby Tuesday 163
Sears Portrait Studio 231
Stroller Strides 187
TGI Friday's 163

Mattapan
Boston Nature Center and Wildlife
Sanctuary 119
Brigham's Inc 167

Medfield

Friendly's 161
Gymboree Play & Music 113

Medford

Bertucci's Brick Oven Pizzeria 148
Clayroom 104
Friendly's 151
Great Cuts 218
Harvard Vanguard Medical
Associates 204
Kohl's 29, 82
Maternal Glory Photography 230
Medford Family Network 196
Music Together 106
Mystic River Yoga 183
Toys R Us 34

Melrose

Gymboree Play & Music 105
Klassy Kids 28
Melrose Common 131
Melrose-Wakefield Hospital
(Breastfeeding Support Center) 212
Melrose-Wakefield Hospital
(Family Education) 183, 196
North Suburban Family Network 198

Methuen

Borders Books 103
Bugaboo Creek Steak House 149
Chuck E Cheese's 104
Friendly's 151
KB Toys 28
Merrimack Valley Mothers of
Twins 196
Not Your Average Joe's 154
Old Navy 31, 84
Reel Moms (Loews Theatres) 107
TGI Friday's 156

Milford

Applebee's Neighborhood Grill 157
Bugaboo Creek Steak House 159
Children's Orchard 41
Holliston Pediatric Group 205
Ninety Nine Restaurant 163
Target 50, 88

Milton

Blue Hills Trailside Museum 119
Music Together 122
Newcomb Farms Restaurant 169
Nutshell 59

Natick

Baby Depot At Burlington Coat
Factory 37, 85
Baby Place, The 37
BabyGap/GapKids 38
Barber Bros 39
California Pizza Kitchen 159
Casey's Diner 160
Charles River Medical Associates 205
Children's Orchard 41
Children's Place, The 41
Chuck E Cheese's 111
Clayroom 111
Cochituate State Park 134
Destination Maternity 86
Family Rhythms Inc 205
Fitness Etcetera For Women 185
Friendly's 161
Gym Fit 113
Gymboree 43
Haircuts Ltd 219
Janie And Jack 44
Johnny Rockets 162
Jordan's Furniture 44
KB Toys 45
Kid To Kid 45
Macy's 46, 87
Mimi Maternity 87
Motherhood Maternity 88
Music Together 115
Planet Gymnastics 116
Portrait Simple 231
Pottery Barn Kids 48
Right Start, The 48, 212
Sears 49, 88
Sears Portrait Studio 231
Stride Rite Shoes 50
Stroller Strides 187
Talbots Kids 50
Vinny T's Of Boston 164

Needham

Baby Matters 193
Bertucci's Brick Oven Pizzeria 166
Clayroom 120
Creative Movement Arts Center 120
Defazio Tot Lot 137
Family Music Makers 120
Friendly's 168
Isis Maternity 57, 90, 121, 175,
189, 195, 211
Michelson's Shoes 59
Music Together 122
Needham Pediatrics 207
Needham Youth Commission 223
Not Your Average Joe's 170
Perry Park 137
Supercuts 220
YMCA 124, 189

Newburyport

Anna Jaques Hospital (Birth Center) 174
Anna Jaques Hospital (Women's
Health Care) 192
Children's Orchard 25
Music Together 106
Not Your Average Joe's 154
Supercuts 220

www.lilaguide.com 245

Newton

- Applebee's Neighborhood Grill 157
- April Cornell 36
- Barn 39
- Bella 40
- Bertucci's Brick Oven Pizzeria 158
- Blue Ribbon Bar-B-Q 158
- Boston Baby 40
- Boston Nanny Centre.................222
- Center Pediatrics.....................205
- Cold Spring Park 134
- Green Planet............. 42, 113, 186
- Gymboree Play & Music 113
- Howard King Pediatrcis 205
- Johnny's Luncheonette 162
- KB Toys 45
- Kids Place, The.......................114
- Lactation Care 211
- Memorial-Spaulding Elementary School Playground 135
- Mommy Chic Maternity 87
- Music Together......................115
- My Gym Children's Fitness Center 115
- Newton Wellesley Hospital (Wellness Center & Childbirth Education) 187
- Pediatrics At Newton-wellesley 205
- Stride Rite Shoes......................50
- Supercuts 220
- Warmlines Parent Resources .. 116, 200
- YMCA 117, 188

Newtonville

- Cabot's Ice Cream 159

North Andover

- Baby Boot Camp.....................181
- Bertucci's Brick Oven Pizzeria 148
- Children's Medical Office of North Andover 203
- Fuddruckers..........................151
- Joe Fish Seafood Restaurant............152
- Music Together......................106
- Ninety Nine Restaurant 154

North Attleboro

- Babies R Us......................52, 210
- Borders Books.......................119
- Build-A-Bear Workshop 119
- Children's Place, The....................56
- Gymboree 56
- JCPenney..........................57, 90
- KB Toys 58
- Kiddie Kandids........................230
- Motherhood Maternity 91
- Ninety Nine Restaurant 170
- Old Navy..........................60, 92
- Picture People........................231
- Sears Portrait Studio 231
- Target.............................64, 92
- TGI Friday's...........................171

North Chelmsford

- Shakti Yoga & Healing Art.............. 183

North Easton

- Ann Elias Dreiker Photography 228
- Children's Museum 120
- Sheep Pasture 123
- Village Toy Shop................................ 64

North End

- Christopher Columbus Waterfront Park 127
- Joe's American Bar & Grill 143
- Philip's Total Care Salon 219
- Tia's On The Waterfront................ 145

Norwell

- Gymboree Play & Music.................. 121
- TGI Friday's 171

Norwood

- Bertucci's Brick Oven Pizzeria 166
- Children's Orchard 55
- Dedham Medical Associates 207
- Family Music Makers 120
- Friendly's..................................... 168
- Kids Club Fun Land 121
- Music Together 122
- Norwood Hospital (Me & My Baby) 198
- Parents' Pride 60
- Rugged Bear 61
- TGI Friday's 171
- Westbury Farms 172
- Wow! 189

Peabody

- Babies R Us 21, 210
- Baby Depot At Burlington Coat Factory 22, 81
- BabyGap/GapKids 22
- Barnes & Noble 102
- Bertucci's Brick Oven Pizzeria 148
- Bonkers Fun House........................ 103
- Borders Books 103
- Bugaboo Creek Steak House 149
- Build-A-Bear Workshop 104
- Children's Place, The 25
- Dede's Dide's Diaper Service 216
- Friendly's..................................... 151
- Gymboree 27
- Gymboree Play & Music.................. 105
- Harvard Vanguard Medical Associates 204
- Joe's American Bar & Grill 152
- Johnny Rockets 153
- Kiddie Kandids 230
- Kids En Vogue 28
- Macy's 30, 83
- Motherhood Maternity...................... 83
- Peabody Pediatric Healthcare Associates 204
- Sears 33, 84

Sears Portrait Studio	231
Snip-its Haircuts For Kids	219
Stride Rite Shoes	33
Sylvan Street Grille	155
Talbots Kids	34
Toys R Us	35

Pepperell

Music Together	106

Quincy

Children's Orchard	55
Friendly's	168
Frozen Freddies	168
Great Cuts	219
Gymboree Play & Music	121
Ninety Nine Restaurant	170
Quincy Family Network (Community Care for Kids)	199
Roseann's	61

Randolph

Bertucci's Brick Oven Pizzeria	167
Friendly's	168
Not Your Average Joe's	170
Piccadilly Pub	170
Showcase Cinema (Baby Pictures)	123

Raynham

Friendly's	168
Little Gym, The	122

Reading

Baby Furniture Warehouse Store	22
Dowd Medical Associates	203
Goodhearts	26
Jordan's Furniture	28
Music Together	106

Revere

Friendly's	151
Great Cuts	219
Mgh Revere Health Care Center	204
Ninety Nine Restaurant	154
Toys R Us	35
Uno Chicago Grill	156

Rockland

Ninety Nine Restaurant	170
North River Collaborative	198

Roslindale

Music Together	101
Sullivan's Medical Supply	213

Roxbury

Garden Of Eden	142
Tremont 647	146

Salem

Brujito's Play Cafe	103
KB Toys	28

Ninety Nine Restaurant	154
North Shore Children's Museum	107
Salem Hospital (Birth Place)	199
Salem Hospital (Lactation Services)	175
Salem Willows Park	107
Target	34, 84

Saugus

Applebee's Neighborhood Grill	147
BabyGap/GapKids	23
Barnes & Noble	102
Border Cafe	149
Build-A-Bear Workshop	104
Children's Place, The	25
Friendly's	151
Fuddruckers	151
Great Cuts	219
Gymboree	27
KB Toys	28
Kohl's	29, 82
Motherhood Maternity	83
Ninety Nine Restaurant	154
Panera Bread	154
Picture People	231
Priceless Kids	32
Sears	33, 84
Sears Portrait Studio	231
Target	34, 84

Sharon

Wards Berry Farm	124

Somerville

Amelia's Kitchen	147
Harvard Vanguard Medical Associates	204
Harvard Vanguard Medical Center Yoga	182
Johnny D's Uptown Restaurant	152
Mario's Salon	219
Music Together	106
Ninety Nine Restaurant	154
Renee's Cafe	155
Somerville Pediatric Svc	204
Stoughton St Park	132
Target	34, 84

South Attleboro

Priceless Kids	60

South Boston

Barking Crab	140
No Name Restaurant	144
Payless Shoe Source	19
Wellspace	180
Joe Moakley Park	127

South Easton

Kidz Planet Gymnastics	121

South End/Bay Village

Charlie's Sandwich Shoppe	142

South Weymouth
Friendly's 168
South Shore Hospital (Women's Family Health) 199, 212

Stoneham
Friendly's 151
KB Toys 28
Learning Tree Store 29
Ninety Nine Restaurant 154
Stone Zoo 108

Stoughton
Applebee's Neighborhood Grill 166
Friendly's 168
Hourigan, Philip MD 207
Jewish Community Center 121
Kohl's 58, 90
Priceless Kids 61
Town Spa Pizza 171

Sudbury
Atkinson Pool 109
Fairbanks Community Center Playground 134
Friendly's 161
Haskell Tot Lot Playground 135
Music Together 115
Rugged Bear 49

Swampscott
Baby Boot Camp 181
Bertucci's Brick Oven Pizzeria 148
Borders Books 103
Friendly's 151

Wakefield
Baby Boot Camp 181
Hadi's Studio-Art-Photography 229
Lake Quannapowitt 131
Music Together 106
Stroller Strides 184
Sullivan Park 132
XerStroll 184
Yoga East 184

Walpole
Barnes & Noble 118
Clayroom 120
Clyde's Roadhouse Bar & Grille 167
Ninety Nine Restaurant 170
Old Navy 60

Waltham
Bertucci's Brick Oven Pizzeria 158
Brigham's Inc 159
Costco 42
Great Cuts 219
Gymboree Play & Music 113
John Brewer's Tavern 162
Maxima Art Center 47
Music Together 115

Ninety Nine Restaurant 163
Supercuts 220
Watch City Brewing Co 164
Wow! 187
YMCA 117, 188

Watertown
BabyGap/GapKids 38
Bugaboo Creek Steak House 159
Carter's 40
Casey Park 134
Children's Place, The 41
Deluxe Town Diner 160
Fillipello Park 134
Friendly's 161
Gap Maternity 86
Great Cuts 219
Harvard Vanguard Medical Associates 211
Kid's Foot Locker 45
Lady Grace 87
Living Yoga 186
Motherhood Maternity 88
Music Together 115
Not Your Average Joe's 163
Old Navy 47
Ruby Tuesday 163
Target 50, 88
Tumble Kids USA 116
Watertown Family Network 117, 200

Wayland
Finagle A Bagel 161
Music Together 115

Wellesley
Abigail's Children's Boutique 36
Bellini 40
Brigham's Inc 159
Family Music Makers 112
Foot Stock 42
Jacadi 44
Laughing Dog Yoga 186
Marcie & Me 114
Music Together 115
OrgagaGanics 199
Periwinkles 48
Perrin Park 135
Rugged Bear 49
Talbots Kids 50
Vidalia's Truck Stop 164

West Bridgewater
Friendship Park 137
Good Days Restaurant 168
Pediatric Associates Inc of Brockton 207

West Roxbury
Baby Belle 14
Bertucci's Brick Oven Pizzeria 141
Fitness Etcetera For Women 179
Friendly's 142

Kids R Kids	17
Millennium Park	127
Music Together	101
Stroller Strides	180

Westborough

Bertucci's Brick Oven Pizzeria	158
Music Together	115
Ruby Tuesday	163

Westford

Applebee's Neighborhood Grill	157
Butterfly Place At Papillon	111
Music Together	115
One Stop Fun Inc	115
Pediatrics West	206

Weston

Dairy Joy	160
Music Together	115
Pediatric Associates of Wellesley	205
Village Barber	220
Weston Pediatric Physicians	206

Westport

| Music Together | 122 |

Westwood

| Marcie & Me | 122 |

Weymouth

Applebee's Neighborhood Grill	166
Friendly's	168
Ninety Nine Restaurant	170
Tufts Library Park	138

Winchester

Ginn Field	130
It Rains Fishes	152
Pediatricians, Inc.	204
Tumble Kids USA	108
Winchester Hospital (Lactation Services)	175
Yoga Mandala	184

Woburn

Bertucci's Brick Oven Pizzeria	148
Chamberi Shoes	24
Clayroom	104
Fantastic Sams	218
Friendly's	151
Great Cuts	219
Joe's American Bar & Grill	152
Kids Playground	105
Kohl's	29, 82
My Gym Children's Fitness Center	107
Ninety Nine Restaurant	154
Target	34, 84
Target Portrait Studio	231
TGI Friday's	156
Toys R Us	35
Woburn Pediatric Associates	204

Wollaston

| Brigham's Inc | 167 |
| Friendly's | 168 |

Wrentham

April Cornell	52
Best Fed Associates	174, 210
Carter's	55
Children's Place, The	56
Friendly's	168
KB Toys	58
Motherhood Maternity	91
OshKosh B'Gosh	60
Ruby Tuesday	170
Strasburg Children	62

www.lilaguide.com

Notes

YOUR RECOMMENDATIONS MAKE THE LILAGUIDE BETTER!
PLEASE SHARE YOUR NOTES WITH US AT WWW.LILAGUIDE.COM

Notes

YOUR RECOMMENDATIONS MAKE THE LILAGUIDE BETTER!
PLEASE SHARE YOUR NOTES WITH US AT WWW.LILAGUIDE.COM

Notes

YOUR RECOMMENDATIONS MAKE THE LILAGUIDE BETTER!
PLEASE SHARE YOUR NOTES WITH US AT WWW.LILAGUIDE.COM

Notes

YOUR RECOMMENDATIONS MAKE THE LILAGUIDE BETTER!
PLEASE SHARE YOUR NOTES WITH US AT WWW.LILAGUIDE.COM

Notes

YOUR RECOMMENDATIONS MAKE THE LILAGUIDE BETTER!
PLEASE SHARE YOUR NOTES WITH US AT WWW.LILAGUIDE.COM

Notes

YOUR RECOMMENDATIONS MAKE THE LILAGUIDE BETTER!
PLEASE SHARE YOUR NOTES WITH US AT WWW.LILAGUIDE.COM